LATITUDE ZERO

Tales of the Equator

Other titles by Gianni Guadalupi

The Dictionary of Imaginary Places
(with Alberto Manguel)

The Discovery of the Nile

The World's Great Treasures

America Discovered (with Antony Shugaar)

Other titles by Antony Shugaar

Niccolo's Smile: A Biography of Machiavelli
(translator)

Western Medical Thought from Antiquity to the Middle Ages
(translator)

Portrait of Venice (translator)

America Discovered (with Gianni Guadalupi)

LATITUDE ZERO

Tales of the Equator

GIANNI GUADALUPI
AND ANTONY SHUGAAR

CARROLL & GRAF PUBLISHERS
NEW YORK

LATITUDE ZERO
TALES OF THE EQUATOR

Carroll & Graf Publishers
An Imprint of Avalon Publishing Group Inc.
161 William St., 16th Floor
New York, NY 10038

First Carroll & Graf edition 2001

Special thanks go to Thomas Suarez
for his front cover and interior illustrations

Library of Congress Cataloging-in-Publication Data is available.

ISBN: 0-7867-0901-4

Printed in the United States of America
Distributed by Publishers Group West

CONTENTS

Introduction

The history of the world has almost always been written from a point of view situated around forty-five degrees north latitude.

London lies just above fifty-one degrees, Paris is around forty-nine degrees, Rome stands at forty-two degrees north latitude. If we consider a swath of territory bounded on the south by Cairo (thirty degrees north latitude) and on the north by Saint Petersburg (sixty degrees north latitude), we are looking at the stage on which Western civilization has developed.

Asia lies a little further south: Beijing stands at forty degrees north latitude, Tokyo at thirty-five degrees north, Seoul at thirty-seven degrees.

North America lies at nearly the same latitude as Asia: Washington, D.C., at thirty-nine degrees, Philadelphia at forty degrees, New York at forty-one degrees, Boston at forty-two degrees, Chicago at forty-one, San Francisco at thirty-eight, Los Angeles at thirty-four degrees north latitude.

The distinction has been made that New York City it is not the capital of American culture, but rather that it is the capital of the

American culture business. Similarly, the band of territory between thirty and sixty degrees north latitude may not have had a monopoly on the world's history, but it has had a virtual monopoly on the world's history writing.

Most of the Earth's publishers, broadcasters, universities, and libraries look on the world from this relatively narrow swath of territory. Latitude, then, is destiny.

Interestingly, the band we have described lies almost exactly midway between Latitude Zero (the Equator) and latitude ninety (the North Pole). It is as if we lived in a big room, and our culture's attention were fixed firmly at eye level, not on the ceiling (Arctic) or the floor (Equator).

Great stories have been told in recent years about the exploration of the rooftops of the world (South and North Poles). But the tales of the Equator have largely been told piecemeal or overlooked entirely.

In this book, we shall recount tales of the Equator. By no means are we presenting an exhaustive account of life at Latitude Zero over the past several thousand years. But we are telling some of the most exciting, adventurous, surprising, and paradoxical tales from the Line.

The Equator is, in a sense, the largest man-made object on Earth (the Earth is flattened at the Poles and bulges outward at its midsection). Because of this equatorial bulge, the imaginary line drawn along Latitude Zero is longer than any other straight line that can be drawn on the Earth's surface. Because of its size, the Equator is moving faster than any other point on Earth (like the outer edge of the terrestrial merry-go-round, the Poles being that same merry-go-round's motionless centerpoint). It gets more sunlight than any other point on Earth, and the equatorial sun stands still, straight overhead. (A few years ago one inventive photographer decided to make a very extended multiple exposure of the sun, every day at noon, for a year; the result was a luminous figure-eight in the sky. The same sequence of photographs shot at the Equator would have shown a single intense dot of light at the zenith.)

The Equator may be in a certain sense a man-made construct, but in another very real sense things are different at Latitude Zero. The world's wind and current systems are organized into northern and southern systems. The South Equatorial Current brushes westward against the eastward-pushing Equatorial Countercurrent in the Pacific Ocean and the Indian Ocean; similar boundaries between current occur in the South Atlantic along the Equator. The Equator marks the boundary between the northeast trade winds and the southeast trade winds; without venturing into too much detail, other prevailing wind systems are divided by the Equator (the Mauritius cyclones and the Bengal cyclones in the Indian Ocean, the willy-willies and South Sea hurricanes off Australia, the cordonazos off Central America).

As a result, the Equator is home to all sorts of interesting phenomena. Now, it is questionable whether the Coriolis effect actually results in water swirling down the drain in a sink clockwise north of the Equator and counterclockwise south of the Equator, but the Equator does mark the world's navigational dead zone: the Doldrums, an equatorial belt of calms and light baffling winds in both Pacific and Atlantic Oceans. The way that mariners in the Age of Sail felt about the Doldrums may be seen in the etymology of the name: a hybrid of "dolt" and "tantrum." In any case, mariners sometimes died horrible deaths caught in this no-man's-land between the northern and southern trade winds.

Indeed, the bizarre pagan pageantry that sailing ships engaged in for centuries upon crossing the Line—King Neptune and his mermen, ceremonial dunkings and hazings—may have been more of a celebration of surviving the Doldrums than any real interest in marking Latitude Zero.

A similarly baffling but relatively new threat to our collective survival is generated by the powerful greenhouse-effect and the convergence of northern and southern deep-ocean currents along the Line in the Pacific. El Niño is a perturbation of the deep equatorial waters of the central Pacific, affecting in turn the equatorial winds, and the past ten years have shown how far-reaching its effects can be.

Lastly, the Equator's sheer speed is attested by the decision of the European Space Agency to launch all its satellites from Kourou, in French Guiana. The nations that make up the European Union all lie between thirty-five and sixty degrees north latitude, but a colonial legacy allowed the ESA to add one thousand miles per hour to the liftoff velocity of their rockets by launching eastward along the Equator. The southeasternmost point—hence the highest over-water takeoff velocity—that Americans possess is found at Cape Canaveral in southeastern Florida.

One mystery of the Equator had been the flow of the Congo River. Early explorers were mystified by the river's constant flow, its lack of dry-season ebb and rainy-season spate. The first few hundred miles of the river's course were broken by rocks and rushing cataracts, and so explorers were unable to venture upriver to understand the reason. Only when the great Victorian explorer, Henry Morton Stanley, walked the length of the Congo from its source to the Atlantic Ocean was an explanation provided. The river snakes northwestward from its source, south of the Congo, looping north of the Line. Thus, along the Congo, the dry season north of the Equator corresponded to the rainy season south of the Equator, and vice versa. It was always raining somewhere along the Congo, and so its flow never dropped.

If the behavior of water and air along the Equator is interesting, equally interesting are the landmasses. If we limit ourselves to the Equator itself, running eastward from the international date line (distant cousin to the Equator), we find the thousand-mile sweep of the Line Islands, Darwin's Galápagos Islands, mile-high Quito and the Ecuadorian Andes, another thousand miles of the northern basin of the Amazon River, and then the mighty Amazon delta itself. Just a little north lies French Guiana, and the notorious penal colony, Devil's Island. Then we run directly across the Atlantic Ocean at its narrowest point to the Gulf of Guinea (the inlet on the

African coast that, according to Pangaea theory, once snugly accommodated the eastward-jutting landmass of Brazil) and to the small coastal island nation of Saõ Tomé and Príncipe. Then the Line runs through Libreville, capital of Gabon, through Equatorial Guinea, and five hundred miles of Congo jungle. Interestingly, the Equator crosses the three thousand-mile-long Congo River not once but twice, once at Mbandaka and once five hundred miles east, at Kisangani. Then, in quick succession, Lake Edward and the mist-shrouded Ruwenzori Mountains (made famous by the late Dian Fossey), Uganda with its capital Kampala; the world's third-largest lake, mighty Victoria, source of the Nile; Africa's second-highest mountain, Mount Kenya; Nairobi; and a swatch of Somalia. Then come the blue Indian Ocean, the coral atolls of the Maldives, Sumatra, Malaysia with Singapore, Borneo, the Makassar Strait, Celebes, the Molucca Sea, the tip of New Guinea, the island nation of Nauru (whose flag is a blue field with a yellow stripe representing the Equator, and a white star for the island itself), and finally the Kiribati Islands, once known as the Gilberts; the Line Islands, of course; and the Pacific Doldrums.

Along this line in the sand and the water, across the mountains and through the great lakes and rivers, went some of the great explorers, dreamers, con artists, and lunatics of history. Some of their stories are familiar and some are obscure, but we think it is fair to say that the Equator has never before been taken as the organizing principle for a collection of astonishing tales of adventure. If the Equator is a land, the longest, narrowest land on Earth, it is a land of extreme stories.

The stories reach back to the earliest times, tales of giant birds seizing elephants to feed to their young, boiling seas under a noonday sun, the riches of Punt and Ophir, and strange narratives of huge benevolent serpents and floating dragon-islands.

These legends of the Equator make way for historical accounts only slightly less fantastic and evocative: just before the dawn of the Great Age of Exploration, for instance, an ambitious Chinese emperor and a venturesome eunuch admiral launched one of the great fleets in history. This great flotilla of majestic, luxurious junks sailed out from the southern ports of China, through the Indonesian archipelago, and all the way across the Indian Ocean to touch land at distant Mombasa in what is now Kenya. After seven great voyages, the fleet returned home for good; the emperor died, and jealous viziers and courtiers destroyed maps and logbooks to ensure that no future emperor could venture out into the great equatorial seas to the west.

The great wave of Chinese exploration along the Equator retreated just as the Portuguese were getting started, and it has been observed that a citizen of Goa, in southern India, who had seen the magnificent Chinese fleet in harbor as a little boy or girl might have lived to see the first Portuguese explorers docking in that same harbor.

Most of the tales of the Equator that are told in this book date from the four centuries that followed, the great age of European exploration. They are stories of various quests for glory and wealth. They range from the magnificent voyage of Magellan, who discovered a western route into the great Southern Sea, the Pacific Ocean, to the spectacular madness of Lope de Aguirre, the crazed conquistador who built a floating republic based on violence and anarchy on the waters of the Amazon and Orinoco. The characters include such cunning publicists as Henry Morton Stanley, who was constantly leading huge expeditions armed to the teeth through equatorial Africa to rescue people who were not entirely sure they needed rescuing. They range from Sir Richard Burton, Orientalist extraordinaire and translator of the *Arabian Nights,* to Emin Pasha, the mild-mannered, shortsighted entomologist who was also the brilliant governor of Equatoria during the wars with the Mahdists of the Sudan.

The tales of the Equator often seem to involve obsessive quests: for the lost Dr. Livingstone, for the elusive Westward Passage, for the long-suffering Penelope of Riobamba, and in one amazing South

American saga, for the kingdom of El Dorado, the Golden One, who was said to live in a city of gold set on a lake that glowed each morning in a second sunrise that rivaled the real sunrise in glory and intensity. One after another, Gonzalo Pizarro (brother of the conquistador of Peru) Francisco de Orellana, Lope de Aguirre, Sir Walter Raleigh, and many, many others chased after El Dorado, a name that has become synonymous with vast and illusory wealth.

There is the story of the nude baroness of the Galápagos Islands, an Austro-Hungarian aristocrat and temptress who tried to create a luxury tourist resort on the Equator, only to create a weird little utopia of free love that finally declined into murder and mystery. There is the story of the White Raja, a Victorian Englishman who set out to find a kingdom of his own and became the absolute monarch of the island kingdom of Sarawak.

Some of the stories tell of harsh conflict between European adventurers and the equatorial lands they came to explore and subdue. Some are emblematic of the rift between two worlds: the pathos of the story of the Joan of Arc of the Kongo, a not-entirely-forgotten eighteenth-century heroine and martyr to a syncretistic religion, burned at the stake through the machinations of Capuchin monks, jealous of her power and popularity.

Some of them are less stark, and certainly the story of Robert Louis Stevenson's extended stay on the Gilbert Islands is one of the most enchanting: the convalescent teller of tales won over a South Sea tyrant, the feared King Tembinok', and was given a small enclave on an island at Latitude Zero in which to live: Equator City.

In any case, here they are: tales of the Equator, a treasury of amazing stories, linked by the longest and most central line on Earth.

PART I

Antiquity

The Rukh was a feature of much of the mythology concerning the Equator; it was said to feed its young on elephants. —British Library, London, UK/Bridgeman Art Library

To the people of the ancient world, the sun in the sky overhead, the changing seasons, the idea of north and south, were all much more substantial and concrete concepts than they are to us today. To a modern sensibility, for instance, cerulean might be an attractive designer color, a number in a Pantone book, a crayon from one of the larger Crayola packs. To the ancient world, cerulean had a very specific definition: it was the color of the sky reflected on the surface of the sea.

Just as we take the color cerulean for granted, and for the ancients it was a composite of sky and sea, two vital and immediate factors in daily life, so the very idea of the Equator necessarily played a different and far more momentous role in ancient cosmology than it does for us.

We take the Equator for granted: it is a line on a globe in our elementary-school room, perhaps, later in life, a big roadside sign in Kenya or Ecuador offering a photo opportunity for our scrapbooks. We know a great deal more than we understand. We "know" what the Equator is, but we would unlikely be able to plot our latitude by observing the sun and stars.

The Greek philosopher Eratosthenes compared the noonday shadow at midsummer in Alexandria with its counterpart at what is now Aswan, and from the difference he was able to calculate the curve of the Earth between those two points.

Clearly, the ancients knew more than a few things about the shape of the Earth and the location of the Equator.

Still, what one or two great men knew and wrote on scrolls may not have been widely communicated. And so the facts that the heat clearly increased as one headed south, the sun stood straight overhead, and the animals and people one met were different and often fierce led many to assume that seas must boil if one reaches far enough south, that crocodiles had much larger equatorial cousins that might well be dragons, that the sea must at some point pour over in a torrent, vanishing into the void.

The section that follows, a collection of tales of the Equator that were current in the ancient world, is amusing and astonishing, and we offer it in that spirit. But we should not turn up our noses at the gullibility of the ancients. After all, they got a lot of things right, and mariners who were venturing into the unknown were incredibly brave, if not always as well documented as we are today.

But let us make some comparisons: even a great scientist such as Galileo wore blinders. He was so determined to resist the temptations of astrology that he refused to believe that the tides could be caused by the gravitational force of the moon. That would be *actio ab distans,* akin to magic, and so Galileo preferred an explanation that looks like lunacy to us. He assumed that the Earth must turn with a fair amount of creaking and lurching, like a cart wheel, or like a bucket being carried on a pole. The tides, then, were nothing other than a giant, global, sloshing effect.

And even now, it is part of the received wisdom of most readers that the Coriolis effect causes water to spin down the drain counterclockwise north of the Equator and clockwise south of the Equator. Go to a sink and run the water: the odds are equally good that you will see it go spinning down the drain clockwise, whichever side of the Equator you may be.

So let us look on our ancient forebears with tolerance and understanding. And there is one story that may help to give us a little humility in our greater understanding of the Equator: a squad of U.S. fighter jets using computer-guided navigation crossed the Equator not too many years ago, flying in perfect formation, wingtip to wingtip, autopilot engaged. As they crossed Latitude Zero, their navigational systems flipped them over, still in perfect formation. Half a dozen pilots hung head down, safe and sound, but frightened and quite confused.

I

The Secrets of the Southern Seas

Possessors of an age-old wisdom, the priests of ancient Egypt were the only humans who knew the composition of the planet. They knew that in the exact center of the world there ran a river, the Nile, along either side of which were strips of rich black earth, the silt that gave life to all creatures. Beyond these two strips of dark soil, toward the rising sun and toward the setting sun, there lay vast expanses of red dust, the desert that gave only death. And if you followed the course of the river itself, once you made your way upstream past the roaring cataracts, there was an infinite land of sucking mud and canebrakes, and beyond that, a weltering labyrinth of forests, a region of shadows that was home to powerful spirits and dancing dwarves that travelers or generals would bring downstream from time to time, offering the little men as gifts to the almighty Pharaoh. Even further on, beyond the cataracts and the canebrakes and the jungles, there towered a mighty mountain, out of which issued the great river Nile. This mountain was one of the four pillars of the vault of the heavens. All around it stretched the great circle of water that the bark of the sun plied daily. The rest was darkness.

This, at least, was the worldview offered by the scholarship of the day. In the port cities of the Red Sea, however, people knew a rather different version of world geography. Every so often, sailors would venture out beyond the relatively tranquil waters of the Red Sea, pushing southward toward the sun itself, and so close did they come to it that often they would return home, their skin scorched and baked. These mariners told tales: in the great circle of water crisscrossed by dizzyingly huge waves, beyond the strait on whose shores grew aromatic plants, there were many unknown lands. Some had visited them, and some had even lived to return home and tell.

There was one fortunate sailor, for instance, who survived a shipwreck. His boat had been tossed by the waves onto an island, and there he roamed for three days without laying eyes on another living soul, eating wild figs, grapes, cucumbers, berries, melons, fish, and birds. On the third day, he lit a bonfire to invoke the pity of the gods. All of a sudden he heard a roaring sound, like thunder, and as the trees shook and the earth rocked, he saw coming toward him a serpent that was a hundred cubits long. The serpent had a beard two cubits in length; its body was the color of lapis lazuli, and seemed to be inlaid with gold. The huge reptile reared up before him and—as he lay prostrate on the ground in terror—asked him: "Who brought you here, who brought you here, o little one, who brought you here?" After the shipwrecked sailor told the serpent of his adventures, the giant creature was moved to pity. He seized the mariner in his serpent mouth and slithered home with him. There he lived with seventy-five other great serpents, all members of his considerable family.

The good reptile foretold that the Egyptian would be rescued four months hence by a ship. And in fact, exactly four months afterward a sail appeared on the horizon, standing in toward the mysterious island. The shipwrecked sailor clambered up into the branches of an especially tall tree, trying to make out the crew of the ship, then ran to give the news to the huge snake. His scaly host, however, knew all about it and simply wished him a safe journey. Moved to gratitude, the stranded Egyptian fell to the ground before the benevolent serpent in thanks. The serpent gave him gifts of the scents and aromas in which the island abounded, and predicted that in just two months' time he would be safe and sound back in Egypt. The stranded sailor then hurried down to the shore, where the Egyptian crew took him on board, and the ship then set sail. As the crew looked back at the island, it sank out of sight and vanished under the waves.

In waterfront taverns, tales were told of another island, inhabited not by serpents but by men. These men, however, had soft and pliable bones and were beardless. Strange as these features may seem, they had another, even more pronounced oddity: their tongues were forked, divided in two right down to the root. They could use their forked tongues to imitate not only all human voices, but even the twittering song of birds and the cries and roars of all animals. They could even speak with two different people at the same time, answering one person with one tongue, another person with the other. On that island, day was always the same length as night in every season throughout the year, and at noonday bodies cast no shadows, because the rays of the sun fell straight down from the sky overhead.

There were lands under that noonday sun that were less elusive than the island of the giant serpent or the island of the two-tongued men. The island of Punt, for instance, was synonymous with treasure. The Egyptian queen Hatshepsut had sent an entire fleet to collect the riches of Punt: ebony, gum, myrrh, incense, ivory, gold, pelts, apes, panthers.

Or Ophir, where the monarch of another land—the same King Solomon who had transformed the little realm of the Hebrews into a great and splendid dominion, who had loved the queen of Sheba, and become in his old age the wisest man on earth—had sent an expedition manned by Phoenicians, the teamsters of the sea. He chose Phoenicians because the Hebrews did not know how to sail.

Ophir was incredibly distant. The journey required three years of sailing under a scorching sun, three years without shade. Finally, when Solomon had given up his Phoenician explorers for dead, they returned from the southern waters, the holds of their ships crammed with gold and an aromatic wood that had never been seen before. This was sandalwood, and the king of the Hebrews ordered zithers and harps to be made out of sandalwood to accompany his cantors.

The centuries passed, countless other ships set sail from countless other ancient ports. As these ships returned home, the southern seas gradually filled up with new wonders. Tales were told of flying fish, showering onto deck or hurtling past in airborne flocks. Others told of the "undersea market," a spectral apparition that frightened even the saltiest dogs. At night—sometimes even in broad daylight—the sea beneath the ship would change color, and it seemed as if many torches were glimmering in the depths. Monstrous shapes would appear; the waters below would reveal towers and pavilions; sarcastic laughter would echo over the waves, followed by an indistinct muttering and the tinkling of gold coins.

Bassora, the great harbor town at the southern end of the Persian Gulf, terminus of the Route of the Indies in the centuries when Baghdad was the City of Califfs—teemed with loquacious Sinbads. They told of huge fish that carried great flaps on their backs like the sails of a ship; other fish that had human faces; an amber that grew on the seabed and floated to the surface after a storm, taking the shape of gourds or truffles; white clouds that unleashed a long narrow tongue that reached down to the surface of the sea, making the waves boil and swallow up ships; islands ruled by women, with mountains of solid silver, where strangers were eaten almost raw after being hung out, upside down, to ripen in the sun, and where crayfish emerging from the surf were turned to stone as soon as they touched dry sand.

On one island lived the *rukh* bird—or roc—a giant avian whose eggs were as large as the dome of a mosque; another island was inhabited by the *karkadann,* which could spear an elephant on its horn and go on grazing without even noticing the added weight; a third island concealed the copper urns into which Solomon had sealed the evil spirits; and a fourth island was home to teeming myriads of apes, capable of lifting large feluccas drawn up on the beach, vanishing with them into the jungle.

It was in the port town of Bassora, around 1170, that Benjamin of Tudela, the Jewish traveler, met one of these fanciful veterans of the watery labyrinth of the southern seas. This mariner told Benjamin that the hottest of the many seas scorched by the equatorial sun was Niqpa, constantly buffeted by windstorms.

> At times the helmsman cannot govern his ship, as a fierce wind drives her into this Sea of [Niqpa], where she cannot move from her place; and the crew have to remain where they are till their stores of food are exhausted and then they die. In this way many a ship has been lost, but men eventually discovered a device by which to escape from this evil place. The crew provide themselves with hides of oxen. And when this evil wind blows which drives them into the Sea of [Niqpa], they wrap themselves up in the skins, which they make waterproof, and, armed with knives, plunge into the sea. A great bird called the griffin spies them out, and in the belief that the sailor is an animal, the griffin seizes hold of him, brings him to dry land, and puts him down on a mountain or in a hollow in order to devour him. The man then quickly thrusts at the bird with a knife and slays him. Then the man issues forth from the skin and walks till he comes to an inhabited place. And in this manner many a man escapes.

Perhaps Chou Ch'ü-fei, the zealous Chinese official of the maritime customs office of Canton who compiled in 1178 a sort of questionnaire entitled *Answers Concerning What Exists Outside the Borders,* questioned those same garrulous storytellers of the southern seas for his material. In *Answers,* Chou Ch'ü-fei retold each and every tale about distant lands that he could gather from the mariners of every nationality who passed through the great port where he worked.

Not far from Java, one sailor told him, there was a great sandbar surrounded by reefs that extended for miles and miles; nearby was the Wei-lü, a vast hole in the ocean where the water tumbled down toward the Nine Worlds. Many centuries before, a junk had been driven there by a sudden gale, and had teetered dangerously close to the edge of the maelstrom. The crew could hear the roar of falling water, but no land could be seen. Luckily for the crew, the wind veered suddenly, and they were able to steer their ship back to safety.

In those years, Chinese junks were the largest ships on earth, "as vast as palaces," according to one chronicler, and the Chinese fleet ruled the seas. "When they spread their sails, they seem like so many clouds in the sky." There were junks more than 150 meters in length, with nine and even ten masts, and crews of several hundred. Hogs were raised on board these immense junks; rice wine was distilled. The wealthiest passengers and senior officers had luxurious cabins, complete with baths. These majestic Oriental ocean liners even ventured out in the face of mighty typhoons and the great sea monsters that made those waters especially perilous. If they happened to land on an island where the vegetation had been burnt, then they knew perfectly well that that was no real island, not terra firma at all, but actually the back of the serpent dragon, and they should set all sails and flee immediately. All the sailors would cut their hair; after collecting the scales of the fish netted that day, they would burn the scales. Only these measures could ensure that the great sea monster would disappear.

Skirting around dangers such as these, the ships of the Celestial Empire ventured as far as the coasts of India, the Persian Gulf, and the African mainland, plying the trade routes of the unpredictable Southern Sea that stretched between Sumatra and the Malacca

Straits (between the Equator and five degrees north latitude), dotted with labyrinthine expanses of islands and strange—sometimes terrifying—lands.

Those who landed in Lo-ch'a, for example, encountered men with black bodies and tawny hair, sharp beastly fangs and claws with talons. Their cities were surrounded by walls as black as ink. The grand chamberlain of that realm of shadows had ears that were set backward on his head, a nose with three nostrils, and eyebrows that he could lower over his eyes like a sunshade. Progressively, as one descended the hierarchy of court officials, the deformities lessened and finally vanished.

In San-fo-ch'i (now Palembang, on the island of Sumatra; three degrees south latitude) the king was forbidden to eat grain; if he did, the harvest would certainly be a poor one. He was therefore required to eat palm flour. The king could wash himself only with water extracted from rose petals. If the king were ever to wash himself with ordinary water from a running stream, the entire land would surely be overwhelmed by terrible floods.

The monarch inherited an exceedingly heavy head-covering made of solid gold spangled with precious gems. The king alone was strong enough to wear it. If the throne was left vacant, the sons of the late king were summoned to the palace, and the son who was capable of carrying such a great weight on his head was proclaimed king in his turn.

Africa abounded in a great wealth of zoological oddities. In the land of Pi-p'a-lo (modern-day Somalia) there lived a camel-crane that stood more than two yards tall. It could fly, but only inches above the ground. Local wizards could transform themselves into birds, beasts, and marine creatures. If any of the natives were to have a disagreement with a foreign merchant, then they would avail themselves of the services of these wizards or sorceresses, who would cast a curse upon the ship. The merchants would then be unable to set sail until the disagreement had been resolved.

On the seashores of that part of the world, enormous fish would sometimes lie stranded, gasping and writhing, eventually dying. These sea creatures were as long as twenty yards, and larger than a ship. These fish were inedible, but the natives would obtain an oil from their carcasses that was good fuel for lamps. Also, the poorer native families used the dried skeletons of those enormous beasts as frameworks for their huts.

In 1349, many scholars of Europe were reading (with considerable skepticism) a book about the wonders of Asia written (actually, dictated) by one of the few Europeans ever to have been there, a Venetian merchant named Marco Polo. At the same time in China, a former sailor named Wang Ta-yuan was writing an account of his travels through the bramble-patch of small and large islands that nowadays we call Indonesia. The title of his book, *Notes on the Barbarians of the Islands,* at once conceals, beneath an apparently dispassionate scientific approach, and betrays the author's enormous relief at having survived those equatorial regions where the heat was as great as the dangers and irritations. Dangerous they may have been, but they were also profitable: China imported from the Southern Seas such rare and expensive products as sandalwood, nutmeg, the so-called "dragon's blood" (the juice of a leguminous plant, used to make a special enamel), and a great number of parakeets, a particularly prized creature, found in that period in almost every household in China.

To obtain these goods, the merchants and navigators had to barter with people in the most dangerous and savage regions of that myriad of archipelagos, sailing up bandit-ridden rivers, pushing through tangled reaches of jungle infested by snakes the size of dragons, braving the poisoned arrows of the "barbarian" headhunters, risking the most virulent tropical diseases. All the same, those waters were frequented by numerous Chinese vessels. And it was here that the first of seven great Chinese naval expeditions to explore the equatorial regions sailed in 1405. These impressive expeditions were first prompted by the desire of the new Ming Dynasty to increase its imperial prestige in the eyes of peoples near and far, even though the official reason set forth in the *Dynastic History of the Ming* was quite different and rather bizarre. According to that account, the emperor Yung-lo mounted the expeditions to search for his predecessor Chien-wen, who had been dethroned and subsequently vanished.

In 1405, command of the Chinese fleet was given to the chief eunuch, Cheng Ho, who had been born in 1371 of Muslim parents in the southern province of Yunnan. With the title of San-Pao t'ai-chien, or Great Eunuch of the Three Jewels, Cheng Ho was given command of a fleet the likes of which had not been seen since the times of Kublai Khan: sixty junks, large and small, with a total crew of twenty-seven thousand men. The junks bore names such as *Blessed Navigation*, *Pure Peace*, and *Eternal Harmony*.

Admiral Cheng Ho had at his orders an impressive general staff, comprising two generals, about a hundred other officers, two masters of ceremonies, a geomancer, four meteorologists, a hundred or so physicians, and a great number of interpreters, speaking all of the languages used in eastern Asia, from Arabic to Burmese. There were also seven imperial eunuchs who were to act as ambassadors, assisted by another seventy or so eunuchs serving as chamberlains and chancellors. Lastly, there was an official chronicler, a Muslim named Ma Huan, who was an Arabic interpreter and who wrote an account of the first expedition with the impressive title of *Ying-yai sheng-lan*, or *The Triumphant Vision of the Boundless Ocean.*

Launched from the shipyards of Lung-chiang near Shanghai in the summer of 1405, the ships waited till the end of the year to set sail, heading south with the favor of the winter monsoon. Ten days later the entire fleet was anchoring in the port of Hsin-chou in Champa, the present-day Qui Nhon, Vietnam. Then, coasting along Cambodia, Siam, and the Malacca Peninsula (also known as the Malay Peninsula, which extends down to about one degree north latitude), the fleet entered the Indian Ocean, laying over along the way on the Nicobar Islands (approximately seven degrees north latitude), whose "savage and nude" inhabitants seem to have tickled the fancy of every sailor who ever plied those waters. Even the normally sensible Ibn Battuta claimed that they had the snouts of dogs. Ma Huan writes that they could not wear clothing because their bodies would soon have been covered with sores and rashes. The reason was this: their ancestors had stolen the garments of the Buddha who bathed on their shores during his voyage of return from Ceylon (modern-day Sri Lanka, about three degrees north latitude); the Buddha, in response, had laid a curse upon them and their descendants.

Once it had passed the island of Ceylon, sacred because of the time that the Buddha spent there, the fleet split up into two squadrons. The first one sailed for the Malabar Coast (southwestern tip of India, from eight to twelve degrees north latitude), while the second made directly for Aden, crossing the ocean, and touched land at Hormuz, and continuing from there toward India. The two squadrons rejoined and then sailed up the Bay of Bengal and back south along the Burma coast as far as the Andaman Islands (twelve degrees north latitude). They returned to the ports of South China after visiting the island of Sumatra and overwhelming a few incautious pirate fleets. It was October 2, 1407.

That lengthy voyage, two years long, was followed by a briefer expedition, which set sail at the beginning of 1409 for Malacca, Sumatra, and southern India. In Ceylon, the fleet was forced to fight because the ruler of the island, "scornful and arrogant," demanded tribute of silver and gold. When Cheng Ho refused to pay, the king attacked. He soon repented his foolhardiness, however, because the admiral landed with two thousand elite warriors, captured the palace, and took the king of Ceylon prisoner, leading him in chains before the emperor Yung-lo in the autumn of 1411.

The chronicler of this second voyage and nearly all those that followed, the court functionary Fei Hsin—whose book's title intentionally echoes Ma Huan's earlier title, *The Triumphant Vision of the Star-Spangled Vessel,* spoke with nostalgia of the island of Java (eight degrees south latitude), which he visited during the third expedition (1412–1415): "The inhabitants of Java are rich and elegant. . . . The island is renowned for its popular festivals. In the tenth month, the Javanese celebrate the spring festival, and every month in the period of the full moon they hold a festival known as the Dance Under the Moon. Dozens of the loveliest maidens on the island dance beneath the moon, holding hands; one sings a verse and the others answer her in chorus, dancing all the while in a ring." But the Javanese also seemed to him to be terribly touchy: "If any one should dare to jest with them, and perhaps touches their hairdo, unfailingly they will fly into a rage, drawing a dagger and challenging the incautious one to a duel. Whoever wins the duel is considered innocent. They truly have a strange way of thinking." It seems plausible to the modern reader that this story may reflect the author's own personal experience on Java.

On the fourth expedition, which set out in 1416, the chief eunuch ventured all the way to the coast of Africa. The Chinese already had trading relationships with the port towns of Mogadishu (in present-day Somalia, two degrees north latitude), Brava, and Malindi (on the coast of modern-day Kenya, three degrees south latitude); In 1415 Malindi had sent a number of "tributes" to the Son of Heaven, including an astounding giraffe. It appears that fanciful zoology was the prime objective of this expedition: Cheng Ho had been sent all the way to Africa in search of a unicorn, a mythical animal that symbolized wealth and longevity. Cheng Ho's junks anchored off Mogadishu, which was inhabited by "quarrelsome people," and inland of which there was "nothing other than sand." The fleet continued on to Brava, "intolerably hot," but, fortunately, inhabited by "very beautiful women, who adorn themselves with earrings and necklaces and wrap their long black hair in a towering coif."

In August 1419, Cheng Ho returned home without unicorns, but with a number of African emissaries. The chief eunuch took to the sea again in March 1421 to take the emissaries back home to Somalia.

The admiral's sixth expedition, in 1424, was a quick round-trip journey to Palembang (three degrees south latitude), the most important trading town of Sumatra, for the official installation of a new governor of the island.

The seventh expedition cost the chief eunuch his life. He was ordered to undertake this expedition by the new emperor, Hsuan-ti, successor of Yung-lo, who had died in 1424. The chief eunuch was now sixty years old, and he set sail at the beginning of 1431. Over the course of two years he visited twenty lands, including Arabia. Good Muslim that he was, he finally took advantage of the opportunity to make his pilgrimage to Mecca. On the way back, he died, in the middle of the ocean across which he had sailed so many times before. The great imperial fleet docked at its home port in 1433, and it never sailed again. The junks eventually rotted at dockside. The isolationist faction of the imperial court prevailed, for reasons that are still not clear to historians. With the shift of the capital from the southern river town of Nanking to the northern, landlocked Beijing, Ming China shut itself up in a splendid isolation. Half a century later, in 1480, when the eunuch Wang Chih, who enjoyed the emperor's favor, began investigating the possibility of imitating the achievements of his predecessor, he went to the archives to search for the reports on Cheng Ho's travels, but he found nothing. Functionaries opposed to maritime expansion had destroyed everything in order to nip in the bud any dangerous attempts to begin those explorations once again.

PART II

South America

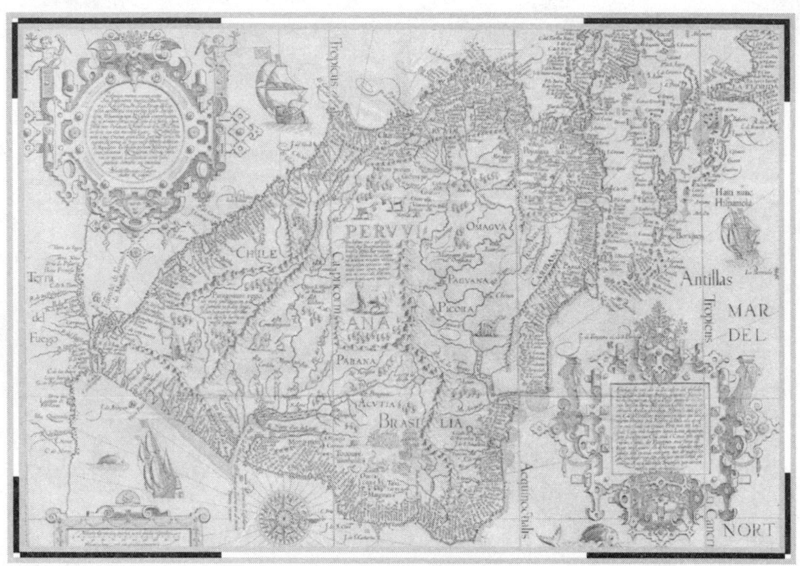

This remarkable early map of South America depicts the continent from north to south, instead of from west to east. Therefore, Central America is found to the right, and Tierra del Fuego is on the left, the Pacific is at the top, and the Atlantic lies at the bottom.
—Courtesy of Thomas Suarez

In many ways, the story of equatorial adventure and exploration moves directly from the Old World to the New World, leaving Africa aside until the nineteenth century.

Africa was, deplorably, a source of slaves and ivory, but Europeans were content to deal with Arab slavers and ivory merchants on the coast, venturing no farther inland than port towns and occasionally along the larger rivers.

A far different situation occurred in equatorial America. One reason was certainly the Amazon river basin, which pours into the Atlantic Ocean square athwart the Equator.

The stories that we offer in this section almost all focus on a quest for El Dorado, the Golden One. This mythical king was said to live in a town of pure gold in the center of a great lake; at sunrise, the walls of El Dorado's golden city shone so brightly that it seemed there was a second sunrise.

Armies of conquistadors came marching over the Andes repeatedly from their base in Peru. The first expedition was in the mid-sixteenth century, and is told here in the story of Francisco de Orellana, the "Unfortunate Conquistador." Twenty years later came the astonishing black tale of Lope de Aguirre, the "Mutinous Conquistador," a man who seemed to prefer treason and violence to the other options available.

If Aguirre was a protonihilist, the men who followed him were a more orthodox group of conmen, rogues, scoundrels, and dreamers. One of them was Sir Walter Raleigh, who believed that El Dorado reigned in the present-day country of Guyana. So certain was he that he staked his life on returning to England with the spoils of the city of gold; failing to do so, he was beheaded. Others carried on the search for El Dorado, and one in particular, an Irish nobleman named Bernard O'Brien, claims to have met with a woman chieftain in a city on an island where there may have been gold. This merging of the legend of the Amazon women warriors and the city of El Dorado is a fitting end to a saga of fruitless trekking and quests after phantoms that marked a full century of South American exploration.

We have included other tales of the American Equator here: in the eighteenth century a great French scientist, Charles Marie de La Condamine, traveled to the Equator with an expedition from the French Academy. The goal of the expedition was to measure the Earth at its broadest point. Scientifically, it was of questionable value, but in terms of sheer adventure, we feel it bears telling.

The story that serves as a coda to de La Condamine's story is one of the great tear jerkers of the eighteenth century: the Penelope of Riobamba. It is the story of how a Frenchman, a member of de La Condamine's expedition, waited almost two decades to rejoin his bride, a lovely Quechua maiden he met in what is now Ecuador. He descended the length of the Amazon, she waited for him back in her Andean hometown, and years and years passed as European wars, the plotting of missionaries, and the natural obstacles of the Amazon basin separated the star-crossed lovers.

Closing this section on equatorial America is the story of the Nude Baroness, a surviving member of the Austro-Hungarian aristocracy in the aftermath of the First World War. She fell in love with the idea of creating a haven for the indolent wealthy on the Galápagos Islands, on the Equator just west of the Ecuadorian coast. It, like all the other stories in this section, is a tale of obsession, misguided energies, dreams vanishing in the bright equatorial sunlight, and a certain dose of madness.

2

The Unfortunate Conquistador

In 1540, in the town of Quito, still devastated by the fires set by the last of the Incas and the further destruction wrought by the Spanish conquistadors who had followed, a new governor arrived: Gonzalo Pizarro.

Gonzalo was the brother of Francisco Pizarro, who had begun his life as a pig herder in a small town in Spain's Estremadura, and had risen to the giddy height of lord and master of the fabulously wealthy Peru. Gonzalo was a typical Spanish soldier of those adventuresome times: physically robust, plainspoken, charming, an excellent rider, courageous in battle, beloved by his men, ignorant as his horse, and completely scornful of anything that was not Castilian. The post of governor of those Andean highlands, the northernmost province of the defeated Inca empire, had made him supremely happy, not so much for the honor itself, as much as because he secretly considered this to be the stepping-off point for a much grander and more important undertaking: the conquest of the vast and unexplored lands to the east of the great mountain chain, where the Spaniards all believed that there lay hidden a second Peru, perhaps even richer than the first.

Already, a few years before, someone had ventured into those forests and had returned with reports of cinnamon trees. Cinnamon was one of the most precious of spices of the day, and till then it was believed that cinnamon grew only on Asian islands occupied by Spain's rivals, the Portuguese.

This was the same cinnamon, said the experts who had examined specimens. It left the same wonderful aftertaste; it gave the same fragrance to meat. In those times, when spices were the most important merchandise in the trade between Europe and the East, and when profits from the spice trade were incredibly high, the discovery of a Land of Cinnamon in the Spanish Indies was already a major event.

But the discovery of cinnamon, important as it may have been, began shrinking into insignificance as other rumors began circulating about the amazing lands that lay to the east of the Andes. The Spaniards who had already plundered the astoundingly rich coffers of Peru were ready and willing to believe that all of the rest of the South American continent was one vast treasure chest. Word had filtered back that many days east of the mountains there lay a kingdom whose ruler was so fabulously rich that the Inca emperors had only been a clan of mendicants in comparison. This king was literally covered with gold from head to foot, because a golden powder was scattered over him every morning, adhering to his skin with an aromatic resin. Each night, he would wash off the golden covering in the waters of a lake, and since his wardrobe was an inexhaustible goldmine, he would be clad from head to foot again in gold the next morning. The entire kingdom was worthy of the king's apparel: El Dorado, the Golden One, as the Spanish called this fabled king, lived glittering in the midst of a capital—called Manoa—filled with metal palaces. The town covered all of an immense island at the center of the salty Lake Parima, also known as Lake Guatavita, two hundred leagues in length. The walls of the city of Manoa were sheathed in slabs of gold, it was said. At sunrise, the gold would reflect its light so brightly that the entire island glowed in the middle of the lake, appearing to be a second sun rising from the lake waters. Temples and palaces were all sheathed in gold, inside and out. The poor covered the walls of their houses with mere silver. The cobblestones in the streets were diamond; the bed of the lake was carpeted with pearls.

Actually, this mineral chimera seemed no more incredible than the first rumors that had attracted Cortés to Mexico or Pizarro to Peru; and after those two incredible conquests, the Spanish plunderers of American empires were predisposed to credulity. Three months after he took office in high Quito, Gonzalo Pizarro was leaving again, marching eastward at the head of an expedition to find cinnamon and the gilded lakeside king. The expedition comprised 340 Spaniards (according to some chroniclers, 220; the sources differ), four thousand Indios, 150 horses, a thousand ferocious fighting dogs (these had been the conquistadors' secret weapon), a flock of llamas, and a vast herd of pigs, to be eaten along the way.

The first obstacle that the expedition had to overcome was just a few miles out of Quito: the eastern cordillera of the Andes, terribly high passes that could only be reached along goat tracks, swept by icy winds and covered in permanent drifts of snow. More than a hundred men froze to death, nearly all of them Indios. When the expedition headed down the eastern slope of the Andes, they encountered a new obstacle: the intense heat of the lowlands and the relentless tropical rains. They trudged through an interminable deluge that soaked them for six weeks without interruption. They pushed forward through ankle-deep, knee-deep, and finally hip-deep muck, stung by swarms of mosquitoes, chopping their way with machetes through dense vegetation, sleeping on tree branches. As they advanced, they were caught up by a rear guard that had left Quito sometime after them. It was commanded by another warrior from Estremadura, a relative of the Pizarros: Francisco de Orellana, thirty years old at the time, five years younger than his commander Gonzalo.

Gonzalo Pizarro decided to split off from the main body of his men, venturing along a valley that seemed slightly less impracticable and pushing forward with a squadron of about seventy men—all on foot, because the horses sank into the mud up to their bellies—in search of the cinnamon trees. And they found them, too, after many days of marching under the pouring rain: they were beautiful, very tall, they yielded cinnamon of the very finest quality, but they were scattered, few in number, located in a region that was so remote that they could never be harvested profitably. Where were the glittering cities and the gold-dusted king? The infrequent local Indios, when questioned, replied that they had never heard of such a thing.

Gonzalo Pizarro thought that they were lying. Tortured with fire, bitten savagely by the fighting dogs, those hardheaded Indios refused to talk. After watching them die under torture, the furious Spaniards decided to head back toward the main camp and to try to find another route. A few days later, however, when they reached a river bank, they happened upon a small flotilla of canoes heading downstream. The Spaniards stopped the Indios with friendly gestures, offered them knives and combs in exchange for food, and then asked the chief—whose name was Delicola—if he knew anything about these golden marvels hidden somewhere in the endless jungles. Delicola, who must have been nobody's fool and who may have been aware of the torture and death that had been visited upon his countrymen a few days before, understood that the only way out of this situation was to tell the Spaniards what they most wanted to hear: pointing into the distance, eastward, he spoke of the realm of gold. He even showed them a narrow spot where they could easily build a bridge, hoping that they would go away and leave him and his men alone. But when Pizarro heard the long hoped-for description, he felt certain that he was finally on the right path. He ordered the main body of men to join him there. Delicola was taken hostage; he would lead them to El Dorado.

When the rest of the men arrived, the expedition began

marching along the course of the river, which was probably the Coca, a tributary of the Napo. Walking in chains, Delicola and his men led the column. It was a brutal march: every few miles there were deep rushing streams to be forded, swamps to be traversed. Men and horses were swept away or sucked under, Indio porters vanished into marshes under the weight of their loads. There were no natives to ask the way or rob of food. Their provisions exhausted, the Spaniards began to eat their dogs. One day, Delicola and his men managed to escape into the forest. None of the Spaniards or Indios were able to track them through the labyrinthine jungle. How could they continue, without guides or bearers? Pizarro ordered his men to build a boat, and to load the cargo and the sick on board.

It took them days and days. They cut down trees, built a forge, made charcoal, melted down horseshoes to cast nails, used tree sap in place of pitch and old blankets in place of oakum. When the brigantine was finally launched, it sailed along the river while the men advanced on the bank. Food became increasingly scarce, and the land looked more and more deserted as the river grew wider. Delicola had said, vaguely, that the Kingdom of the Golden One began where the river flowed into a larger river.

At this point, Pizarro decided he would turn back with most of the men and retrace his steps two or three days' march. When they reached a less deserted area, they would camp. In the meanwhile, the brigantine, under Orellana's command, would sail downstream until it reached the kingdom of El Dorado. There, with kindness or with force, Orellana was to obtain provisions to bring back to the rest. Then, all together, rested and well fed, they would swoop down to conquest like so many hawks upon their prey.

Orellana set out with fifty-seven men, the strongest and most capable, along with most of the expedition's harquebuses and crossbows. Gonzalo Pizarro and his men waited and waited for his successful return. They ate the last few horses and the last remaining fighting dogs. "They wasted nothing, neither the viscera nor the hides nor any other parts," as one chronicler of the expedition duly noted. At last, impatient and concerned, Gonzalo Pizarro resumed the march along the river, only to discover the path blocked by impenetrable swamps.

And so, when a few native canoes were captured, a small group of men was sent downstream in search of Orellana. The search party returned a week later empty-handed: they had found not a trace of their comrades and no sign of golden cities. Pizarro ordered a second attempt made. This time the search party pushed farther downstream, as far as the long-sought confluence with the Napo River. Once again, nothing. No Spanish soldiers; no gold or buildings. There were small signs that Orellana had passed that way: marks cut into the bark of a tree with a knife. But where was the brigantine? The leader of the search party guessed that perhaps Orellana might have mistaken the Napo for the Coca, and so the party paddled upstream along the Napo for a good distance. They had the good luck to stumble across a large plantation of manioc (or cassava) that had been abandoned by the Indios. The party loaded its canoes with manioc right up to the gunwales and returned to the main encampment, where in the meanwhile their starving comrades—after devouring the last scraps of horse and dog, with side dishes of grass and leaves—had been forced to boil and eat their saddles and whips. Pizarro listened to the reports that arrived along with the life-saving manioc, and decided that Orellana and his party must have either drowned or fallen prey to some native ambush. The brigantine was gone; the men were all dead.

At this point, Gonzalo Pizarro ordered his soldiers to march to the manioc plantation; here at least they were able to eat their fill and recover. Then they marched to the confluence of the two rivers. And there, like a ghost emerging from the tangled jungle, there appeared a gaunt and tattered vision: all that remained of Hernán Sánchez de Vargas, one of the fifty-seven strapping warriors who had set out with Orellana. This was the story that he told: He had been abandoned when all the others, including Orellana, decided it was impossible to sail back upstream to rejoin Pizarro and the main party because of the powerful current. And so they put themselves in the hands of providence and sailed downstream, hoping to reach the ocean. He alone had opposed the plan, and so they had left him to die of hunger in the jungle.

The revelation of that act of base treachery—for that is how Gonzalo Pizarro, and every subsequent historian of the *conquista,* viewed Orellana's decision—unhinged Pizarro's wavering determination. All hope was lost. Nothing remained but to try to get back over the Andes alive.

They marched upstream along the Napo; it seemed to run from the general direction of the cordillera. A small advance party scouted the river by canoe, building a huge signal fire each evening to mark its position, so that the main party, on foot, could reach them. They consumed the remaining store of manioc and the wild fruit that they found in the jungle. "In these conditions they pushed forward, half starving, naked and barefoot, covered with sores, cutting a path with their swords, as it rained endlessly, so that for days on end the sun was obscured and they could not dry themselves. They cursed themselves repeatedly for having placed themselves in this situation, expos[ing] themselves to these privations and hardships, which they could so easily have avoided."

At last they happened upon an Indio village, where they were given a little food, and directions for the shortest way back to Quito. The shortest way, but still anything but easy: more jungle, more swamps, more rivers to bridge and trees to cut down in order to bridge them.

One night, Gonzalo Pizarro dreamed that a dragon was ripping his heart from his chest. He summoned one of his men who had a reputation as an astrologer and soothsayer. This man explained that, once they made it back to Quito, Gonzalo Pizarro would learn that the one he loved best was dead. It was true: his brother, Francisco Pizarro, governor general of Peru, had been assassinated while Gonzalo wandered through the forests.

The odyssey ended in August 1542, two years after it began. The survivors—just a few more than a hundred—hobbled into Quito. One eyewitness recalled: "All of them, the general and the officers and the ordinary soldiers, were half naked, because their clothing had rotted under the constant rainfall, tattered and shredded. The only garments that covered them were animal skins, tied on front and back, and a few headpieces made of the same material. Their swords were scabbard-less, and were scored and pitted by rust. Their feet were bare and pocked with sores and cuts, from stepping on thorns and tree roots. They were all so weak and gaunt that no one would have recognized them."

As for Orellana, perhaps it is fairer to say that he was a victim of circumstance than that he was a traitor. Fra Gaspar de Carvajal, the future archbishop of Lima, was a member of Orellana's party, and he wrote the only firsthand account. According to Carvajal, when Orellana and his party reached the confluence of the Coca River into the Napo River, they found some food in a native village. At this point, the commander of the party had decided to try to get back upstream to Gonzalo Pizarro, but his men came close to mutiny. They had the expedition notary draw up a petition, which they all signed, declaring that it was impossible to fight against the current to get back upstream. Fearing an outright revolt, Orellana yielded to their demands. He offered one thousand gold pieces to any man who might walk back upriver to inform Pizarro of the decision. Three men volunteered to undertake the mission—and to win the cash—but in the end, none of the three actually set out. As for Hernán Sánchez de Vargas being abandoned in the jungle, Carvajal makes no mention of this detail. Did he overlook Vargas because he had been the only witness to a group act of treason, and Carvajal believed (and hoped) that he lay dead in the jungle? Or was it simply that Vargas had straggled and lost his way, and the others, after waiting for him, had set out downstream? We shall never know.

In any case, Orellana replied in writing to the petition signed by his men (forty-nine out of the original fifty-seven). He declared that he was ready, if reluctant, to lead them to safety by another route, and that he would obey their collective will. The only other route available was down the Napo River.

They loaded the boat with more foodstuffs obtained from the Indios, including many turtles, and then set sail. They kept to the center of the river, and eventually the Napo flowed into another much larger river. The banks of this river stood far off on the horizon like an inky shadow. The natives seemed peaceful and hospitable; they landed at one village and decided to build a second brigantine.

In April 1542 they set off once again, this time in two vessels—duly christened the *Victoria* and the *San Pedro*—and then things started going horribly wrong. First and foremost: hunger. This stretch of the river was uninhabited, and the banks were so tangled and steep that it was impossible to land. Fishing was almost impossible. In the end, they had nothing to eat but grass, a bit of flour, and the leather of their belts. Then, when they finally saw some natives again, these proved to be implacably hostile, and they attacked immediately. The Spaniards were forced to fight for their lives, for two days and two nights, as they sailed downstream through a heavily populated and fiercely warlike region.

Then they entered the territory of the Omagua, people who had great quantities of porcelain in their houses, "the finest porcelain that was ever seen in this world, enameled and embellished with all colors, so shiny and gleaming as to astonish the viewer." Here was a good sign, a sign of wealth. The Spaniards thought once again that they might be on the track of the long-sought-after El Dorado. Their hopes redoubled when they learned from the natives that "every object in their houses that was made of clay, inland, in contrast, would be made of gold and silver."

Orellana and his men decided to head toward that glittering inland region. But they had not advanced half a league before the narrow forest tracks that they were following widened and became majestic, arrow-straight boulevards. This sign of an advanced civilization frightened them. They feared that they might come face-to-face with a well-organized imperial army, and they scampered back to the brigantines, to head downstream. They would postpone conquest for some other time.

In the land of Paguana, after they sailed past the mouth of a broad and powerful tributary with water that ran black as ink, they landed at a village where they saw "something absolutely worth seeing": a tree trunk some three yards across, upon which had been carved a city, surrounded by walls, supported by two jaguars. The courteous natives explained that this was a sacred symbol, dedicated to a race of women warriors to whom the village paid tribute in the form of parrot feathers and palm fronds to use as roof thatching.

Further downstream, as they passed by riverbank villages whose inhabitants proved to be increasingly hostile, the Spaniards "suddenly found themselves in the excellent territory and realm of the Amazons."

They found themselves surrounded by canoes loaded with warriors, and though they killed many of them, with harquebus fire and hails of crossbow shot, they were still in clear danger of being overrun. The Indio warriors, midway through the battle, called for help from the Amazons, their mistresses. A dozen of the women warriors came to their assistance, "fighting as if they were in command." According to Carvajal, "These women are very white and tall, and have hair very long and braided and wound about the head, and they are very robust and go about naked, [but] with their privy parts covered, with their bows and arrows in their hands, doing as much fighting as ten Indian men, and indeed there was one woman among those who shot an arrow a span deep into one of the brigantines, and others less deep, so that our brigantines soon looked like porcupines."

As it turned out, the Spaniards succeeded in killing several of those formidable women, whereupon the Indios seemed to lose heart. Seeing, however, that fresh reinforcements were arriving, the judicious Orellana decided that the time had come to break off the battle, and he set off downstream as fast as he could.

The days that followed brought new battles with flotillas of native canoes. It was not until he had made it out of that rich but dangerous stretch of the river that Orellana found time to interrogate a prisoner, and of course he asked him about the Amazon warrior women. The prisoner replied that the Amazons lived, without men, in some seventy villages. Their houses were made of stone, and they had furnishings of gold and silver (surprise, surprise!), they worshiped idols made of gold and silver, they wore jewelry made of gold and silver, they ate off of dishes of gold and silver.

> These women would couple with men from time to time, and when the desire took them, they would assemble a large force and they would set off to wage war against a powerful lord who resided not far away. They would carry off men and hold them captive in their own land as long as they wished, using them to satisfy their desires. When they found that they were pregnant, they would send them back to the villages where they had seized them, without hurting them in any way. Later, when they gave birth, if the babies were male they would kill them, and send the bodies back to their fathers. If the babies were female, they reared them with great solemnity and taught them the art of war. (from *Descubrimiento del Rio de la Amazonas* by Gasper de Carvajal)

Carvajal, a learned man, added that these women should not technically be called Amazons because, though they did fight with bows and arrows, they did not cut off a breast to use them more efficiently, "and in the Greek language, the word 'Amazon' means, she who is without a breast."

After various other adventures among hostile Indios and friendly Indios, at the end of August 1542—roughly while the tattered remnants of Gonzalo Pizarro's army was entering the gates of Quito—

Orellana's two brigantines reached the mouth of that infinite river that the Portuguese had previously called the Maranhao. From that day on, it would be known as Rio de las Amazonas, literally River of the Amazons—the Amazon River.

A few months later, Orellana traveled to Spain to inform Charles V, Holy Roman Emperor and king of Spain (among other titles), of his discoveries, and to defend himself against the accusation of treachery with the evidence of the invaluable documents he carried with him.

He met with a chilly reception, particularly because the river he had traveled entered the sea in Portuguese territory, and international complications were feared. But in the end the Council of the Indies decided that upstream of the river mouth, the Amazon was still free territory. According to Orellana's reports, that territory was quite rich. Orellana was named governor of what was meant to become the Spanish province of Nueva Andalusia and assigned the task of conquering and colonizing the new land.

He set out in May 1545 with four ships, many hundreds of colonists, and the wife he had married back in Spain. The voyage was a disaster: one ship was lost in the mid-Atlantic, the other three actually sailed up the mouth of the Amazon but were wrecked among the river islands. Orellana himself vanished, lost in some recess of the great river; he had been the first to travel its enormous length, and the first to assign it a name and a legend.

3
The Mutinous Conquistador

Twenty years later, the mirage of El Dorado, the Golden One, harvested a new bumper crop of victims.

The tale actually begins in 1559, but the events leading up to it cover the previous decade. The first distant seed of the tale of Lope de Aguirre comes in 1549: a few hundred Indios reached the eastern borders of Peru, following the course of the Huallaga River, the end of a journey that had started at the Atlantic coast, near the mouth of the Amazon River. These few hundred Indios were the sole survivors of a mass migration that had begun two years before. According to some sources, more than ten thousand Indios had set out under the command of their tribal chief, Viraratu, abandoning an overpopulated territory where they were forced constantly to war against neighboring tribes for the scarce food and resources available. Viraratu had decided to take his people in search of a free and welcoming land. They built a fleet of large canoes and began to paddle up the Amazon, but every time they tried to land and settle, they met with fierce opposition from local tribes. In the end, having been thwarted in every attempt to find a new home, they had been forced all the way up the Amazon to Peru, and there they arrived exhausted, their numbers decimated.

In their accounts of their voyage up the Amazon, these Indios described great villages overlooking the river, whose inhabitants possessed gold and silver in great quantities; indeed there were entire streets inhabited by goldsmiths who worked those metals, and they would gladly exchange them for objects made of iron. The survivors even displayed samples: jewelry, necklaces, and bracelets.

These reports revived the nebulous geography of golden empires and kingdoms of women warriors that, in the fervid imagination of the Spaniards who had colonized Peru, filled the unexplored regions of the Great River to the east. Dreams of golden cities along the Amazon had been set aside but not forgotten. Gold fever flared up once again: all the talk was of El Dorado, the Amazons, Omagua, and Manoa. "All of this," wrote one chronicler, Fra Pedro Simón, "so overheated the souls of all those restless men who filled Peru, who were always ready to give credence to idle rumors, that the Viceroy deemed it best to find some way to occupy this great mass of turbulent men."

Indeed, whether he believed in them or not, these dreams of new lands to conquer were extremely convenient for Don Andrés Hurtado de Mendoza, marquis of Cañete, who was then governor of Peru, in the name of the king of Spain. Peru was just emerging from long years of civil war, and the country was still rife with malcontents, misfits, drifters, brigands, and adventurers of every sort. Law and order was constantly threatened by this small army of potential troublemakers, a mass of bloody-minded individuals always ready to unsheath their weapons, too many to be arrested and too riotous to be placated. If it were only possible to enlist them all—or nearly all—in a fine new expedition eastward, through those same jungles that swallowed up the army of Gonzalo Pizarro, spitting out a few tattered bones two years later, then the governor would have successfully rid long-suffering Peru of their annoying presence. And no matter the outcome, the Spanish crown would benefit: either through the elimination of those die-hards, by Indio massacre or tropical disease, or else—if by some fluke they should prove successful—by the addition of another magnificent dominion to the holdings of His Majesty Philip II of Spain. The miscreants, in that case, would become wealthy hidalgos, conquistadors, and heroes of the Spanish empire. Otherwise, they would remain what they were: jailbirds, and, ideally, lost or dead jailbirds.

Governor Mendoza also had just the man to lead the expedition, or at least he thought he did: the young hidalgo, Pedro de Ursua, a thirty-year-old native of Pamplona, a daring son of Navarre who had already covered himself with glory in numerous campaigns conducted with the sort of bloody ferocity that in those days passed for military virtue, campaigns waged against rebellious Indios or mutinous African slaves.

Ursua accepted the command without objections, enthusiastic at the prospect of following in the footsteps of Hernán Cortés and Francisco Pizarro, and flattered by the parchments covered with flowing script that named him governor of the realms of Omagua and El Dorado, pending conquest. He immediately published the calls for recruitment, and they were welcomed with unanimous fervor by the very scum of Peru.

Among the new recruits was a man who was to become the damned soul of the expedition, usurping and perverting its goals and final destination: Lope de Aguirre, variously remembered as Aguirre "the tyrant," Aguirre "the madman," the bull's-eye target of all the invective and scorn of every chronicler of the tragic events that were to ensue.

The physical and psychic portrait drawn of him by one of his fellow adventurers clearly depicts a latter-day Caligula of the Indies, waiting only for the opportunity to perpetrate every sort of infamy:

> He was short in stature, average in appearance, with an ugly face, small and emaciated; his eyes, when he stared at something or someone, would glitter in his face, espe-

> cially if he was angry. When he was in the company of others, he was turbulent and resolute; he could readily withstand hard work, and especially lack of sleep; rarely was he seen to sleep, save only for a few moments by day, at night he was always found awake. He could march for hours carrying enormous burdens, he was capable of wearing and bearing numerous arms, often he wore two coats of chainmail, a sword, and a dagger, a harquebus or a lance, and at times a breastplate as well. By his nature, he was an enemy of the good and the virtuous; he looked unfavorably on any expression of holiness or virtue; he was a friend and henchman to any man who was wicked, vile, or infamous; the more you were thieving, criminal, or cruel, the more he would be your friend. He was always cunning, deceitful, treacherous, and fraudulent; it rarely happened that he would tell the truth, and he would never keep a promise, save by miracle. He was given to vice, the pleasures of the flesh, and greed; he was often drunk. He was a bad Christian, perhaps a Lutheran heretic or even worse; indeed, he would commit the crimes that we have mentioned above, such as murdering priests, monks, women, and innocent men, and he would never confess these sins, even when urged to do so. He was accustomed to recommending his soul to the Devil; he entrusted to Lucifer as well his entire body and person—his legs, his arms, and even his genitalia. He could not open his mouth without rejecting the Lord and all His Saints. He never spoke well of anyone, not even of his friends.

This filthy and sleepless fount of profanity, armed to the teeth—more a character from a Gothic tale than from the chronicles of the *conquista*—was about fifty years old when he responded to Ursua's call for recruits, with a rich career of brutality behind him. He had fought in all the civil wars that had bathed Peru in blood, he had served as assistant executioner under Gonzalo Pizarro, and he had earned the sobriquet of El Loco, the Madman.

In 1548, having exploited a group of Indios beyond the standards of even the conquistadors, he was sentenced by Alcalde Esquivel to a whipping of two hundred blows, an infamy for the gentleman that he claimed to be and technically was. He stoically took his punishment, but he swore vengeance. For three years and four months, he followed Esquivel implacably, tracking him down wherever he might take refuge: from Lima to Quito, from Quito to Cuzco, until he saw his opportunity and seized it, stabbing the former alcalde, or mayor, to death in his home. A cold-blooded killing: when he realized that he had left his hat lying next to his enemy's corpse, he went back and got it.

This at least is the version recorded by the historian Garcilaso de la Vega, who wrote long afterward; it may well have been just another black legend concocted after the fact.

Ursua took a couple of years to gather men and materials. He was well aware of the terrible experiences of his predecessor Gonzalo Pizarro, and he decided to travel only by water. He set up a boatyard on the banks of the Huallaga River and sent ahead carpenters and blacksmiths to build an entire fleet: eleven vessels, small and large. He finally set out from Lima in September 1559 with four hundred Spaniards, five hundred horses, two thousand Indios, and a number of women. Two of the women were to be protagonists—and victims—of the most tragic episodes of the expedition: Lope de Aguirre's young mestiza daughter and the lovely Doña Inés de Atienza, Pedro de Ursua's lover.

When the numerous brigade reached the banks of the Huallaga, ready to take ship and start downstream, it was discovered that most of the vessels had already rotted and were no longer riverworthy, in part because of the hot, damp climate, or because of the poor quality of lumber used in their construction, or else because of the sheer incompetence of the boat builders themselves. They were forced to build rafts, which finally set out in September 1560, heading downriver to the confluence of the Huallaga with the Marañon, which, after receiving the waters of the tributaries Ucayali and Napo, swelled and broadened, becoming the Amazon River.

Ursua soon proved himself a despotic and incapable leader; the combination of arrogance and lack of skill quickly generated discontent among the already undisciplined mass, and a lurking mutinous bent came quickly to the surface, even more quickly than it might have at the hands of more capable leadership.

The provisions were inadequate, and after months and months of navigation through regions lacking food and, more significantly, the slightest hints of wealth, the men began to mutter, accusing Ursua of spending all his time making love to the alluring Doña Inés instead of working to ensure the success of the expedition. Word spread that Doña Inés was the true commander of the expedition and that the fate of the most outstanding warriors of Peru depended on the caprices of a harlot.

When they reached Omagua, where they had expected to find gold and silver by the shovelful, they found miserable huts thatched with palm fronds, inhabited by hostile paupers. Ursua gave the order to establish a solid encampment where they could wait for the end of the rainy season; from there they could push inland, toward one probable site of El Dorado. Now the mutinous sentiment grew: those proud conquistadors, all hidalgos or would-be hidalgos, "coming as they did from Peru, which is one of the richest and most fertile lands on earth, were far more willing to stuff themselves with bread and meat than they were to work hard."

The mutiny finally broke out on New Year's Eve of 1561: the incompetent and now openly despised Ursua was murdered by a group of conspirators in his hut; within hours all of his few faithful supporters lay dead as well. "Long live the king, death to the tyrant," cried the mutineers; and in the name of the king of Spain they elected a new governor in the person of Fernando de Guzmán, a lightweight aristocrat, clearly a pawn and a puppet. According to the accounts given by the eyewitnesses—all of them with reasons to cast as much responsibility as possible upon him—the true mastermind of the mutiny had been Lopo de Aguirre. He received a promotion and was named *maestro de campo*.

Shortly thereafter, Guzmán ordered that a document be drawn up addressed to the king—all the conquistadors had a thing about setting down even their most objectionable deeds on paper—justifying Ursua's murder with instances of his incompetence and stating the expedition's determination to continue the search for El Dorado. Aguirre, signing the document ironically, "Aguirre the Traitor," explained to his naïve comrades that the document would do little to help them. You are all outlaws now, he told them; King Philip II of Spain would never forgive them for their mutiny, and as for El Dorado, quite simply, it did not exist and never had. Or to be more precise: El Dorado did exist, but it was the land they had left behind them, Peru, rich in gold and silver, abounding in "bread, wine, meat, and pretty women." And so, said Aguirre, instead of suffering like fools in these "savage and deserted" lands, it would be best to complete the rebellion they had already irrevocably set in motion by seizing Peru and declaring independence from their sovereign.

Aguirre must have had at least some formidable qualities, for he succeeded in gradually persuading the majority of the men to accept his audacious plan. On March 23 the figurehead Guzmán was proclaimed prince of Peru, and a new document was drawn up in which they all declared that they no longer recognized Philip II as their lord and master.

While the newly elected prince indulged in simple-minded vainglory, demanding that he be served with frills and flounces as befitted his rank and distributing impressive titles to the various lands of South America that awaited easy conquest, Aguirre was leading the expedition. They were no longer heading toward the mouth of the Amazon; they were now directed northward, crossing the Equator and entering the basin of the Orinoco River by means of the Casiquiari River, that remarkable watercourse that connects the two great rivers via the Rio Negro, tributary of the Amazon. Aguirre took this uncharted route by instinct, and to his great good fortune. All he wanted was the shortest way to the Atlantic Ocean and, miraculously, he found it in that labyrinth of waterways.

In the meanwhile, chaos reigned in the expedition. They had launched a revolution and, like all revolutions, this one began to devour its children. No one trusted anyone else, everyone was conspiring against everyone else. Aguirre, however, defended by a zealously faithful bodyguard comprising some fifty harquebusiers, Basque just as he was, always proved to be the strongest, as he skillfully played off one against the other. Perhaps it was simply that he had a single clear idea.

In any case, Aguirre eliminated all his enemies, one by one, before they could eliminate him. Guzmán's lieutenants were the first to go; the next to be killed was Prince Guzmán himself, before he could take revenge for his slaughtered henchmen. Then the beautiful Doña Inés was killed, perhaps because her presence was causing conflict among the men, all anxious to be her next lover. Many simple soldiers, their names lost to history, were killed along the way. The village in which most of these murders were committed was dubbed Pueblo de la Matanza, Village of the Bloodbath.

It seems that at a certain point the wholesale slaughter even took on connotations of an early class war, *avant la lettre.* Aguirre, recounts one chronicler, "decided that he would no longer have with him gentlemen or respectable folk, and so he slaughtered all who fit that description; he took with him only ordinary soldiers, leaving behind all the Spanish women and the sick."

This Robespierre in armor, at the head of a floating republic, occupied the island of Margarita in what are now Venezuelan waters as the first step on his march back to Peru; then he evacuated it after forty days of sacking and plunder, and the murder of all the local authorities.

Aguirre's original plan seems to have been to return to Peru via

Panama; but he then changed direction, landing in present-day Venezuela and seizing the city of Valencia; the inhabitants all fled in terror.

From Valencia he sent a letter to King Philip II. This document has often been interpreted as clear proof of his madness; some scholars have called it a first indistinct and chaotic cry of liberty and independence for the Americas. The sovereign of Spain and the Indies probably never read it.

At last, even though by now he could probably sense that things were collapsing around him, Aguirre marched from Valencia to Barquisimeto. As he marched, however, his men began to abandon him, lured away by the promise of amnesty to all those who surrendered. Aguirre was surrounded by loyal Spanish troops; with the excuse that they were going in search of water, his men disappeared one by one. In the end, only one man remained at his side, Anton Llamoso by name. Bitterly, Aguirre asked him why he had not deserted like the others. Llamoso replied simply that they had been friends while alive, and that they would die together.

Then El Loco performed his last deed, not entirely devoid of a certain dreadful majesty. He entered his daughter's room and told her: "Commend yourself to God, daughter of mine, for I am about to kill you, that you may not be pointed at with scorn, or wind up in the power of any who might call you the daughter of a traitor." With those words, he ran her through with his sword.

Shortly thereafter, soldiers broke into the room and took him alive. He had attempted to fire at them with a harquebus, but then he let the weapon fall from his hands and collapsed on a bed across from the bed in which his dead daughter lay.

He was executed on the spot, at the insistence of his own late followers, who feared that if he stood trial, he might reveal details about their own misdeeds. They executed him themselves, forming a firing squad with their harquebuses. His dead body was then decapitated and quartered; the parts of the corpse were sent to various parts of Spanish America, to serve as a warning and an example.

4
The Man Who Met the Amazons

When Aguirre and his desperadoes, after miraculously emerging from the watery Amazonian labyrinth, raised the banner of open mutiny by first occupying the island of Margarita and then landing on the mainland to begin their march of conquest on Peru, frantic messengers were sent hastily up and over the slopes of the Andes to bring the frightening news to the imperial authorities. In the town of Santa Fe de Bogotá, capital of Nueva Grenada (which he had founded many years before), the now elderly conquistador Gonzalo Jiménez de Quesada had hurriedly organized a small army with which he planned to venture down to the lowlands and confront the mutinous Aguirre.

Quesada had his own personal reasons for resentment against Aguirre, but more specifically against the expedition led by Ursua, which had culminated in a senseless bloodbath. He, too, back in 1557, had officially petitioned His Majesty Philip II to authorize him to set out in search of El Dorado. Quesada had been profoundly offended by the royal preference shown to the young gentleman who had led a valuable expedition to death and catastrophic failure.

The small army that Quesada had assembled to fight Aguirre

proved unnecessary, because Aguirre had been executed and dismembered before it could enter into action. Still, Quesada's prompt action was reported to the king, and the aged conquistador's forgotten petition was taken out of the files to be reconsidered.

Philip II, nicknamed El Rey Prudente, was slow and cautious in his decision-making. Many years went by before the long-awaited response arrived from Spain. It was not until 1568, when Quesada was seventy years old, that he was named governor of El Dorado, with the provision that he should conquer the region that would bear that name, extending for a thousand miles, bounded on the south by the Caquetá River, which runs athwart of the Equator and, broadening, becomes the river Japurá River, flowing in turn into the great Amazon River; and on the north by the Pauto River, which forms part of the Orinoco basin. This vast region is nowadays known as the Llanos of Colombia and Venezuela.

Quesada's renown and his glorious past—as well as the eternal thirst for gold, of course—attracted numerous volunteers, most of them veterans who had previously served under Quesada. The commander, as one chronicler nastily observed, "was so addled by endless fantasizing about El Dorado, the Golden One, that his faculties were practically blunted; indeed, he fell victim to one of the most remarkable delusions ever to obsess the mind of a lunatic in the history of the world." In short, a Don Quixote in his dotage, leading an army of feeble, white-haired veterans. Many of Quesada's men were even older than he.

The army set out in April 1569. It was comprised of four hundred men, a great many women, and various numbers of Indios, black slaves, horses, cows, pigs, sheep, and goats. They marched slowly, not so much because of the generally advanced age, but to keep pace with the unhurried gait of the livestock.

They marched gradually out of the mountains and foothills and on into the lowland prairies, walking day after day through the infinite expanse of tall, dry grass. It was the dry season, and a carelessly watched campfire spread into the grass. The expedition was almost instantly surrounded and beset by a raging prairie fire. Though surrounded by flames, the treasure-seekers survived, miraculously unhurt. The powder kegs, however, exploded, and the expedition's harquebuses became useless.

On they marched, on and on, into the dun-colored distance, marching blindly through an ocean of grass reaching high over their heads, tormented by what seemed like every biting insect in the world. At night, bats descended out of the darkness, vampire bats that sucked the blood of the livestock and did their best to get human blood as well, biting the noses and fingers and toes of the sleeping questers. On they marched, all suffering equally, counting their dead every morning before moving on. They marched ahead through the vegetal emptiness, at the end of which they were supposed to find El Dorado. But there was no end, and when their desperation prevailed over their dreams, they finally turned around and went home. At the end of 1572, Bogotá welcomed back the survivors: twenty-five Spaniards, four Indios, about twenty gaunt horses, ribs plainly visible. The aged Quesada spent his few remaining years writing his autobiography. He was "penniless and oppressed by debts." He left those debts to his last surviving relative, his niece, Doña Maria, and with them, the title of governor of El Dorado, which could be inherited, by royal decree, provided that the heirs committed to continuing the quest for the Golden One.

Doña Maria lived in Spain, where she had married the hidalgo Antonio de Berrio y Oruña, who had distinguished himself in the recent European wars. Once they received Quesada's dubious bequest, the couple set out for Nueva Grenada with their eight children (six daughters and two sons), and arrived in Bogotá in 1580.

Berrio was no spring chicken himself: he had been born in 1520, and was therefore sixty years old when he began the search for his golden inheritance, a realm of thousands upon thousands of square miles of land that no one had ever laid eyes upon, but that every one talked about. Indeed they talked too much, and everything they said was contradictory. Berrio, in contrast, was a single-minded man. He began by ruling out all the regions that had been explored by previous expeditions. They had all returned empty-handed. What remained was a territory as large as Spain, between the Llanos and the mouth of the Orinoco; opinions about this region varied as well. "Some say that this land is awash in waters, dotted with lakes and lagoons; others say that there are great and prosperous kingdoms here, imagining that El Dorado is here, where they say that there are marvelous things to be found," wrote one geographer of the time. Berrio, a tenacious explorer, roamed widely through that promising blank portion depicted in maps of the New World; he never found anything, but by some perverse trick of destiny, or perhaps due to his own endless gullibility, he continually met people who supplied him with abundant information on El Dorado. Each new informer pointed him in a new and different direction. Toward the end of all his wanderings, which lasted from 1584 until 1590, the possible location of El Dorado had shifted to the southeast, near the source of the Caroni River, a southern tributary of the Orinoco that flowed northward from the heights of the Sierra Pacaraima. This time, Berrio felt certain that he had found the right place, especially because of his meeting with a Spaniard named Martín de Albujar who claimed actually to have visited Manoa, the capital of El Dorado. He was a soldier who had been captured by Indios during an expedition in 1576. He had lived with them as a prisoner for ten years, until he finally managed to escape.

As if the astounding true adventures that he had actually experienced were not sufficient, Albujar felt called upon to tell a story of having been marched all the way to Manoa, blindfolded so that he would not know the way. His captors removed his blindfold as he stood poised to enter the gates of the city; it then took him a full day and a half to walk through the city as far as the royal palace, where he was given comfortable lodgings and treated well. There he remained for seven months, until he told his captors that he wished to return home. The king not only immediately granted his wish, but also gave him a parting gift of a huge trove of gold, with native porters to carry it home for him. As soon as they had reached the banks of the river, unfortunately, the wicked river Indios had stolen it all.

Like his predecessor Quesada, Berrio needed to believe, and believe Martín de Albujar's story he did. A few years later, pure happenstance brought him and his beliefs into contact with another European gentleman who was just as obsessed with chimerical American treasures: Sir Walter Raleigh.

Raleigh's fortunate career was said to have begun many years before with a renowned deed of gallant chivalry: he had supposedly spread his cape across a puddle to keep Queen Elizabeth I of England from muddying her shoes. If this well-known story was not true, as the phrase goes, it ought to have been. In any case, Raleigh had somehow won his queen's favor, and he soon enjoyed a privileged status at court. But Raleigh was much more than a brilliant courtier: he was a man of great and versatile genius, a farsighted politician, a talented and subtle poet and author. He had undertaken numerous successful military expeditions against the Spanish; he had founded the first English colonies in North America, in the territory of Virginia that he had named after Elizabeth, the Virgin Queen. Then he had fallen out of royal favor when he secretly married Lady Elizabeth Throckmorton, one of Queen Elizabeth's royal maids of honor ("my dull ladies," as she called them). He had been imprisoned for several weeks in the Tower of London, until he won his release.

In 1595, he appeared with a fleet of four ships off the Venezuelan island of Trinidad, and swiftly occupied it. England was at war with Spain, and Raleigh hoped to return to royal favor through a successful military enterprise. But on Trinidad he found even more than he had hoped for: He captured Berrio and, with him, El Dorado. An El Dorado of words: Berrio told Raleigh everything he knew, and a great deal that he did not know at all, but that he imagined or hoped. Raleigh, in turn, wrote and wrote. When he returned to London, after having sailed some distance up the Orinoco delta, daring the "river's wrath" without finding anything more than reptiles and insects, he published a book with a clearly propagandistic title: *The Discoverie of the Large, Rich, and Bewtiful Empyre of Guiana, with a relation of the great and Golden Citie of* Manoa *(which the Spanyards call* El *Dorado).* The book was published with a handsome map of the labyrinthine Lake Parima, on the shores of which stood the fabulous capital, "that for the greatnes, for the riches, and for the excellent seate, it farre exceedeth any of the world." Now the goal of Raleigh's life was to return to conquer this empire for his queen. But Elizabeth died in 1603, and Raleigh quickly fell into disgrace with the new king, James I. Before long he was back in prison, and this time he remained in the Tower for thirteen long years. He passed the time writing a history of the world. In 1616, the king finally yielded to his entreaties and his lavish promises to bring ships laden with gold from Guiana. Raleigh was freed and given command of the long-awaited expedition that would give England a colonial empire ten times as rich as Mexico and Peru put together. But the king also gave him extremely strict instructions: he was absolutely forbidden to harm a hair on the head of any Spanish subject or to damage any Spanish possession. James I was interested in gold, but he also wished to keep the peace.

The task was impossible: how could Raleigh hope to penetrate into the interior of the continent without overcoming the certain opposition of the troops at the various Spanish forts guarding the coast? Sure enough, when the ten English ships sailed into the Orinoco delta, sending out launches to row up the course of the river as far as the confluence with the Caroni, and then up that river to reach El Dorado and the fabulous trove of gold, they soon found their way blocked by the little fort of San Tomé. They had no choice; they attacked and overwhelmed the Spanish fort. They needn't have bothered: there were no riches of any sort, there or anywhere along the course of the Caroni, and when the launches returned to the flagship after a month and a half, it was immediately evident to the anxious Raleigh that the enterprise was a failure.

Worse than a failure: Raleigh's son, Wat Raleigh, had been killed in the attack on the fort of San Tomé.

The fleet sailed home practically empty-handed, carrying only two pathetic gold ingots found in the smoking ruins of the fort. Raleigh stubbornly insisted that they were samples of the treasures of Manoa. In the meantime, the king of Spain had already lodged vociferous protests over the wanton destruction of his American holdings. King James was implacable; perhaps he had even hoped for this outcome. Sir Walter Raleigh was accused and tried for piracy and treason. Found guilty, he was beheaded on the morning of October 29, 1618, after greeting, "smiling and perfectly composed," the many lords of the realm who had come to witness his execution.

Still, the book he had written continued to make men dream. Two years after Raleigh's harsh death, one of his officers, Captain Roger North, who had taken part in the expedition up the Caroni River, made an attempt to take El Dorado by surprise by sailing up the Amazon. The official purpose of the expedition was not to find Manoa, but rather to establish a colony of 120 aspiring New World farmers, Englishmen and Irishmen together. Among the Irishmen was an enterprising youth named Bernard O'Brien, son of a Catholic gentleman whose lands and money had been confiscated as punishment for taking part in a revolt against the English occupiers in 1595. Bernard had come to the Americas to seek his fortune, in hope of regaining the family lands. He had read everything about the equatorial region that he could lay his hands on, and he believed that the hidden empire so highly praised by Raleigh must lie somewhere to the north of the great river.

Leading an expedition of sixteen men—twelve Irishmen and four Englishmen—O'Brien arranged to be landed at a point that the natives called Pataui, that is, "Coconut Grove." The local natives were members of the Sipinipoia tribe, and they soon proved friendly, especially because the colonists were generous gift-givers and gladly used their terrifying harquebuses to fight the Sipinipoias' enemies. "By so doing," wrote O'Brien, "I won their devotion, and they felt obliged to cultivate tobacco and cotton for us, as well as to supply us with food and beverages."

Still, a small plantation lost somewhere in the vast South American wilderness was not what the daring Irishman had been dreaming of. He had completely mastered the local language, and his Sipinipoia friends assured him of the existence of the Amazons, and they agreed to accompany him on a quest to find these fabled women warriors upriver. Fifty Sipinipoias and five harquebusiers joined him aboard four enormous canoes, and they paddled upstream for hundreds of miles. Every time they met a new tribe, O'Brien hired one of them as an interpreter, and so they advanced, slowly but peacefully, until at last O'Brien understood that he had reached the long-sought goal. At last, a tribe of Indios showed him the way to a large island, possibly in the Lake of Erepecu, where a queen ruled, not a king. They called her Cuña Muchu, which meant Great Lady; and O'Brien, who was practically jumping out of his skin in his impatience, asked one of the Indios who was accompanying him to take the queen the finest gifts O'Brien possessed. Though these gifts were nothing more than a mirror and a shirt made of Dutch cloth, they must have made a good impression. The queen agreed to receive him.

And so Bernard O'Brien, Irish gentleman, presented himself at the court of the Amazon queen, the first and only European ever to enjoy that coveted honor. It should have been a memorable conversation, but apparently it was no more than a conventional exchange of compliments and bromides. According to O'Brien's own account, the meeting sounded like nothing more exciting than an afternoon visit with a seldom-seen aunt in Cork. "She asked me if I had sent the gifts, and I assured her that I had indeed. Then she asked what I wanted, and I said that I wanted peace and permission to travel through her realm and trade with her people. She said that she would grant my requests, and in exchange for my gifts, she gave me three of her slave girls. I gave her a shirt to wear; it looked very noble on her. After a week, I asked permission to leave, promising to return, and she and her vassals expressed great sadness at my departure."

Was that all? No, O'Brien insisted on adding that he had seen decisive proof that he had visited the legendary Amazons: during his stay, he had seen only women; there was not a man to be seen. Moreover, those women had "vestigial right breasts, not much bigger than that of a man, artificially shrunken in order to shoot better with bow and arrow. Their left breasts, in contrast, were entirely normal, like the breasts of European women."

The expedition decided to venture no farther westward because the Indios appeared hostile, and so they marched upstream along one of the great tributaries of the Amazon, either the Trombetas or the Paru de Oeste, which flowed out of the exact region where Raleigh's Golden One was said to rule. Having crossed over the watershed without so much as a glimpse of gold, they marched down along the Suriname River until they reached the Atlantic Ocean. They completed their trip by returning to Pataui via the Amazon River.

O'Brien went back to Ireland in 1624 and, good son that he was, he spent most of the money that he had managed to earn in Amazonia to buy a pardon for his father who lay in prison. He was, however, able to repurchase only a sixth of the family lands that had been confiscated. This restless soul set off immediately in search of new adventures: "I wanted to see new lands, and I traveled to Denmark, Muscovy, Poland, Germany, Italy, and Portugal."

In 1629, he was back on the Amazon River, though in the meanwhile the Portuguese, who would not countenance outsiders on what they considered their river, had destroyed Pataui.

O'Brien built a new fort, gathered his friends, the Sipinipoias, and fought the Portuguese. He finally had to admit defeat, and agreed to terms of surrender that the Portuguese swore to on a copy of the Holy Gospels. The victors immediately broke the terms, stripping the vanquished of all their possessions and killing those who resisted. O'Brien himself was thrown into chains for a year, and then exiled to live with a tribe said to be practitioners of cannibalism. Clearly, the Portuguese hoped to see him wind up in a cookpot, but the Irishman was more resourceful than they knew. He won over the cannibals, teaching them "a better way of life"; unfortunately he writes nothing more on the subject, and so we are left to wonder at what marvelous adventures and close escapes he experienced.

In 1634, he made his way back to Europe, bringing with him the son of a tribal chief. Once he set foot back in the Old World, he sent a petition to King Philip IV of Spain—who was also king of Portugal—requesting compensation for the treatment he had suffered at the hands of the sovereign's subjects back in Brazil. He received no reply, but the document remains in the files of the General Archives of the Indies, in Seville. And so, three and a half centuries later, we can read an account of an Irishman who lived among the mythical *cuñantensecuima,* the "women without husbands," as the natives called them.

5
Measuring the Earth

In 1719, the French army was laying siege to the Spanish fortress of Roses, which blocked the road through Catalonia to Girona. Among the French troops was a baby-faced officer experiencing combat for the first time, a daredevil eighteen-year-old named Charles Marie de La Condamine. So indifferent to danger was this young officer that he would openly expose himself to enemy fire, wearing a garish and easily discernible scarlet cape. In time, the Spanish gunners learned to seek out the bright red speck, using him as a handy point of reference as they calibrated their cannon fire. When de La Condamine's superiors complimented him for his courage but begged him to refrain from risking his life for no good reason, the young officer explained that he was simply indulging his scientific curiosity. He wanted to determine precisely how long it would take the Spanish artillery to adjust their aim. *Curiosity* is the word that best summarizes the life and the personality of the future scientist de La Condamine. Indeed, his curiosity gave rise to a substantial body of legendary anecdotes; nowadays it is hard to tell fact from exaggeration with regard to de La Condamine.

Among the choicest stories: Once, in Constantinople, de La

Condamine witnessed the administration of a particularly harsh Ottoman torture, the bastinado, which consisted of caning the soles of the feet of a number of miserable paupers guilty of various minor crimes. Curious to know whether the bastinado was as painful as he had been told, de La Condamine walked into a shop, ostentatiously pilfered some piece of bric-a-brac, and was pleased to find himself sentenced to twenty-five blows.

In Paris, in the salon of Madame de Choiseul, de La Condamine's hostess was seated at her ecritoire penning a letter. Stealthily rising from his easy chair and peering over the shoulder of the grande dame as she wrote, he made out the words: "I would tell you more on the subject, but just now Monsieur de La Condamine is reading every word that I write." "Oh, Madame de Choiseul," he exclaimed, "your suspicions are unjustified. I assure you, I was not reading at all!"

At the public execution of Damiens—who attempted to assassinate King Louis XV and had been sentenced to quartering by four horses, one tied to each limb and then whipped off at a gallop—de La Condamine tried to pass himself off as one of the executioner's assistants in order to observe from a closer vantage point. The other assistants unmasked the infiltrator, and were about to hustle him back into the crowd. "Let him watch, gentlemen, let him watch!" cried the executioner. "He is an enthusiast!"

In the end, as we might well have expected, de La Condamine's curiosity cost him his life, though only at the ripe age of seventy-three. Learning that a young surgeon was offering to perform a novel and terribly risky operation for the first time that was a potential cure for one of the infirmities that plagued the elderly scientist, he volunteered as a subject and died under the scalpel.

This man, remembered as an emblem of the *Siècle des Lumières,* or Enlightenment, would stop at nothing to join the expedition sent to the Equator by the French Academy of Science in order to determine the true shape of the Earth.

Sir Isaac Newton had set forth the theory that the planet was slightly flattened at the North and South Poles and bulged at the Equator. The French astronomer Jean-Jacques Cassini, the high priest of the French scientific establishment, disagreed. The Earth, maintained Cassini, was a spheroid elongated toward the Poles and slightly concave at the Equator, like "a man with a fat belly who has tightened his belt at the waist." The controversy grew protracted and, in time, bitter. Cassini sought proof: he sent the young Jean Richer to Guyana (c. five degrees north latitude) in search of evidence. Richer brought a pendulum-driven clock with him to determine whether the clock would run more quickly at that equatorial latitude. Instead, Richer reported, the pendulum swung more slowly, which supported Newton's hypothesis. Instead of accepting the results of the experiments, Cassini flew into a rage and insulted Richer, calling him a liar and a traitor.

The French Academy of Science decided to resolve the question once and for all. In 1734, it organized two major expeditions: one, commanded by Maupertuis, would travel to Lapland, the closest accessible point to the Arctic Polar Circle. The other would travel to New Spain, to the Equator.

The equatorial expedition was comprised of ten persons: the astronomer Pierre Bouguer, the mathematician Louis Godin, Godin's cousin, Jean Godin des Odonais, Captain Verguin of the French navy, the artist and draughtsman Morainville, the botanist de Jussieu, the surgeon and physician Senièrgues, the clockmaker Hugot, a Monsieur Mabillon and a Monsieur Couplet, and the tirelessly curious de La Condamine, who had contributed a sizable sum out of his own pocket toward the cost of the expedition in order to be allowed to participate.

The expedition set sail in May 1735 from La Rochelle aboard a French warship; in November they landed at Cartagena de las Indias, in what was then the viceregal province of Nueva Grenada. Here they were joined by two Spanish colleagues, the mathematicians Don Jorge Juan y Santacilia and Don Antonio de Ulloa. Together they set out for Puerto Bello—a port town that had been, notoriously, pillaged and burned to the ground by the famous pirate Henry Morgan—and from there traveled upriver along the Chagres, by canoe, to the far side of the isthmus of Panama. Covering the last stretch of the journey by mule, they reached the town of Panama, another illustrious victim of Morgan's rampage. In Panama, they were forced to wait several months, until late February of the following year, when a Spanish vessel finally set sail, bearing the expedition southward, toward the Equator, docking in the harbor of Manta. In the distance the scientists could see the towering peaks of the immense cordillera, or mountain chain, of the Andes.

The expedition had reached the Audiencia of Quito, but the final destination was still far away, high atop the distant mountains. Two members of the expedition, Bouguer and de La Condamine, detested each other from the ground up. The pair had quarreled furiously about everything from the day they met, for the simple reason that Bouguer was a straitlaced and pedantic moralist while de La Condamine was a carefree libertine, a coddled product of the Parisian salons. Imagine their mutual surprise, then, when they agreed that they alone would stay in Manta. The place struck them as an ideal spot in which to begin surveying and triangulating. They were both wrong: they had failed to take into account the almost constant fog. They discovered their mistake too late, because the other members of the expedition had already set sail for Guayaquil, and from there would proceed up the cordillera to reach Quito.

Amid incessant bickering, the pair began their astronomical observations and pendulum experiments; but the eternal mist made it practically impossible to see the sun by day and the stars by night. De La Condamine suggested moving north to the Equator itself, some seventy miles away. After the inevitable dispute, Bouguer agreed. They loaded the delicate scientific instruments onto mules and set off, accompanied by the Indio guides provided by the viceroy. They traveled through the cactus of the coastal desert, along shorelines broken by the skeletons of whales and sea lions, until they reached Cape Pasado, or Cabo Pasado (perhaps thirty miles south of the Equator), where they stayed for two weeks. It was an earthly inferno: miserable food, vicious biting insects, cockroaches and red ants that devoured the provisions, mosquitoes, bloodsucking flies, bees that worked their way into one's hair, fleas that dug under the flesh between one's toes and laid eggs. This daily torment was hardly designed to calm the nerves or spread balm on the hostility between the two scientists. Finally, one night, amid the infinite silence of those equatorial latitudes, they heard the sound of horses approaching. There were three horsemen; they came to a halt and one horseman leapt to earth, executing a perfect courtly bow. At the sight, de La Condamine lowered the cocked pistol that he was aiming at the horseman's head, positive that these were bandits. It emerged that the courtly horseman was His Excellency Pedro Vicente Maldonado y Sotomayor, governor of the city of Esmeraldas, who had traveled all this way to place himself "at their service."

De La Condamine could not have imagined a more welcome visitor, because Don Pedro was the New World doppelgänger of de La Condamine himself. Don Pedro was driven by an insatiable curiosity. He spoke French, Spanish, and Quechua; he had studied at the Jesuit College of Quito; he was an accomplished mathematician; he had drawn the best map available of his province; lastly, he had built a road from a point on the shore of the Esmeraldas River all the way to Quito, reutilizing an ancient, pre-Columbian track. Don Pedro suggested that the two Frenchmen use this road to reach Quito, the capital of the Audiencia, instead of the long and roundabout way through Guayaquil. Old World curiosity immediately found an affinity with New World curiosity. Don Pedro and de La Condamine became instant friends. The disagreeable Bouguer freed them of his presence by choosing to take the Guayaquil route, of course, and the two new friends instead set off for Esmeraldas.

The town was populated by Africans, survivors and the descendants of survivors of the wreck of a slave ship fifty years previous. They loved their governor, they were unfailingly cheerful, and it was with laughter and song that a party of townspeople launched a small fleet of dugouts to ferry Don Pedro and his guest upstream along the Esmeraldas River. As they traveled, de La Condamine took advantage of the time they spent on shore to venture into the sub-Andean jungle that lined the river, and there he discovered many things: a gummy sap that bubbled out of cuts made in a tree called the caoutchouc; emerald mines; the remains of a long-forgotten civilization of giants, the *colorados* Indians, whose bodies were smeared with red pigment; a strange metal, neither gold nor silver, called platinum. When the river ceased being navigable, the party continued on foot through the muggy jungle, until they finally emerged into the Andean foothills. They continued to climb, struggling uphill as the cool air became chilly and then intensely cold, and their ears began to ring, their heads began to spin, and their breath came in short, shallow puffs. Upward they continued, until they reached an altitude of thirteen thousand feet. They topped the crest of the Andes, and at last they headed downhill into a high valley, where they found pasturage and tilled fields. Here they were able to buy horses, and comfortably, on horseback, they at last entered Quito.

De La Condamine's colleagues had arrived some time earlier, and they had been welcomed with full honors. They roundly deserved such honor, for they were "measurers of the Earth," a description that sounded vaguely of sorcery, not only to the Indios of the town but also to the many Spanish colonists. And as soon as the scientists set to work, scaling icy cliffs and wandering off over remote high plains with their newfangled instruments, the general astonishment and admiration began to be veined with suspicion and fear. Before long, the entire Audiencia of Quito began to believe that the enigmatic outlanders were actually searching for the treasure trove of the Inca. Even the new governor became distrustful of the French scientists; unfortunately, the former governor, who had accorded them a triumphal welcome, had been replaced. The new governor began to hinder their work, sending guards to keep an eye on the supposed treasure-hunters at all times, secretly questioning the Indios who were serving them. In the end, the scientists decided to send a message to the viceroy in distant Lima, a thousand miles south. They sent none other than de La Condamine, together with Don Jorge Juan y Santacilia, and the grueling journey was a delight to him: it afforded him a chance to see Peru. Don Jorge and de La Condamine returned eight months later, with letters from the viceroy ordering the governor to stop interfering with their work. The measurement of the Earth resumed, from peak to peak, from volcano to volcano, from arid plain to high valley, in the chill of the night and the broiling heat of the day. Nearly every member of the expedition fell ill at some point, they worked feverishly, and in time they were all exhausted. They had almost completed the work of triangulation in June 1739, and were just beginning to work out the mathematical results that would show the true shape of the terrestrial globe, when a letter arrived from Paris informing them that Monsieur de Maupertuis and his comrades had returned from Lapland after completing their mission. Their results proved that Newton was right: the Earth was flattened at the Poles. The French scientists of the equatorial expedition were disappointed at having been beaten by their Arctic colleagues, but in response they simply redoubled their scientific efforts.

Their surveying and observations took them, at last, to the city of Cuenca, three degrees south of the Equator, an isolated and backward place, wrote Don Jorge Juan, inhabited "by a rough and vengeful people, truly wicked in every sense." The scientists' reputation as hunters of Inca treasure, though officially countered by the high-flown letters from the viceroy, had preceded them, and here found even more credence than elsewhere. Local mistrust was exacerbated by the behavior of the expedition's physician Senièrgues, who took an interest in matters that he might better and more safely have left alone.

Senièrgues offered his medical skills to a prominent local family, the Quesada. The family's twenty-year-old daughter, the lovely

Manuela, had been engaged to a member of another illustrious and powerful local family, Don Diego de León. Don Diego, however, had jilted Manuela in order to marry the daughter of the alcalde, or mayor. The Quesada decided to ask the advice of their doctor, Senièrgues: after all, he had lived in the world capital of refinement and elegance. Surely he would know what to do.

Senièrgues suggested, and they agreed, that the solution was to wash away the affront with money. The doctor offered to act as intermediary, and suggested to Don Diego that he pay a certain sum to the family as indemnification for his behavior. Don Diego, the unfaithful suitor, deeply resented this threat to his wallet, and he began to spread shameful rumors linking the worldly doctor Senièrgues with the enchanting Manuela. One day, the French doctor happened to meet Don Diego in the streets of Cuenca and challenged him to a gentlemanly duel. Initially offended by the rumors, Senièrgues became doubly incensed when Don Diego accepted the challenge but insisted on pistols. "A gentleman uses a sword," cried the doctor, and drawing his own he lunged at Don Diego, fully intending to run him through on the spot. He lost his footing, however, on a loose paving stone, and tumbled ignominiously to the ground. The crowd separated the two men; feelings began to run high in the city against the French interlopers, seekers of local treasure and debauchers of local womanhood. Even the priests began to instigate unrest, preaching every Sunday against the French sinners.

Tensions were white hot, and the situation was triggered on August 29, 1739, at a bullfight attended by the entire populace of Cuenca. Senièrgues had dared to attend. At the sight of the Frenchman sitting next to Manuela in the Quesada family box, the owner of the arena, a close friend of Don Diego, could not contain himself. The owner of the arena rode directly below the box and, rearing up in his saddle, insulted Senièrgues openly and at length. The Frenchman stood up suddenly, and the owner interpreted this indignant reaction as a prelude to a physical assault. He wheeled his horse and announced to the crowd that because of the Frenchman's vile aggression, the bullfight was suspended indefinitely.

"Death to the French interloper!" cried the mob, deprived of its spectacle. Senièrgues managed to draw his sword and pistol, but he never used them. He was knocked to the ground, pelted by flying rocks, and finally hacked to death by the enraged audience. His fellow scientists tried to save him, but they were overwhelmed and pummeled, and were quickly forced to take refuge behind the stout walls of a monastery.

The aftermath of the tragedy dragged on for months; the main instigators—the alcalde, the owner of the arena, and Don Diego—were finally found guilty of murder, but the sentence was a dead letter, and the three men walked free.

Then came de La Condamine's turn to commit a grave diplomatic error. The instructions of the French Academy of Science had been clear: "The geodetic base of the measurements should be marked by permanent monuments." De La Condamine ordered such monuments to be built: two brick pyramids, one at Ayambara and one at Caraburo, with commemorative inscriptions. The inscriptions, however, failed to mention the names of the two Spanish members of the expedition: the mathematicians Don Jorge Juan y Santacilia and Don Antonio de Ulloa. Even worse, the French fleur-de-lis was clearly depicted atop each monument. These were matters that, to the authorities of the Audiencia of Quito, smacked of the crime of lèse-majesté, wanton insults to the Spanish crown. There were accusations, diatribes, and, in the end, court trials. In 1742, a sentence was handed down: add the names of the Spanish mathematicians, eliminate the French fleur-de-lis. Six years later, from Spain itself, the Council of the Indies found that the Audiencia had been overlenient. The Council ordered the complete destruction of the pyramids.

In the meanwhile, the expedition, its task complete, was dissolved. Louis Godin remained in Lima, where he had been named astronomer of the university. The botanist Jussieu stayed in Quito.

As for Godin des Odonais, we shall tell more of his adventures in the chapter that follows. The other members of the expedition marched north along the Andes mountain chain to Bogotá, descending the course of the Rio Magdalena to Cartagena, and there taking a ship back to France.

De La Condamine, on the other hand, following his inborn curiosity, took a much more circuitous route: he decided to follow the course of the Amazon River; he had seen a map in the Jesuit archive of Quito drawn by a Jesuit explorer, Father Samuel Fritz. De La Condamine left Cuenca on May 11, 1743, and landed in Cayenne, in French Guiana (five degrees north latitude), on February 26, 1744.

He observed tirelessly: the regime of the vast river, the fauna, the flora, the Indios, the Portuguese colonists. He saw a Carmelite missionary successfully vaccinate his native converts in Pará against smallpox. He brought back to France not only a personal crusade against smallpox and in favor of vaccination, but also quinine and rubber; he carried on a vicious polemic with Bouguer, who had got back first and who tried to seize all the laurels for the expedition's scientific achievements.

In 1757, deaf and partly paralyzed, he married a niece twenty years younger than him. Then his paralysis became total, leaving only his restless brain to carry on, still active, still thirsting after new knowledge. He offered a sizable reward to any physician who could determine the cause of his illness, but the medical science of the time was too primitive. De La Condamine died in 1774, during the operation that he had decided to risk, his last hope and the final impulse of his prodigious curiosity.

6
The Penelope of Riobamba

The French scientific expedition led by de La Condamine in 1741 to measure the Earth's circumference at the Equator had a memorable and romantic aftermath, often narrated under the title of "The Penelope of Riobamba." This almost unbelievable sequence of events served European publishers over the next fifty years as a rich vein to be mined for heartbreaking stories; publishers printed and reprinted this tear-jerking saga, embellishing it with new and increasingly dramatic twists and turns, anxious to satisfy the tastes of a growing reading audience, avid for astounding or tragic tales. A cousin of the astronomer Louis Godin, a strapping young man named Jean Godin des Odonais, was entrusted with the modest and grueling—yet essential—task of carrying the expeditions's surveying chain and of clambering up various Andes peaks to erect the surveying staffs used in making accurate measurements. But young Jean Godin's real love was linguistics, and he spent all his free time with the Indios, trying to learn their language. Destiny, cunning manipulator of lives, acquainted Jean with a wealthy Creole gentleman of French descent who had settled in the small town of Riobamba, on the slopes of Mount Chimborazo, a certain Don Pedro

Manuel de Grandmaison. Don Pedro had a thirteen-year-old daughter, Isabela; she was equally fluent in French, Spanish, and Quechua. Isabela cheerfully agreed to help the fervent scholar with his pronunciation. The willing teacher, however, was more than a versatile linguist—she also possessed a pair of gleaming dark eyes, long black tresses, and a pretty mouth that inspired thoughts of kisses in Jean Godin, rather than Quechua phonemes. It was a short hop from philology to courting, and the father of Jean's intended gladly gave his consent. A long caravan of French scientists and surveyors set out from Quito to attend their compatriot's wedding.

A small tragedy disturbed the festivities—and for decades to come authors narrating the story read it, in hindsight, as an unhappy bellwether. Just a few days after the wedding vows, one of the guests, a draftsman named Morainville, clambered up onto the scaffolding surrounding the construction site of a church for which he had drawn up the plans. Carelessly, he stepped onto a faulty plank and fell to his death on the ground below. This combination of happy and ominous events took place in 1741. One year later, after the expedition had completed its appointed tasks, de La Condamine set off down the Amazon, reaching Paris after lengthy travel in the spring of 1745.

Jean Godin remained behind in Riobamba, but he had asked the French scientist to alert the various Jesuit missions scattered along the shores of the mighty river that he too would soon be traveling the same route, in the company of his young bride. De La Condamine asked the hospitable missionaries to arrange logistic support for the upcoming journey of the new family, but Godin's departure was delayed for years, instead of months. Indeed, it was not until the end of 1750 that a letter was delivered to de La Condamine in Paris from his former chain-bearer. The letter had been sent from Cayenne, capital of French Guiana, in April of that same year. Godin wrote de La Condamine that he had been obliged to put off his departure continually due to Isabela's "frequent pregnancies," and that he had finally decided to descend the Amazon on his own because his father's death in 1748 had made it necessary for him to hurry to Cayenne to wrap up family affairs. He thanked de La Condamine warmly for the hospitality he had received from the various Jesuit missions along the Amazon; even after so many years the missionary brothers still expected him, and he asked La Condamine to act as intermediary with the French minister of the navy, Rouillé, to make formal request of the king of Portugal to allow him to travel back up the course of the Amazon and to descend it once again with his entire family. The scientist hastened to obtain an audience with Rouillé, who had himself received a letter from Godin in the meanwhile. De La Condamine also paid a call on La Cerda, the Portuguese ambassador to France. Everyone involved seemed busily at work; letters were sent back and forth between Paris and Lisbon and Pará and Cayenne so that the impatient Odysseus of Guiana might receive the necessary passports to rejoin his legitimate bride, his Penelope pining in distant Riobamba.

Something, however, went wrong in the slow and unreliable network of transatlantic communications. Perhaps someone lied. In any case, Lisbon claimed it had sent the proper documents to Pará, and in Pará they claimed they had received nothing. Long months went by and Godin, stranded in Cayenne as if in some equatorial Land of the Lotus Eaters, had plenty of time to complete a massive study of the alimentary flora of Guiana, and then another exhaustive study of its timber. He even went on to make efforts to acclimate the cinchona and cinnamon plants to Guiana. As the months turned to years, he wrote and wrote again, increasingly discontented and despairing requests for the necessary passports. And the tone of his letters veered increasingly from discontentment to despair because, with all the delays and miscommunications, the Seven Years' War had broken out. France and Portugal were now formally enemies, and the idea of allowing a Frenchman to travel freely along the course of the Amazon was entirely out of the question. It was, moreover, well known—and everybody knew everything in those equatorial colonies of the eighteenth century, news traveled slowly but it traveled, how it traveled—that the capable but incautious Godin had sent to France, along with a bountiful array of botanical samples for the Jardin des Plantes, a thorough and detailed study on the navigability of the Amazon River, with indications of the various anchorages that might accommodate a fleet. The staff of the colonial office of Pará thanked their lucky stars that the passports had never reached Godin. At the governor's palace everyone agreed: Godin's story of yearning after his distant wife is a ploy, quite clearly; this Frenchman is a spy! He would have led the French navy right up into the heart of Amazonia, if given half a chance.

Finally, in 1763, the Seven Years' War came to an end, and Godin, unflappable, began writing his letters once again, this time to the right man: the count of Hérouville, trusted right-hand man of the all-powerful French prime minister, the duke of Choiseul. And like in some fairy tale, on October 18, 1765, a Portuguese galley of thirty oars dropped anchor in the harbor of Cayenne. The galley had come from Pará, at the command of the king of Portugal; the captain's orders were to convey Godin upriver as far as the first Spanish outpost, to wait while he made his way over the Andes to be reunited with his family, and return with them, and then carry them all back downriver. After long years of frustration and delay, the surprise seemed too good to be true. Godin's mind almost seemed unhinged by the good news. Could this be a Portuguese trap, a trick to take him prisoner and shut him up to rot in some dark dungeon in Pará, to serve out the rest of his life in revenge for his plan for the French conquest of the Amazon river basin? Godin hesitated, he invented excuses, he delayed his departure. The captain of the galley waited patiently—orders from his king. The French governor of Cayenne began to show his irritation, as suspicion dawned that perhaps Godin's entire tale was a fabrication. Had this Frenchman deceived half the crowned heads of Europe? Perhaps there was no Isabel, in Riobamba or anywhere else in the vast expanses of the viceroyalty of Nueva Granada. After an exchange of increasingly insulting letters, the French governor ordered Godin to leave

Cayenne. The galley set off along the coast in late November with its reluctant passenger but after sailing just thirty leagues, still far short of the mouth of the Amazon, it had to set Godin ashore at Oyapock; here was Godin's plantation, and he needed to gather various necessities for the journey. And now the Ulysses of the New World, instead of sailing impetuously on to his South American Ithaca—instead of taking a bench alongside the thirty oarsmen to lend his muscles to speed the galley on its way up the mighty river—simply fell ill and took to his bed. Was he truly ill, or was he malingering? We shall never know. But we do know that he appeared to be at death's door. The Portuguese galley captain, a stubborn man determined to carry out his monarch's orders to the letter, even if it were to take years, lay at anchor in the Bay of Oyapock for six full weeks. Then Godin summoned him to his sickbed and, in a weak voice, said that he was too sick to travel. An acquaintance of Godin's—a certain Tristán d'Oreasaval—would travel up the Amazon and bring Godin's family back to him in his stead. At this point, the captain yielded to Godin's point of view, and with Tristán set sail on January 24, 1766; with every galley slave rowing furiously, the vessel made its way up the course of the Amazon and reached Loreto, the first Spanish outpost, in August of the same year. And here the truly tragic part of the story begins.

According to Godin's instructions, Tristán was to travel as far as the Jesuit mission of La Laguna, where he was to deliver to the father superior a packet of letters from the father general of the Jesuit order, one addressed to the father superior and another to the provincial father of Quito, with a request to organize travel for Madame Godin from Riobamba to the waiting galley. In the packet there was also a letter to Madame Godin, from her husband. With plenty of money to cover all his expenses, Tristán had only to stay at La Laguna and await the arrival of the lady and her entourage, see them aboard the Portuguese galley, and sail back to Cayenne. Instead, Tristán stopped at Loreto to engage in some trade on his own behalf, and cavalierly entrusted the packet of letters to a

Spanish Jesuit he happened to meet there. This first Jesuit was, indeed, returning to Quito, but he handed off the packet of letters to a second Jesuit, who in turn gave them to a third, who relayed them to a fourth, and so on in a chain of traveling Jesuits, until the letters—detoured and delayed—vanished among rivers, jungles, and mountains. If the letters were slow in arriving, rumors were swift. News made its way over the Andean cordillera, and one fine day Isabela Godin learned that a packet of letters addressed to her was making its way over the Andes, and that a royal galley lay at anchor just for her on the Amazon River. The letters, however, were as distant and unreachable as the mountains of the moon; and the ship sent by the king of Portugal sounded suspiciously like an equatorial fairy tale. The cautious lady sent her black servant Joaquim to see with his own eyes. Joaquim made it all the way to Loreto, and there he saw the royal Portuguese galley and he saw Tristán, and he hurried back with the happy news. Preparations were made for the voyage: Isabel sold house, land, and furniture and organized a caravan. All of these things took time. The expedition was not ready until October 1769, after more than three years. In Loreto, the phlegmatic Portuguese captain waited stoically; he knew perfectly well that a trip over the Andes to the Amazonian jungles was a serious undertaking.

With a few servants, Don Pedro Manuel de Grandmaison, father of the happy bride who was yearning to see her husband once again after a separation of twenty years, set out about a month ahead of the larger expedition to arrange for supplies, housing, bearers, litters, canoes, and paddlers. Isabela—who had watched all four of her children by Jean Godin die off of tropical diseases—was accompanied by a twelve-year-old nephew, her two brothers, her trusted servant Joaquim, and by three mestiza serving women, as well as the customary horde of Indio bearers. Three French gentlemen also joined the group; their names are lost to history, but one of them passed himself off as a physician, a precious qualification for travel in that part of the world.

When a letter arrived from Don Pedro informing her that all lay ready, that canoes and paddlers awaited in the village of Canelos on the river Bobonaza, Isabel finally set off. She felt sure that the hardest and most exhausting part of the trip consisted of the ascent and subsequent descent of the mountain chain. Once the party reached Canelos, the current of the Bobonaza River would carry them quietly along to the confluence with the Pastaza River, which would in turn float them down to the Amazon, where the long-awaited galley would whisk them off downriver to the coast.

It was seven days' grueling march from Riobamba to Canelos: trails that were little more than semiliquid rivulets of bottomless muck (it was the rainy season), jungles sopping with suffocating humidity, teeming with roaring beasts and hissing serpents. At long last, Canelos. Surprise: the village lay abandoned. A sudden and virulent outbreak of smallpox had swept through the population and the few survivors had fled into the jungle to escape further contagion. The expedition fanned out and managed to find four survivors, Madame Godin spoke to them in Quechua, she loaded them down with gifts, she persuaded them to help ferry the party downriver aboard a canoe and a raft loaded with provisions and baggage. Their bearers, terrified, had deserted in the night. The remaining members of the party floated down the Bobonaza to the confluence with the Pastaza. But the Pastaza was in full flood, its waters crowded with dangerous flotsam. It was impossible to sail down the river at night, said the native oarsmen. It would be best to stop and spend the night on the riverbank. By morning, all four had vanished.

There was no turning back now. They would have to do their best to navigate the treacherous waters of the Pastaza on their own. They pushed out into the rushing water of the river, running at five knots between solid walls of compact jungle vegetation. Incpt paddlers, the men did their best to guide canoe and raft among drifting logs and jutting crags and boulders. One of the Frenchmen lost his hat and, when he leaned overboard to snag it before it washed out of reach, he fell in and was drowned. Toward nightfall the canoe ran head-on into an underwater obstacle of some sort. The fragile craft overturned and the whole party was dumped unceremoniously into the river, fortunately close to shore. The raft overturned and was washed away downstream.

The group straggled out of the water, pulling the overturned canoe to shore, and even managed to save some provisions. As they sat around a campfire that night, the self-proclaimed physician suggested a plan of action: he would go ahead in the canoe with the other surviving Frenchman and with Joaquim to the village of Andoas, about five days downstream. From there he would send help. The plan was discussed and approved, and the next morning the trio set out.

The days crept by, but no help arrived: five, ten, fifteen, twenty days, an entire month. Food was becoming scarce, and the unfortunate city-dwellers were unable to make use of the jungle bounty that surrounded them. Every night was an unending torment of buzzing, whining, bloodsucking insects, the terrifying rustling of leaves and branches, the sounds of animals in the dark. At last the little party decided that they had waited long enough; perhaps the three men never made it to Andoas, perhaps they drowned in the river.

The little group fashioned a primitive raft from the available materials and clambered on board. As soon as the fragile craft floated into the center of the river and began to move along with the current, it collided with a submerged log. Caught on the snag, the raft was tattered and torn by the onrushing waters. The last provisions tumbled into the river and were lost, and the members of the expedition just barely managed to clamber onto the riverbank, safe and sound.

This was the end: they were exhausted, weak as kittens, they were starving, they had no more food, and they hadn't the strength or knowledge to find food in the jungle or river.

The first to die was the twelve-year-old nephew. Later, looking back on events, Isabel—the only survivor—was unable to say whether the three mestiza serving women died a few hours after the nephew or a few days. Finally, both her brothers breathed their last. Delirious and feverish, Isabel Godin lay amid six rotting corpses, rapidly decomposing in the steamy jungle heat. Somehow, she came to her senses and pulled herself upright. She fashioned a pair of sandals from the shoes of one of her brothers. Seizing a fallen tree branch with which to hobble along, she stumbled off into the jungle, without the slightest idea of where she was headed, like a somnambulist, like a phantom. By this time her gleaming raven locks had turned snow white.

Hours or days after Isabel had wandered away from the charnel site on the riverbank, her trusted servant Joaquim finally arrived, aboard a large dugout canoe paddled by four strong Indios from the Jesuit mission of Andoas. He was late, but it had not been his fault: all blame lay with the fraudulent French physician, inept or dishonest, who had wasted weeks in organizing a rescue party until Joaquim had managed to persuade the Jesuits to allow him to go. Horrified, Joaquim looked at the badly decomposed cadavers, unrecognizable, devoured by ants, scattered and dismembered by scavenging beasts, among the vines and underbrush. Convinced that there had been no survivors, he climbed back into the canoe and traveled downriver to La Laguna, where he gave the tragic news to Don Pedro, who in turn sat down and wrote a sad letter to Jean Godin, in Cayenne.

But the indomitable Isabel, the Penelope of Riobamba who undertook an Amazonian odyssey to regain her somewhat reluctant Ulysses, was still alive. She had wandered through the jungle labyrinth for nine days, feeding herself on fruit and birds' eggs, until she finally happened on two Indios launching a newly carved dugout canoe. She managed to ask them to take her to the mission at Andoas, and then, overcome by exhaustion and relief, she collapsed in a dead faint.

The odyssey culminated in an apotheosis: for the entire vast length of the Amazon, for years, people spoke with amazement of the ordeal of Madame Godin. In Loreto, the miraculous survivor of Amazonia finally set foot aboard the Portuguese galley. The faithful captain, true to his sovereign's command, had remained at anchor despite the tragic news that had filtered downstream with the river current. In July 1770, Isabela finally embraced Jean Godin once again on his plantation in Oyapock. Three years later, the happily reunited couple landed in a French port, where they were greeted by Monsieur de La Condamine.

7
The Nude Baroness

Paris 1932. Late one evening, in a bar in Montmartre, a lovely and elegant woman smoked Turkish cigarettes with a long amber cigarette holder, listening in fascination as a man spoke to her with uncommon intensity. It might seem like a classic scene of seduction, and in a way it was, because the man's words would soon make the woman fall in love.

But not with him. Instead, with a distant equatorial archipelago that the man was describing as an earthly paradise. He was a diplomat working at the Ecuadorian embassy to France, and he was depicting the beauty of the Galápagos to the woman: a lost world comprising about fifty islands, large and small, only two of which were inhabited. A latter-day Eden where time stopped in prehistory, a place where there were two thousand volcanos and eighteen hundred people. The Galápagos were inhabited by animals found nowhere else on Earth, such as marine iguanas and giant tortoises that attained weights of 650 pounds and ages of five hundred years. It was here that Charles Darwin, who visited the islands in 1835, first conceived the ideas that developed into his theory of evolution.

These islands were pounded by Pacific rollers, shrouded by

trailing mists and dense banks of fog, illuminated by flaming volcanic eruptions. The first man to see them, a Spanish navigator in the sixteenth century, called them the Encantadas, or Enchanted Islands. Herman Melville was enchanted by them as well, and wrote about them in lyrical terms.

The woman was so fascinated by the words of the Ecuadorian that she took notes with a small gold pencil on a cardboard coaster. She was already thinking of the archipelago of the Galápagos as a kingdom for her to conquer, an opportunity to turn her life around once and for all. And she needed to: she had been caught up and stranded in the great collective disaster that had destroyed the Austro-Hungarian empire fourteen years earlier.

Elisa von Wagner was born in Innsbruck in 1896, to a wealthy family of the petty nobility, the baronial dynasty of the von Wagner Wehrborns. Like all the girls her age born to her station in life, she had been raised in luxury and refinement. She attended the exclusive Marie Thérèse College. After coming out into society at the usual spectacular debutante ball, she had danced and flirted, waiting for a young aristocrat to ask her hand in marriage. But the First World War had slaughtered most of the available Prince Charmings; defeat had split up the empire and led to revolution, culminating in the loss of the family fortune. Elisa's world collapsed. Both her parents died. At the age of twenty-three, the baroness Elisa von Wagner, lovely and exuberant, decided to leave Austria and a certain future of poverty. She went off in search of fortune with the small nest egg that remained, and especially with her undeniable beauty and charm. The Orient Express, the train of dreams and adventures, took her straight to Constantinople, where the Ottoman empire also lay in ruins. In the Turkish capital, a femme fatale—which is what she had decided to become—could easily find marks among the officers of the Allied armies of occupation (English, French, and Italian) and among the White Russians who were fleeing the Bolshevik revolution.

Just like in a film by Erich von Stroheim, another illustrious émigré from the lost world of Hapsburg Austria, there were rivers of champagne, spinning roulette wheels, intimate boudoirs in luxury hotels, revolver shots and wheeling sabers. Amid all this, the Austrian man-eater ripped through men's hearts and wallets. A captain in the British army asked her to marry him; she rejected him and he committed suicide, shooting himself in the mouth. "What a mooncalf!" commented the imperturbable Elisa. Two Russian aristocrats fought a duel over her; the loser was disfigured by a saber slash to the cheek. A third Russian aristocrat, seduced by her and then abandoned, could not stand the idea of losing her. He stabbed her, but the wound was minor, leaving only the tiniest of scars.

In the end, her high-society suitors began to feel that Elisa was taking things just a tad too far. Little by little, they turned their attentions elsewhere. She ran out of money and began to slide down a slippery slope, just like in the cabaret songs of those giddy years. Before long she had run up dizzying bills that she could not even begin to pay off. She bounced from step to step on a downward progression, from the Grand Hotels of Pera and Galata to the flophouses and dives of Turkish Stamboul. She wound up working as a waitress in a Turkish restaurant; to make ends meet, she seduced the owner and, from time to time, a customer. In any case, she had long decided that she needed to leave Turkey entirely. She was just waiting for the right sucker to happen along. And happen along he did, dining one evening at a corner table in the person of Monsieur Bousquet, a French businessman in Constantinople on business. To seduce the short, stout, middle-aged Monsieur Bousquet was the work of an evening, and a few weeks later, Monsieur and Madame Bousquet, apparently happy newlyweds, boarded a passenger ship heading back to France. As soon as they reached Paris, however, the unfortunate Monsieur Bousquet was in for a bitter surprise. Accusing him of being an "impotent pervert," Elisa demanded an immediate divorce. She got the divorce and, more important to her, a solid alimony to go with it. The alimony, however, was not enough. Money, after all, is never enough, and so the baroness sought out a new victim. This time she found a rich industrialist, becoming his secretary because of her perfect mastery of numerous languages and the excellent and convenient education she had received at the Marie Thérèse College. In short order, she was a kept woman. Kept she might have been, but faithful she definitely was not. She had plenty of other lovers, including a strapping blond young Jewish American named Robert Philipson. He was her current lover the evening that she met the Ecuadorian diplomat.

Just one month after that fateful meeting, the baroness Elisa von Wagner held a press conference in the hall of a Parisian hotel. She informed the assembled journalists that she would soon be leaving for the Galápagos Islands, where she would found the Paradise Retrouvé, a beach resort unlike anything on earth, exclusively dedicated to elite tourism, available only to a wealthy and sophisticated clientele. There would be a huge hotel with swimming pools, tennis courts, and golf courses, stables, a little marina for the many yachts that would be mooring there . . . perhaps, in time, even a casino, which would become the Monte Carlo of the Pacific. The whole project enjoyed the support of the government of Ecuador, which wanted to make the deserted Galápagos Islands into something comparable to what the United States had created in the Hawaiian Islands.

And then, accompanied by Robert Philipson and a German friend with an adventuresome bent named Lorentz, Elisa sailed across the Atlantic Ocean and through the Panama Canal. They disembarked in the Ecuadorian port of Guayaquil, where they hired a carpenter named Chamuso, who would build a temporary residence in which they would live while construction began on the main structure of the hotel. The government provided them with a boat, the *Cristobal,* which took the whole troupe to the island of Floreana. The boat steamed for seven days and, as it prepared to anchor off the island, the baroness—in a quasi-pagan rite—doffed all her clothes and dove, nude and spectacularly lovely, into the sparkling blue water. She then swam to shore and emerged, like Venus, to take possession of her island realm. The climate in this latter-day Eden was so fine that she did not bother to dress again for the whole time she remained there. She wore only a sapphire ring and a .12-caliber revolver strung around her neck with a red satin ribbon.

The three men and the various animals they had brought with them landed in a less theatrical manner. There were donkeys, cows, and calves, and an imposing heap of equipment and supplies. The first order of the day, in theory at least, was to select the ideal site for the future hotel with all its annexes and attractive features, and then to begin to survey the land. Instead, the days passed and no one lifted a finger, except for Chamuso the carpenter, who cobbled together a little shack and then put down his tools to join the rest of the crew in idleness. And who can blame them? Did Adam toil in the original earthly paradise? This was Eden, and if there was only one Eve for all three Adams, she was perfectly reasonable about sharing her charms with each.

And with others as well. It turned out that the island was not entirely uninhabited. There was an Austrian family pursuing a radical return to nature: Gerhard and Margret Wittmer with their two teenaged sons, Franz and Klaus. There was a Berlin dentist, Sigmund Ritter, with his lover, Dora Hilde Koerwin; they were both complete vegetarians. Sigmund clearly had no patience for half-measures: he had had all his teeth extracted before leaving Germany, because teeth are unnecessary if you are eating only vegetables, and they can always develop cavities. And after the baroness and her companions had been on the island for just a few months, a veritable stampede arrived: twenty-two Norwegians unloaded on the island by two con men who had persuaded them of the ease with which they could colonize the island and farm its fertile soil.

All twenty-two were men, and they had brought everything they might need on a desert island, except women. But there was the baroness, stark naked, who welcomed all arrivals. And as the days slowly passed in that equatorial Eden, the baroness took a turn with one—and sometimes two—after the other: the Norwegians, Dr. Ritter, his fifteen-year-old son, Franz, and even the younger Klaus. Dora Koerwin, caught up in the contagious erotic fever, took consolation in the arms of Philipson and Lorentz and the occasional Norwegian. Floreana became an island republic of free love, where jealousy was banished entirely.

Or perhaps not entirely. Around New Year's Day of 1934, a series of strange events began to unfold. In the late fall of 1933, Chamuso the carpenter had been found at the foot of a tree, with a fractured skull. Everyone placidly assumed that he must have fallen out of the tree while gathering fruit. Since there was no police force on Floreana, the case was immediately closed. And the case was not even opened for Dr. Ritter, who began to feel excruciating stomach pains and to run an alarmingly high fever on January 1; he died sometime on the night of the third. When his lover, Dora Koerwin, returned to Europe years later, she wrote that he had died from eating meat that had gone bad, which seems odd for a vegetarian, indeed a vegan. Next came the Norwegians. Nineteen of them fell ill all at once, suffering the same symptoms as the late dentist: fever, vomiting, abdominal pains, cramps, cold sweats. There were no doctors and there was no medicine, at least no medicine for whatever was ailing them. Terrified that they would meet the same unpleasant end as Ritter, the sick Norwegians decided to leave the island aboard the dilapidated fishing boat on which they had arrived. If they could reach one of the other islands, maybe they could find some help there. Nineteen feverish and miserable Norwegians set sail, all weak as kittens, all delirious and hallucinating. When the fishing boat finally landed in a little Ecuadorian port near Guayaquil, there were only sixteen left. Within three days, there were only four survivors. The other twelve had died in the hospital where they were taken. Questioned by the local authorities, the survivors said that the other three Norwegians had died at sea and had been thrown overboard. But they were lying. Eight months later, a patrol boat of the Ecuadorian coast guard motoring past the island of Genovesa was attracted by a thin plume of smoke. It was the three Norwegians, still quite alive and terribly hungry. They had been abandoned by their companions, who had assumed that the three were goners. Left on the island with scanty rations, the three had survived on iguana meat, and perhaps that diet cured them, because their sickness vanished.

And the three Norwegians who had remained on the island of Floreana? Two died in the course of the three weeks that followed. Only one survived; his name was Nuggard, and he was a beast standing six feet six inches, weighing 230 pounds.

One evening, at the end of February 1934, the Wittmer family was eating dinner outdoors when Lorentz arrived, ashen-faced, sweating, panting in terror. He asked if he could stay with them for the night. He said that he was afraid, and he swore that he was going to leave the island in the morning. He would not, however, say why. The Wittmers thought that he was delirious and that he too had come down with the strange illness of Floreana, or else that he had quarreled with Philipson and that the blond American had threatened to kill him. They let him sleep there. At dawn, the baroness came to see him, spoke with him at length, and when she left the German seemed less afraid.

That evening brought a new and dramatic development: Franz, who had gone to Elisa's hut in search of his usual ration of love, found the door swinging wide open. There was not a trace of the woman or of Philipson. The pair seemed to have vanished. The island was big, full of caves and woods. They could be anywhere.

Lorentz, in the meanwhile, went to see the last Norwegian, the giant Nuggard. In the whole island of Floreana, there was only one boat left, a ten-foot skiff. Lorentz, however, did not know how to launch a boat, so he needed a sailor, like Nuggard. He had to convince him to flee the island with him. And so Lorentz told Nuggard that the baroness, whose hobby was to gather herbs and certain mysterious berries, had poisoned the other Norwegians with a potion in which she had mixed—horrifying detail!—iguana saliva. Reluctant and incredulous at first, Nuggard finally yielded to Lorentz's persuasion. He agreed: they would take the skiff and set their course for Marquena, just sixty nautical miles away, along a route dotted with islets where they could land in case of emergency. Then, with a second trip, they could reach Chatham, where there was a fishing village and a police station. Lorentz and Nuggard went down to the beach together and added a rudimentary mast and sail to the boat, stocking it with supplies and water.

The following morning they returned, intending to launch it and set sail. As the pair struggled to shove the heavy vessel into the water, a pistol shot rang out, echoing from the rocks that surrounded the little inlet. Lorentz fell, dead or dying, into the skiff. Nuggard desperately redoubled his efforts, gasping and shoving to get the boat into the water, but Philipson was on him in a flash, stabbing him over and over with a hunting knife. Then he climbed aboard, with the baroness, and set sail.

Or at least that is how one author reconstructs the events. Little is known for certain about what happened that fateful day, but in April 1934 a fishing boat found the skiff drifting about forty nautical miles from the island of Marquena. In it were two cadavers, practically skeletons by this point, picked almost clean by sea birds. The identification papers indicated that these were the bodies of Lorentz and Nuggard. At the bottom of the boat was a ring with a large sapphire, the baroness Elisa's ring.

In December 1934, the Dutch explorer and writer Victor von Hagen was sailing past the island of Santa Cruz (or Indefatigable) and saw something white high atop a peak that overlooked the little Bahía Negra. He landed, curious to see what it might be, and climbed the mountain. He found a skeleton tied to a tree. There were no clothes, but from the vertebrae of the skeletal neck there hung a red satin ribbon fastened to a .12-caliber revolver.

Thus ended the reign of the Queen Bee of the Galápagos, surmised the Ecuadorian authorities, immediately alerted by the crew of the fishing boat. But they were wrong; the autopsy showed that those miserable remains had once been the body of a man. But no one ever searched for the baroness Elisa von Wagner, who had vanished into the waves of the Pacific Ocean.

A few years later, in February 1946, Floreana was finally searched thoroughly, by American and Ecuadorian soldiers. But they were not looking for the lovely missing Austrian, as they noisily rummaged through the island's forests and caves. They were searching—in vain—for Adolf Hitler. The dictator, according to rumors that had been printed repeatedly by the Panamanian press, had escaped by submarine to the Galápagos Archipelago, the last earthly paradise.

PART III

Africa

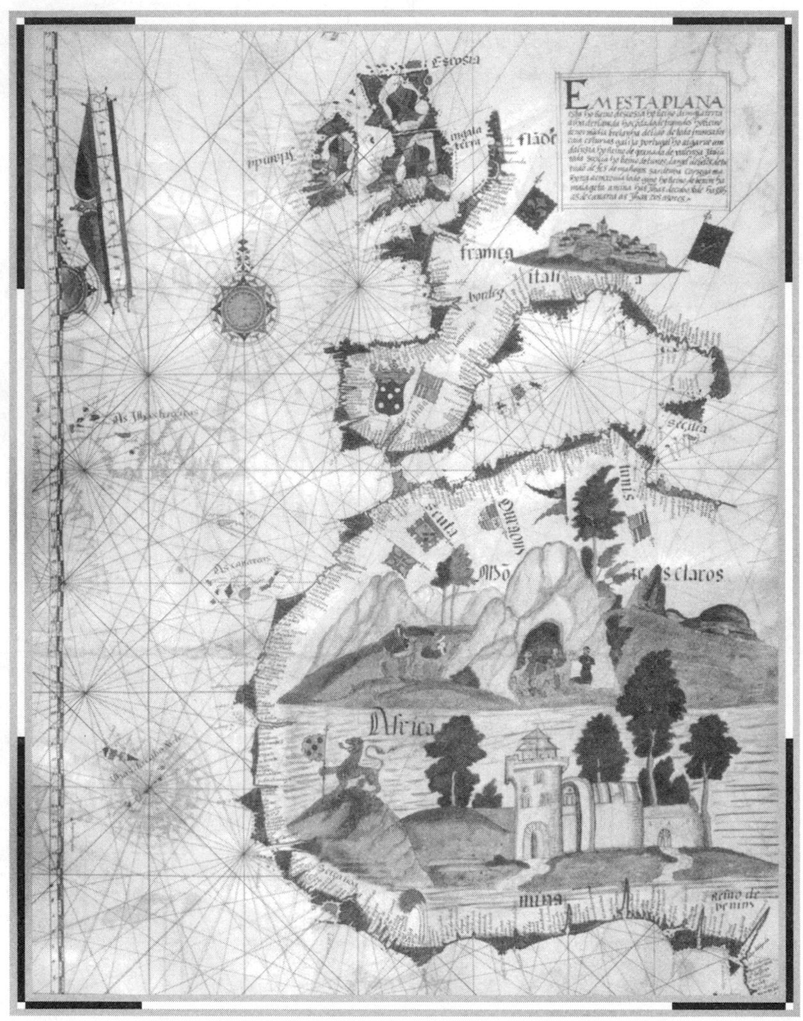

This lovely map of Western Europe and West Africa dates from 1563, and depicts the discoveries of Fernao Gomez in the late fifteenth century. —Academia das Ciencias de Lisboa, Lisbon, Portugal/Bridgeman Art Library

Ironically, most of the tales from the Dark Continent of Africa are later in time than those from South America. Full-fledged colonial fever broke out in the New World first, and in particularly grandiose and virulent forms; it was not until Victorian times that Europeans began to wreak the same kind of devastation in Africa that their "exploration" had visited upon equatorial America in the sixteenth, seventeenth, and eighteenth centuries.

Aside from an initial story set in the eighteenth century—Joan of Arc of the Kongo—all the tales of the African Equator date from the 1800s.

If the lure for armies and expeditions marching endlessly along the South American Equator was gold, or at least the illusion thereof, the bait for the expeditions in equatorial Africa was more modern: fame.

If the conquistadors were out to conquer and to enrich themselves, the Victorians in Africa were, ostensibly, in search of knowledge. If their explorations resulted in best-selling books and large contracts with newspapers, with lucrative if bloody trade in rubber and ivory as a fringe benefit, then that was purely accidental.

Some of the names in this section of our history of the Equator are Sir Richard Burton, Sir Henry Morton Stanley, Dr. David Livingstone, Sir Samuel Baker, Lord Gordon of Khartoum, Emin Pasha, and King Leopold II of Belgium, emperor of the Congo. Some of the sites of exploration are the Congo River, the Nile River, Lake Victoria, Lake Albert, and Lake Tanganyika.

And if there is a spirit hovering over it all, that spirit is unquestionably Mr. Kurtz from Joseph Conrad's *Heart of Darkness,* a figure modeled upon people that Conrad may have met during his time as a riverboat pilot on the Congo.

8
Joan of Arc of the Kongo

In 1483, *annus fatalis* (Latin for "fateful year"), an immense canoe, unlike anything that had ever been seen before, topped by vast white wings that glittered in the strong African sunlight, emerged from the crashing rollers of the great western ocean and slowly began to sail up the estuary of a broad and majestic river. The onlookers lining the riverbanks stood rooted to the spot in amazement.

They gazed wonderingly as they made out creatures in the great canoe, human in semblance but white of skin, pale and colorless like the shades of the dead that lived beneath the salt water, in the realm of the spirits. Perhaps these living dead, these animated specters, were simply messengers from the world of the ancestors.

If so, they were not very good messengers: they spoke in a tongue incomprehensible to one and all. But they did bring gifts with them: exceedingly strange fabrics, bizarre articles of clothing, glittering objects. And so the watchers on the riverbank welcomed the pale new arrivals with righteous awe and a vague but pervasive sense of dread, as was appropriate to vistors from the afterlife.

These messengers from the land of the dead were Portuguese

mariners under the command of Diogo Cão, and their caravel ventured upstream to a distance of almost thirty leagues (ninety miles), until they reached the cascades of Yelala. There they chiseled an inscription into the wall of living rock, to be read by passersby even today. That great river, the mightiest stream that the Portuguese had ever seen, was called the Zaire (the present-day Congo River; six degrees south latitude), and lining both its banks were the provinces of a vast kingdom called the Kongo. The monarch, Nzinga Nkuwu, heaped the newcomers with gifts and honors.

Less than ten years before Columbus sailed west to discover the Americas, the Portuguese were discovering a new world all its own: equatorial Africa. This first, spectacular encounter between Europeans and the peoples of the Kongo resulted in the rapid conversion to Christianity of the royal family and of many notables. Rapid, but short-lived: fewer than three years had passed before Nzinga Nkuwu, rebaptized Dom João I, abjured the new religion and reembraced the old pagan ways, along with many other converts.

It was impossible for them to give up their old polygamous ways. And it was not merely that their many former wives, "seeing themselves ejected from the domestic hearth, seethed in rage and fury," as one missionary wrote at the time. Rather, it was the fact that polygamy lay at the very foundation of the agrarian economy of the Kongo. "A man who has but one wife is haunted by hunger. He has little to eat and is held in low esteem. In these lands, the only ones who work are the women, and they supply the men with food. Now, a single wife cannot feed a husband, feed herself, and feed her children. . . . But now, if a man has ten or twenty wives, or even more, then he is roundly considered a great gentleman."

Still, the new faith had sunk roots here and there. For instance, the firstborn son of the king, Mbemba Nzinga, known to the Portuguese as Dom Afonso, remained a Christian. As such, he was exiled to an outlying province, and when his father died he won the throne in a fierce battle against the official heir, the bastard Mpanzu Nzinga. It was an epic battle that pitched "countless ranks" of pagans and a tiny band of just thirty-six Christians. As the stories had it, Mbemba Nzinga, or Dom Afonso, managed to throw the foe into disarray and rout through the intervention of Saint James, who descended from heaven astride a great white horse, waving a fluttering standard that bore a cross and the legend: *In hoc signo vinces.* Following the battle, the Christian king Afonso I reigned undisturbed for thirty-seven years. During his long and peaceful reign, the Catholic religion spread and was consolidated, reinforced by miracles that were minor, unassuming, but nonetheless very persuasive to the people of the Kongo. All that it took (people said) was a bit of prayer from fervent missionaries, and lo and behold, a plague ravaged the chicken houses of those Kongolese who were unwilling to convert to Christianity. Poor Kongo, made Christian through the manipulation of outbreaks of avian malaria. Next came an epidemic of syphilis, a sickness that—the missionaries explained—notoriously afflicted those who had committed sins of the flesh.

As the religion spread, churches sprang up everywhere; a cathedral was even built in the capital, M'banza Congo, renamed São Salvador. The king had become Christian, the powerful of the land had become Christian: the people shrugged and went along. But the people preserved, at least in secret, their ancient customs, their ancient beliefs. The "fetishes," the "idols" that refused to die, survived in hiding. Since it was dangerous to fight openly against the symbols of a faith imposed from above, those symbols were assimilated, welcomed as new members of the pantheon, imported from overseas. Thus, statues of saints were invoked to ensure good hunting. The crucifix became a particularly powerful amulet to protect against the angry spirits that thronged the nighttime jungles. The years turned into decades, the decades stretched into centuries, and this recondite, subterranean coexistence engendered a pidgin, equatorial version of Roman Catholicism. The contradictions of this pidgin sect emerged dramatically in the late seventeenth century, when the kingdom was rocked by crisis. The Portuguese now ruled in Angola, and they had turned openly hostile against the Kongo. Throngs of pretenders struggled to seize and hold the throne.

In 1665, at Ambuila, the army of the Kongo was routed by the Portuguese of Angola and their allies, the fearsome Yaka warriors. In the wake of the terrible defeat came thirty years of chaos and civil war, the collapse of all organized government, misery, and famine. In 1678, São Salvador was burned to the ground. The churches, the royal palace, the Jesuit college built a century before were razed. The populace fled to the bush. The city stood desolate for twenty years. The "benighted heathen" were enjoying the supposed benefits of civilization and Christianity.

Times of calamity tend to create prophets. A woman saw an apparition of the Virgin Mary, who told of Her Son's indignation at the state of affairs in the Kongo; the Virgin Mary told the woman to invoke heaven three times every day at sunset. A young man roamed through the villages, proclaimed that God would punish those who refused to return to the desolate capital. In 1704 an old woman named Ma Futa discovered "the head of the Christ, all ravaged by the dagger blows of human evil" (it was actually a rock that had been carved by the waters of the Ambriz River). The Madonna had foretold catastrophes—said Ma Futa—if the king did not march immediately to São Salvador. Ma Futa performed miracle cures. The queen thought she was a saint, and persuaded the king to return to the rubble of his ravaged palace. The royal couple protected Ma Futa against the anger and persecution of the European missionaries.

These were only bellwethers, foreshadowings that set the stage for the appearance of the great and true prophetess. She was a young woman, born of noble family. She was named Kimpa Vita, or Dona Beatriz in Portuguese. She was a lovely girl in her early twenties, with a slender and graceful body, delicate features, a devout demeanor, and grave, careful speech. She had her revelation—as is so often the case with second sight—while in the throes of a mortal illness. As she lay suffering on her deathbed, Beatriz saw a man dressed in the robe of a Capuchin monk appear at her bedside. The monk told her that he was Saint Anthony and that he had been sent by God "into her head" to preach to the people and to work for the restoration of the kingdom.

Beatriz "died," or at least she said that she felt her old soul vanish, replaced by the new soul of Saint Anthony, who revived her. Cured suddenly, the young woman rose from her sickbed and explained to her astonished parents that she had received a divine mission. Like the apostles, she gave away everything she owned and, freed of all her earthly possessions, withdrew from the cares of this world and went to live on Mount Kibangu. From the mountaintop, her fame spread through a Kongo anxious for signs and prodigies. She explained to her first followers that Saint Anthony is "the second God," that he held "the keys to heaven," and that he would show mercy to the people of the Kongo. When she came down from the mountain and made her first appearance in the city of São Salvador, she was already venerated as a saint. The city notables held up the hems of their robes for her to wipe her mouth when she ate, her followers fought for the food and drink that she distributed with her own hands, the noblewomen of the city swept the dirt of the paths before her whenever she went walking.

It was said that she followed the custom of "dying every Friday," and on that day of the week she ascended into heaven to "dine with God, defending in his presence the cause of the blacks of Kongo and the rebirth of the kingdom"; then, she would be "reborn every Saturday." She performed miracles and commanded nature: uprooted trees would stand upright once again when she passed by.

São Salvador became the mecca of a new faith, a magical city of the long-heralded golden age. The city's rebuilt ruins would reveal mines abounding in precious gems and metals. The sky over the city would miraculously rain down "the rich goods of the white men." As if by enchantment, São Salvador once again thronged with people. From every corner of the ancient kingdom, pilgrims hurried to venerate Beatriz and to behold such portents and omens. "Thus, the false saint made herself the benefactress, mistress, and lady of the Kongo," wrote one indignant missionary. A black Joan of Arc.

In two years the prophetess had developed a full-fledged alternative theology, with its own sacred geography, entirely African. The true Holy Land was the Kongo, and the founders of Christianity belonged to the black race. Christ was born in São Salvador, and he was baptized in the waters of Nsundi; his Virgin Mother Mary "had been the daughter of a slave or servant of the Duke Nzimba Npanghi"; Saint Francis "belonged to the clan of the Dukes of Vunda." Blacks and whites had profoundly different origins: the whites came from "a soft stone called fuma," while the blacks "were the fruit of a nsanda tree." And so the faithful dressed in clothing fashioned from the bark of the nsanda tree, while the chiefs wore crowns braided from fibers of the same plant, a sign of membership and the insignia of power. They sang Catholic hymns—the *Ave Maria,* the *Salve Regina*—they abhorred sin, vice, and fetishes, just like the missionaries, but they did not venerate the cross "because it was the instrument of Christ's death," and they accused European priests of having distorted divine revelation (and the cornucopia of wealth that came with it) to the exclusive benefit of the whites. It was a nationalistic religion, and it restored some small measure of hope to a desperate people, beaten down by three decades of disasters, a millenarian faith in a mystically rejuvenated Kongo. The hour of the millennium was about to strike, because Beatriz—like the Virgin Mary—gave birth to a son who was to become His people's savior: "I cannot deny that he is mine," said the radiant mother, "but I do not know how he may have been conceived. I know only that he came from heaven on high." It was this divine birth, however, that was to prove her ultimate undoing.

The Capuchin missionaries, fearful that they would soon be swept away by the cresting tide of conversions to Antonianism—for that was the name of the new syncretistic religion founded by Beatriz–Saint Anthony—grasped at that inexplicable birth as their last source of salvation. There were two clans of royal lineage struggling at that time for the throne of the Kongo, the Ki-Mulaza and the Ki-Mpanzu. Both clans were attempting to ride the tiger of religious revolution, and each hoped that the Antonian wave would sweep them along with it. It was the Ki-Mpanzu who prevailed in the inner circle of the prophetess. The reigning sovereign, Pedro IV, however, was a member of the Ki-Mulaza clan, and he sensed that his throne was beginning to totter unsteadily. This was the right moment for the missionaries to act: the Capuchins pointed out to the king that, technically, a saint was supposed to be chaste above all, and that her claim that she had had a child fathered by the Holy Ghost—a male child, moreover, inasmuch as he was a reincarnation of Saint Anthony—might well conceal a devious machination. Dom Pedro hesitated, waffled, fearing the fury of the populace. In the end, however, he yielded to the blandishments of the European missionaries and decided to begin an investigation. At first he wanted to send Dona Beatriz to Luanda, in Angola, to be judged by the Portuguese archbishop there, and he ordered his men to arrest her with extreme caution and care. The Capuchins were alarmed and they protested: the supporters of the "witch," the partisans of the "heretic" might easily free her during the long overland journey. Once again, they worked to persuade the king, and in the end he yielded to pressure: the royal council handed down a sentence of death against the "false Saint Anthony and her guardian angel." The guardian angel in question was the suspected—and now convicted—earthly father of the infant savior. Beatriz was executed on July 2, 1706. An eyewitness to the execution, the Capuchin father Lorenzo da Lucca, one of those who had devoted so much energy on behalf of "the justice and the honor of God," described the scene:

> Two men holding bells went and took up positions in the midst of the enormous crowd, and when they gave a

signal with their bells, the people immediately fell back, leaving a clearing in which the baschamucano, or judge, appeared. He was covered from head to foot in a black mantle and wore a hat, likewise black, on his head. Both mantle and hat were horrendously black, so horrendous that I think it would be impossible to find so horrendous a black anywhere. The guilty parties were led before him. The young woman, who held her son in her arms, now seemed to be filled with fear and alarm. The accused sat on the bare earth and waited for the death sentence to be read out.

We understood at that moment that they had decided to burn the baby along with the mother. This appeared to us to be too great a cruelty. I hurried to the presence of the king to see whether anything could be done to save the life of the infant.

The baschamucano pronounced a lengthy speech, the principal subject of which was a panegyric to the king. He enumerated the king's many titles and listed evidence of his zealous dedication to justice. Finally, the baschamucano pronounced the death sentence against Dona Beatriz, stating that she had deceived the people under the false name of Saint Anthony with her heresies and her falsehoods. Consequently, her lord the king and the royal council sentenced her to be burned at the stake, along with her illicit lover. They were both led toward the pyre. The woman attempted to renounce her convictions, but all her protests were in vain. So great a tumult developed among the multitude that there was no way for us monks to provide comfort to the condemned prisoners. All at once they were hurried over to the pyre. This was an immense stack of faggots, and once they had been thrown onto the stack new bundles of brush were tossed on top of them. The man and

> woman and little baby were then burnt alive. The executioners were evidently still not satisfied, because the next day men were sent to burn the remaining bones, reducing them into the finest cinders.

Thus Joan of Arc of the Kongo, Dona Beatriz, died "with the name of Jesus on her lips." So wrote another Capuchin monk, Bernardo de Gallo, concluding with pious cynicism: "Poor Saint Anthony, accustomed as he was to dying and returning to life, this time died but failed entirely to revive."

It was still not over: two years later King Pedro IV was forced to levy an army of twenty thousand men to put down an Antonianist uprising. The site of the sacrifice of Beatriz, her lover, and their child had been transformed "into two deep wells," above which "appeared two lovely stars."

9
The Impossible Lakes

In 1848, as revolutionaries were erecting barricades in the capitals of Europe and thrones of various antiquity were toppling across the continent, on the distant and tranquil coast of what is now Kenya, two strapping and high-spirited missionaries were making ready for "a tour of the interior." They were German missionaries in the service of a British Bible society. Their names were Krapf and Rebmann, and this would not be their first "tour." They had already made numerous trips inland, and they had glimpsed—though they had not scaled—the snowbound summits of Mount Kenya and Mount Kilimanjaro, ice-clad peaks whose existence most European scholars of geography still roundly denied. Indeed, most geographers were certain that snow could not even exist in the blast of equatorial heat that baked the earth at Latitude Zero. During this new "tour of the interior," the missionaries stumbled on another impossible geographic feature. Arab slave-drivers leading long caravans of captives toward the slave-ports of the East African coast told the two Germans of one—or several—inland lakes that were vast as seas. From these immense lakes issued a river that ran northward, toward Egypt. The existence of these lakes and their role as the primary source of the Nile River had already been posited by the geographers of antiquity, foremost among them Ptolemy. The great scientist and geographer Ptolemy (who lived from A.D. 90 to A.D. 168), in fact, had thoroughly consulted the collection of the great library of Alexandria and had composed an authoritative description of the world, venerated as sacred scripture at least until the Great Age of Geographic Discoveries (beginning in the fifteenth century). Ptolemy stated that the Nile flowed out of the Mountains of the Moon, so named because the glittering mantle of snow that blanketed their summits reminded travelers of the light of the moon, and indeed, after nightfall, reflected that lunar light. The Nile, Ptolemy specified, flowed out of those mountains and out of numerous vast lakes that lay at their feet.

The existence of these lakes—and of equatorial glaciers—was taken as an article of Ptolemaic faith for many centuries, only to be cast in doubt by science at the turn of the nineteenth century. How could the lakes, or the glaciers, withstand the evaporating blast of the withering equatorial heat? The European scholars laughed at these reports: they were clearly just fables of antiquity.

All the same, when an exceedingly sketchy map drawn up by Rebmann reached London, showing a vast inland lake with a sinuous coastline, Great Britain's Royal Geographical Society decided to organize an expedition that would settle once and for all the enigma of the source of the Nile.

Command of this expedition was entrusted to one of the most singular figures of Victorian England: Richard Burton, then thirty-five years old, the veteran of a series of audacious adventures in the Near East and Africa. The son of a colonel in the British army, young Richard had toyed for the briefest moment with the idea of becoming a man of the cloth. But the Church was not for him; instead he followed in his father's military footsteps, enlisting as a soldier in the army of the East India Company. Burton had a gift for languages—by the end of his life he had succeeded in mastering more than forty of them—and an insatiable curiosity. His interests ranged from Persian mysticism to everyday life in the bordellos of the Punjab. This background suited Burton perfectly for one of his greatest achievements; he later undertook and completed an unabridged translation of the *Arabian Nights*, also known as the *Thousand and One Nights*, omitting none of the erotic passages, and equipping the work with a body of critical footnotes that, published alone, would have constituted a sizable encyclopedia of Islamic sensuality.

In 1853, disguised as an Afghan, he had made a pilgrimage to Mecca, risking his life to make his way into the holy cities of Arabia, forbidden territory to infidels. Burton returned home with the exact measurements of the Kaaba (a small cubical building in the courtyard of the Great Mosque at Mecca, which contained a sacred black stone, regarded by Muslims as the House of God, the objective of their pilgrimages) measured in spans, or handbreadths, since it would clearly have been dangerously incautious to carry a measuring stick. A year later, in 1854, Burton penetrated another inviolable sanctuary: Harar (nine degrees north latitude), a city in what is now eastern Ethiopia. In those days it was a wealthy slave-trading town governed by an autonomous emir, who welcomed with lavish and ceremonious hospitality this English adventurer masquerading as an Arab slave merchant. Emerging safe and sound from Harar (a mirage of a city, where Arthur Rimbaud, *poet maudit* and desperate voyager, came to live just a few decades afterward as a gunrunner, later contracting a leg infection from which he died at the age of thirty-seven), Burton joined back up with three other officers of the East India Company army who had originally set out with him to explore those desolate regions: lieutenants Stroyan, Herne, and Speke.

John Hanning Speke, born in 1827, was a zoologist and, before all else, a hunter: he had established quite a reputation in India for his adventuresome hunting expeditions on the slopes of the Himalayas and in the jungles of Bengal. The task assigned him on this present expedition had been to discover the course of an elusive river, the Wadi Nogal. He searched for it, failed to find it, and—wrongly—declared that no such river existed.

Now that the foursome had rejoined ranks, they set out to explore the arid region of Ogaden (eight degrees north latitude); they had just left the port city of Berbera (in present-day Somalia, 10 degrees north latitude) when they were attacked by a band of marauders. Stroyan was killed, Speke was seriously wounded, and a spear sliced through Burton's cheek; Herne came through unscathed. Stripped literally bare, the three survivors, counting themselves lucky to be alive, wandered along the seacoast for several days; badly weakened by hunger and thirst, they stumbled upon a band of British marines, who carried them to safety aboard their ship anchored off Berbera.

That had been in 1854. Now, in 1857, when Burton was entrusted with the quest for the mysterious African lake (or lakes), he chose Speke as a fellow adventurer. In January 1857 the two explorers reached Mombasa (four degrees south latitude), a seaport in what is now Kenya, and from there they set out on a preliminary excursion into the interior. They immediately contracted malaria, however, and returned, weak and feverish, to the coast and to the island of Zanzibar (six degrees south latitude). It was on that island—the marshaling point for nearly all of the trade in slaves captured by Arab raider/merchants in the heart of the African continent—that the explorers organized their great journey. They decided to follow the route used by the slave caravans. This route led to a place called Ujiji, situated—it was said—on the shore of the great lake.

The cooperative sultan of Zanzibar provided them with an escort of Baluch soldiers; the ranks of the exploring party were further swelled by an Indo-Portuguese cook from Goa; a freed slave named Sidi Bombay, who spoke the native dialects of the interior; numerous donkeys; and even more numerous native bearers. These bearers would take up the burdens carried by the beasts once they had been decimated (as was inevitable) by the ravages of the terrible tsetse fly, which infested much of the territory through which they were to pass.

The long, slow procession made its way over the five hundred miles of trail that led from the Indian Ocean seacoast to Kazé—now known as Tabora (five degrees south latitude), a town in the northwest of present-day Tanzania. There the Arab merchants had established a sort of trading post. The trail led through a patchwork of small "sultanates," as the merchants called them, African tribal territories, each of which extended for about twenty miles. In each of the "sultanates," the chief demanded from every caravan a payment of *hongo,* a "tribute for passage." With each negotiation over *hongo,* days were lost in nerve-racking haggling, because the custom was to demand an exorbitant tribute, and then gradually ratchet down the price. Many more days were spent waiting for rain before attempting to pass through areas made impassable by lack of water. At last, however, on November 7, 1857, more than three months from the day they left the coast, Burton and Speke marched (each doing his level best to assume as martial an air as was compatible with a raging fever) into the welcoming town of Kazé, a vast expanse of huts and tiny cultivated fields in the heart of Uniamwezi, the Land of the Moon (certainly an encouraging name for explorers questing after Ptolemy's fabulous Mountains of the Moon).

The Arab merchants who lived in Kazé were well supplied with foodstuffs and goods of all sorts; in those log huts one could find almost the same profusion of luxury that abounded in Cairo and Damascus, and the two white wayfarers were able to rest in comfort and recuperate, amid lavish Islamic hospitality. As they slowly nursed themselves back to health, gathering information about the region, what they heard differed starkly from the accounts carried back to Europe by missionaries. First of all, there were three lakes: Nyasa, Ujiji, and Ukerewe. Out of the largest of the three, Ukerewe, flowed a river that the Arabs called Djub, or Juba, that ran northward. The impetuous Speke immediately decided that this watercourse must be the source of the Nile. He wanted to rush to it instantly. Burton, commander of the expedition, was more cautious and he reined in his subordinate. He decided that they should recuperate where they were for as long as necessary. Then they would continue to Ujiji, where a final decision would be made.

A month of rest improved their conditions but did not entirely restore their health. As they continued their march westward, Burton was plagued by temporary paralysis and partial blindness. Speke too was troubled by a condition of the eyes that clouded his vision, at points rendering him entirely sightless.

When they finally reached Ujiji in December, each of the explorers could see nothing more than a confused glittering of water under the rays of the tropical sun.

Ujiji was a lakeside sister-town to Kazé, another hastily built trading post used in commerce with the lakeshore tribes who called the lake Tanganyika.

The two explorers had traveled all this distance to chart the huge lake and to sail around its entire circumference; but the canoes of the natives were too rickety to contain the necessary cargo of foodstuffs and trading goods. The Arab slavers, ironically courteous and helpful toward Europeans, came to their assistance. On the far shore, there lived an Arab merchant, a wealthy sheikh who had built a dhow, the typical sailing vessel used on the seas of Arabia. He used the dhow to fish, to trade, and for sport. But to ask the loan of the dhow, it was necessary to cross the vast lake: Speke did so in a canoe carved out of a tree trunk, pushed along by helpful winds, after paying the local chief the exorbitant sum of four *dhoti merikani* (strips of American-made linen sheeting) and four *kitindi* (bracelets made of brass wire). Right in the middle of the lake, Speke was caught in a furious storm, and the dugout came very close to sinking. The worst came, however, when Speke landed on an island to spend the night. His tent was invaded by a swarm of cockroaches. Exhausted, he did his meager best to brush them off, but he was bone-tired, and he finally fell asleep in the midst of that black welter of insect bodies. Soon thereafter he was awakened by a piercing pain: one of the insects had burrowed into his ear, digging its way to his eardrum. In a desperate frenzy, driven to the brink of madness by the pain, Speke carved away at his ear with a pocketknife, killing the cockroach but badly wounding his ear in the process. In the days that followed the wound became infected, swelling the side of his head and making it impossible for him to chew. He was forced to subsist on fluids alone.

Once he had overcome his amazement at coming face-to-face with a white man in his black and aquatic realm, the sheikh who owned the dhow proved to be extremely kind and immediately agreed to lend Speke his boat for the advancement of the incomprehensible and probably foolish European science. Sadly, however, he was unable to offer the use of the dhow's crew, because he was just setting out with his trusted and versatile sailors to go "trading" (which is to say, to kidnap unsuspecting human beings into slavery) in the unknown lands to the south, a region still untested by the slave dealers, and, he hoped, abounding in human booty. Since the dhow was useless to Speke without a crew who knew how to sail the vessel, he had to abandon the idea of using it. He also resisted the temptation to accept the sheik's offer to accompany him to lands that no white man had ever seen. Instead, he returned to Burton's camp, lucky that he had done so, because the gentleman Arab slave driver was soon massacred with all his men in an ambush laid by Africans unwilling to become the raw material of a new slave trade.

Once Burton and Speke were reunited, they decided to regroup in Kazé, reentering the town in June 1858. There, they once again enjoyed the company of their Arab friends. Sipping extremely sweet green mint tea, they began to speak of the great lakes of Africa. As described by those Levantine tale-spinners, the immense Lake Ukerewe and the florid empire of Uganda that extended along its shores beckoned, like so many settings from an African version of the *Arabian Nights.* This time, however, Burton listened to Speke's point of view. He allowed his fellow explorer to go and see the waters in question, though Burton was too sick to accompany him.

The little caravan set out: the interpreter Bombay, twenty native bearers, ten Baluchs. Since the Beluchs were Muslims, and hence rigid teetotalers, they cursed the native bearers, who took advantage of every stop to get drunk on *pombé,* the local beer. The main thoroughfare of the Land of the Moon was a little footpath that intermittently vanished in the tall grass. Along this barely visible highway passed all trade to and from the coast: slave caravans, ivory caravans, herds of livestock on the way to market, cloth and glass beads being transported to Arab lands. The path was narrow, and progress was difficult at best. One day, at a turning in the trail, Speke's head bearer came face-to-face with a man carrying an elephant tusk, he too the lead man in a long single-file line of bearers. The two bearers stared at each other with fierce determination; then they suddenly hurled themselves at each other, smashing their heads together like infuriated rams. Soon every other member of the two long caravans was doing the same thing. The white explorer feared that an indigenous feud had suddenly broken out, a war fought by ramming heads together. In an attempt to stop the fighting he rushed forward, ready to lay about him with a gnarly club. But uncertainty stayed his hand: he could not distinguish friend from foe. They all looked the same to his Caucasian eyes. Suddenly the melee ended, one column courteously made way for the other, and all the bearers laughed heartily at the white outlander who had failed to understand a perfectly reasonable manner of establishing the right of way on a narrow road.

Here, too, the rule of *hongo* applied, and Speke found himself in a considerable bind. The local currency consisted of colored glass beads, and he had brought only white glass beads, which nobody would accept as legal tender. Again, the local chiefs, their advisers, and their tendency to haggle endlessly over minor points caused delays that exasperated the impatient English explorer. The most enervating encounter—but also, perhaps, the most charming—was with Ungagu, sultaness of a tribe whose territory lay athwart Speke's route. Ungagu ordered Speke to make a considerable detour to pay a visit on her and to render her homage. Local etiquette required that any visitor to the sultaness spend several days waiting to see her. After that time, an increasingly frantic Speke was ushered into a labyrinthine palace composed of huts and corrals crowded with lowing livestock. He was finally seated on a bench and examined at length and in detail by a lady of the court, who then went to make a report to her queen. A short time later, the sultaness made her appearance, her gait rendered majestic by the pounds and pounds of brass wire wrapped around the elephant tails and zebra manes that hung from her waist, covering her legs. She was a smiling sixty-year-old matron dressed in a much-patched and heavily stained Arab gown. She took Speke's hand, snuggled up next to him on the bench, and began to pat and finger his clothing with a great show of admiration. When she reached his waistcoat, she declared that this would be a proper gift for a sovereign as great as she. Speke readily surrendered his vest, and received a young steer in exchange. The sultaness spoke glowingly of the white explorer's hair, comparing it to a lion's mane, and then withdrew, fingering the vest and dragging her feet through the dirt.

Stripped of an article of clothing but finally free to continue his journey, Speke set out and, on the morning of July 30, 1858, from atop a hill, he saw a glittering light in the distance amid trailing wisps of slowly dissipating fog. This gleaming sheen of light was reflected from the long-sought waters of Lake Ukerewe, which Speke promptly renamed Lake Victoria in honor of his own queen. He was completely out of food. Since he could not afford to travel around the immense body of water, dotted with islands and promontories, he made do with questioning the locals, deducing from their answers that this lake must certainly be the chief source of the Nile. He hastened back to Kazé, triumphant, making a victorious entrance, like a Roman general returning from a conquered province. But Speke's enthusiasm met with Burton's scholarly rigor: it was possible, indeed, quite likely, that the lake was the source of the Nile, but there was only one way to be sure: circumnavigating it, and then following the river that flowed out of it. For now, Burton stated, that this was the source of the Nile could be considered no more than a simple hypothesis. Speke reluctantly agreed and relations between the two explorers cooled sharply. They decided to return immediately to the coast, and during the trek they spoke little if at all. From Zanzibar, they took ship for Aden, where Burton remained for several months to recuperate in the hot dry climate. Speke, instead, hastened back to England aboard a passing warship. He had promised Burton, leader of the expedition, that he would await his return before publishing an account of their discoveries.

10
The Nile Unveiled

As Burton later commented, bitterly, Sir Roderick Murchison, president of the Royal Geographical Society, needed a "lion" to present each year to the public, a lion that would cause the ladies to shudder with its triumphant roar. And so, when Speke broke his promise to Burton that he would not reveal his putative discovery to the British public, and announced to Murchison that he had just come from discovering the source of the Nile, Murchison had no doubts or hesitations. He took Speke at his word, without a shred of proof. The world was promptly informed that a millennia-old mystery had been solved thanks to British enterprise, and Speke, willing and even eager, became the hero of the day. Meanwhile, his unsuspecting chief was still slowly recovering his health under the harsh sun of Aden.

When Burton returned home in May 1859, his indignation at what he considered unethical behavior on Speke's part drove him to even more pointed criticism of Speke's claims. Burton now stated out of hand that the Nile flowed from more than one lake. He was even more deeply hurt at being excluded from a new expedition, whose task was to verify the existence of the still hypothetical effluent. This expedition, naturally enough, was to be commanded by Speke. Victorian public opinion was solidly behind the refined English gentleman Speke, and against the rough and scandalous Irishman, Burton, an habitué of Indian bordellos. The nation was not eager to hear any skepticism expressed concerning a remarkable discovery that redounded to the glory of the queen. After all, if the lake that fed the great river were named Victoria, then the river itself, and all the fecundity it brought to the surrounding valley, would all flow from the queen's greatness. Increasingly embittered, Burton left the poisonous atmosphere of England and went to the United States, traveling among the Mormons of Utah and the prospectors of California.

Speke, in the meanwhile, prepared to set out on his new expedition. He invited an old fellow hunter from the Himalayas to join the expedition: James Augustus Grant, an officer of the Indian army, born in Scotland in 1827.

Together they set sail in April 1860, and in mid-August they landed on Zanzibar, greeted by several veterans of the previous expedition, including the invaluable Sidi Bombay. The new sultan of Zanzibar proved just as helpful as his late father. In the meanwhile, however, the situation in the interior had worsened. There was now a steady state of war among the various tribes and between the African tribes and the Arab slavers. One German explorer had already been killed. Despite this inhospitable situation, Speke and Grant set out, although they knew that the unremitting fighting meant fields were devastated and uncultivated, and that villages stood deserted. There was every likelihood that they would be unable to find enough food to feed their numerous native bearers. Still they headed due west. When, however, they encountered the gaunt and emaciated survivors of a trading caravan hobbling their way back from the interior, and heard the leader of the column describe how they had been forced to boil the leather overalls of the bearers in order to make a little weak broth, they began drawing up an alternative plan. They decided to take a more northerly route through a less-frequented territory, and split up into two groups, following more or less parallel paths. The only tangible result of this plan, however, was that they were obliged to pay twice as much *hongo* because the African chiefs refused to accept the two columns as part of a single expedition and demanded tribute from both.

Everything changed for the better when they entered the territory of Karague, to the west of Lake Victoria. Here they found an equatorial Arcadia rich in pasturage and well-tilled fields, inhabited by a peaceful and courteous people. The kindest of all was the king, Rumanika, who—far from demanding costly tolls for the right to pass through his lands—ordered his subjects to welcome the foreigners and provide them with all the food they needed, free of charge. And when, on November 25, Speke and Grant finally set foot in Rumanika's royal palace, a hodgepodge of huts and courtyards and also equipped with a handsome reception hall built by the Arabs, the ruling family showed a majesty worthy of their European counterparts. The king solicitously inquired after the health of his royal European cousins. Particularly remarkable were the royal wives. In this kingdom, obesity was considered the height of feminine beauty, and the wives downed bowl after bowl of milk, drinking almost without interruption. Their forced diet had in fact made them very beautiful, at least according to the standards of Karague. Speke thought that their rolls of flesh were reminiscent of giant puddings, and it took the assistance of at least two or three slave girls to help each wife rise from a sitting position and walk from place to place, with a hobbled charm that characterized these Pantagruelian ladies in that paradise of pinguidity.

Between grand banquet tables groaning with poultry and goats, the good Rumanika finally revealed the reason for his extreme benevolence toward his white guests: he knew perfectly well that they were powerful sorcerers, and he hoped to obtain from them a spell with which to kill a rebellious brother who aimed to usurp his throne. The explorers denied that they had any such powers, but Rumanika was greatly consoled when Speke gave him a pistol, certainly as good as any spell or enchantment for killing a brother. This was the first firearm seen in Karague, where the prudent Arabs had always been careful not to give such dangerous gifts. The explorers prolonged their stay, as hunting parties were followed by audiences at court, grand banquets, and endless conversations in which they learned of countless new African wonders: to the north lay another immense lake, the Luta Nzige (in time, as careful exploration showed the lake to be relatively small, it was given the name of Albert, Prince Consort to Queen Victoria); there were endless, tangled forests inhabited by monsters who strangled young girls and little tiny men who lived in trees and shot poison darts; there were cannibals who filed their teeth to sharp points and chomped down savagely on human flesh.

Closer to hand, there were other kingdoms in which news of the arrival of white explorers had spread. All the neighboring monarchs wanted them to visit their courts as well. The first emissaries to come were messengers from Kamrasi, king of Unyoro, and they bore a heartening message: other white explorers who were sailing up the Nile in a great vessel would soon arrive. Speke and Grant imagined that this must be John Peterick, an ivory merchant who was also the British consul in Khartoum. He had agreed to meet them partway along the Nile. When they learned of his approach, they wrote him a letter and entrusted it to native runners.

Next came a more solemn and more authoritative invitation from M'tesa, king of Uganda, demanding a visit. Most of Lake Victoria lay within his powerful empire, and his war fleet regularly plied the lake's waters.

Unfortunately, Grant was suffering from a leg wound, and the iron laws of Uganda forbade invalids to enter the realm. So Speke was forced to set off alone. He reached the royal palace on February 19, 1862; the clutter of structures occupied an entire hill. In that Versailles of poles and palm fronds, an extremely intricate etiquette ruled, far more rigid than the seventeenth-century etiquette of the Sun King. In the presence of their ruler, subjects were obliged to kneel on the ground, spreading their arms in prayer and repeating endlessly the words *tuiyanzi-yanzi-yanzi,* a phrase expressing gratitude. No object could be presented to the king unless it were wrapped in some kind of covering. This rule applied as well to human bodies: anyone writhing in the dust at the foot of the throne who showed more skin than was acceptable might be instantly put to death (when Grant finally arrived, the court master of ceremonies examined him carefully and objected to the bare skin between the top of his stockings and the hem of his trousers). As a kingly whim, however, M'tesa had meals served to him by young naked girls; any of his guests who might chance to cast his eyes on them, or on the more fully clad beauties of the king's enormous harem, might quickly be decapitated, as might anyone who ventured to touch the throne or the robes of the king. M'tesa was continually surrounded by young pages ready to dart off to carry orders where desired (and if they darted slowly, the punishment might be a spear through the heart). Fantastically masked sorcerers had dual responsibilities: to ward off the evil eye and to keep their king's goblet brimming over with palm wine.

Speke ran into problems with the court ceremony of Uganda almost immediately after reaching the capital. His arrival was announced in the royal court, and he was quickly shown to his accommodations, because the audience with the king was scheduled for the next day. When the sun rose on that fateful dawn, the explorer donned his finest clothing, had twelve of his men put on the scarlet jackets of the British uniform, and loaded his bearers with gifts for his Ugandan majesty. The procession set off in perfect order, marching behind the Union Jack that fluttered proudly in the breeze. *Irungi! Irungi!* shouted the onlookers who had gathered from every corner of the town.

The snag came when Speke entered the courtyard of the palace: he was invited to sit on the ground and wait for the king. On the ground? Never! The indignant Englishman refused: let a chair be brought, in keeping with his dignity and rank. There was dismay among the courtiers at this flouting of protocol, each side insisted, and in the end Speke turned on his heel and left the palace, followed by his men in a panicky cluster, each of them expecting at any second to feel an assegai pierce his ribs. Instead, nothing happened at all, because when M'tesa learned of the incident, he reasoned that only magical powers could have justified such prideful arrogance. He immediately sent a messenger to Speke, asking him to return, and to bring his own folding chair with him.

Thus, the battle of wills between native etiquette and imperial etiquette culminated in both contenders seated facing each other, on their respective thrones, staring at each other for a solid half hour in perfect silence, awaiting the arrival of the interpreter. Every so often, the king would gesture to the Englishman, indicating that he should remove or put on his hat, open or close his umbrella. When the interpreter finally showed up, the king ordered him to ask the Englishman whether he "had beheld him." When Speke replied that he had, indeed, beheld the king, M'tesa rose from his throne and stalked from the room, imitating the gait of the lion, a gait that in Uganda was a prerogative of the king alone. The king was going to dine, because he had vowed to fast from the moment the white man arrived until the end of their audience, and he was now really hungry.

In the days that followed, the audiences became slightly less rigid and formal. Speke had the further good fortune of winning the protection of the queen mother. The dowager had decided to consult the learned white sorcerer concerning certain supposed illnesses that afflicted her. She was delighted at the cure that was prescribed: abundant and frequent servings of palm wine, her favorite beverage. The stout queen mother even aroused her royal son's jealousy by her continual audiences with Speke: M'tesa wanted the white visitor all to himself. Speke was gratified by the honors paid him, but horrified by the executions ordered in the palace on a daily basis for trivial offenses. If a cook prepared a meal that was less than perfect, he would pay with his life. A concubine who had dared to offer a piece of fruit to her king was spared instant strangulation only through the intercession of Speke himself. When Speke gave the king a carbine rifle as a gift, M'tesa ordered a willing page to try it out on the first passerby; when a man fell dead at a single shot, M'tesa thanked Speke gravely. The rifle, he said, "killed nicely."

Through the good offices of his palm-wine drunkard and patient, the queen mother, Speke persuaded M'tesa to send a group of men to transport Grant to the palace. Grant was still convalescing when he was carried to the palace on a litter, on May 27. Still, the two explorers asked M'tesa for his royal leave to complete their mission: to find and follow the river that flowed out of the lake. M'tesa refused the request, but one day, in a moment of jovial distraction, he agreed; the caravan left the Ugandan capital in great haste, fearful that M'tesa might change his mind. Grant suffered a relapse, however, and decided to head back to Unyoro to recover. Speke continued on his own. On July 21, 1862, he finally gazed down upon the majestic river that poured out of the lake, tumbling down in a spectacular waterfall that Speke dubbed Ripon Falls, in honor of the new president of Britain's Royal Geographical Society. He then made his way down the course of the river to find Grant. When he reached the border of Unyoro territory he was dismayed at the reception that greeted him: a hail of arrows. He was forced to clear the way with rifle fire. And yet King Kamrasi was expecting him—what had happened?

Speke explained later in his written account of his adventures: the king, "untutored, suspicious, and merciless," had been informed that two separate expeditions led by white men were entering his kingdom from opposite directions, and he had immediately surmised that the outsiders were bent on conquest. To add to his suspicion, insistent rumors had reached his ear to the effect that Europeans were cannibals and that they traveled around Africa carrying with them incredibly ferocious white dwarves shut up in trunks. When the time came, the explorers would simply open the trunks and release the presumably murderous and ravenous dwarves. Speke immediately sent runners to deny the rumors and to placate the king. As soon as Speke joined back up with Grant, they marched together to pay their respects in the capital.

Unyoro, too, had its ceremonies and protocols. Here they were required to wait for several days, and during that time the king's emissaries did their level best to extort as much as they could from the two explorers, letting drop veiled threats. At last, Kamrasi—satisfied with a double-edged dagger and a chronometer worth fifty pounds sterling—agreed to receive his European guests. Perhaps this prolonged reception influenced those guests' description of the royal palace: the huts were filthy and stench-ridden, the courtyards were covered with a thick stratum of manure, in which the king splashed around knee-deep, personally selecting the livestock to slaughter for the banquet in the visitors' honor. He seemed to choose the oldest and most emaciated cattle.

Despite the miserly accommodations and filth, this must have been the most prosperous of the three kingdoms that the explorers visited, at least to judge from the royal concubines. The women of the court of Unyoro were so fat that eight strong men could barely lift one.

Speke and Grant enjoyed this dubious hospitality for four long months. It was not until November 9 that they were allowed to depart, by this point stripped of almost every possession they had brought with them. They descended along the course of the Kefu, a tributary of the Nile, anxiously searching the narrow horizon in the constant hope of meeting with Peterick's men, and instead seeing increasingly frequent "traces of civilization": trinkets and beads manufactured in Europe and brought there by traders and slavers. On December 3, in a place called Faloro, they saw a huge encampment. They were welcomed festively by a native soldier in Egyptian uniform. He turned out to be the chief of a band of ivory hunters hired by a Maltese merchant named De Bono, who lived in Khartoum. They had been there for the past three years. The chief knew nothing about Peterick. He was about to head home with his men and the ivory they had gathered and offered to accompany the two Europeans north along the Nile. The British explorers were impatient, however, and decided to push on to Apuddo. When the horde of hunters—some two hundred in number—reached the village, they stripped it like a swarm of locusts. They seized every bit of food in sight and pressed the inhabitants into service, forcing them to carry the bales of ivory and driving them along the riverbank, whip cracks sounding across the broad river until they reached Gondokoro on February 15. Gondokoro, with a little white church built by Austrian missionaries who had been trying in vain for years to convert the locals to Christianity, was the southern outpost of civilization in the Nile basin. Grant and Speke felt as if they were already on European soil. As Speke wandered around the village in search of the elusive Peterick, he suddenly found himself gathered up into a vigorous bear hug by a huge and unquestionably European bearded man. In a daze, he slowly recognized an old friend and hunting companion, Samuel Baker. Baker had ventured this far south, in the company of his young and daring wife, to find Speke. He hoped, Baker said with perfect British irony, that Speke and Grant had gotten themselves into some frightful fix in the mysterious equatorial regions. He would be delighted to rescue them, and thus share in their glory.

A few days later, long after Speke and Grant had given up hope of ever seeing him, Peterick finally showed up, candidly confessing that he had taken his time because he felt certain that he would never see either of them alive again.

After leaving Gondokoro on February 26, Speke and Grant set foot on English soil again after an absence of three years and two months. They proudly announced that the Nile held no more secrets: its chief source was Lake Victoria, just as Speke had always claimed. Public opinion swung wildly in their favor, but controversy had not died entirely away. Another national demigod, the explorer David Livingstone, had his doubts about the matter and a sharply differing view concerning the intricate hydrography of the Nile basin. Burton, in turn, had returned from his American travels, now maintaining that the Nile necessarily sprang from Lake Tanganyika, and not from Lake Victoria at all. Perhaps, Burton added, the Nile was also fed by runoff from the snows of Mounts Kilimanjaro and Kenya—Ptolemy's Mountains of the Moon—after all.

A year later, the British Society for the Advancement of Science held a public debate to settle the matter. The discussion was scheduled for September 16, 1864, in the elegant spa of Bath, Speke's birthplace. On the morning of the debate, a slip of paper was handed from member to member of the huge audience that sat in anxious anticipation of what the popular press was billing as the "duel of the Nile." As the slip of paper circulated, a grim silence fell over the hall. Captain John Hanning Speke had been killed the day before, at four in the afternoon, while hunting on a cousin's estate. He had been found lying dead on the ground, a rifleshot through his chest. The official inquest issued a finding of accidental death: while climbing over a rock wall, Speke must have caught the trigger of his fowling piece on a branch or a piece of jutting rock and died instantly.

Many, however, Burton among them, suspected suicide. The neurotic and hypersensitive Speke, worn down by the controversy and obsessed by the fear of being stripped of the laurels he coveted for purportedly discovering the Nile's source, had perhaps collapsed under the tension and remorse over his betrayal of Burton. We shall certainly never know the truth.

None of the protagonists of this story of exploration that culminated, unexpectedly, in a mysterious death by gunshot was ever entrusted with another major expedition of exploration, even though many questions remained to be answered in the vast and intricate Nile basin. Both Burton and Grant returned to Africa, the former as British consul in the Gulf of Guinea, the latter as a consultant on the expedition that Lord Napier led against the negus of Abyssinia, Theodore, in 1868. Neither of them, however, played the "lion's role," as Sir Roderick Murchison might have said. Burton died in Trieste, Italy, in 1890, where he had been named British consul. In Trieste, Burton spent his last years peacefully, writing numerous books. He worked in a great hall filled with writing desks; each desk held material for one of his books, and he would work at each of the desks, day after day. On each desk stood a water glass; in each glass stood a fragrant jasmine flower.

Grant died two years after Burton, at Nairn, Scotland. He had assumed the role of defender of Speke's memory, and so zealous was he that he refused implacably to make Burton's acquaintance.

11

The Missing Lake

That day in February 1864, at Gondokoro, after releasing Speke from the brotherly bear hug that threatened to choke the life out of him, Samuel Baker asked whether he had left "any laurels to seize" in his travels along the Equator. Speke told him of the lake Luta Nzige, about which he had learned at the court of King Rumanika. Baker thought it must certainly be connected to the Nile river system of tributaries, and it would be an objective worthy of him, an excellent sprig of laurel with which to crown his brow. Less than a month later, the Bakers, husband and wife, set out for Unyoro.

Samuel White Baker was at the time more than forty. He was born in London in 1821 to a family wealthy to the point of opulence, and he had enjoyed a lifetime of gratifying experiences: he founded a farming colony on the island of Ceylon; fought in the Crimean War; supervised the construction of the first Turkish railroad in Dobruja, a region in northeastern Bulgaria and southeastern Romania, between the Danube River and the Black Sea. Above all, however, like his friend Speke, he was a great hunter: among the trophies he had bagged were bears from the Balkans and tigers from

Bengal. He had married his second wife, a blond Hungarian named Florence Ninian von Sass, who was fifteen years younger than he and who, like him, loved adventurous travel and hunting. The happy couple set out in 1861 for the Sudan, traveling up the Atbara, an eastern tributary of the Nile, until they reached the borders of Abyssinia. They hunted, enjoyed spectacular sunsets, made love, and learned Arabic: Baker mistrusted native interpreters and wanted to gain a mastery of the language for himself. After a year of that life, in a roundabout tour that took them to the banks of the Blue Nile, they descended to Khartoum (sixteen degrees north latitude) in early June 1862.

Built about thirty years before at the confluence of the White Nile and the Blue Nile, the capital of Egyptian Sudan then had a population of roughly thirty-five thousand souls, twenty-six of them Europeans, most of them adventurers of the worst kind. To understand much of the equatorial adventures that follow, we must indulge in a brief parenthetical history of the Sudan.

The Sudan was a conquered land: it had been invaded and easily occupied between 1820 and 1824 by the army of Mehemet Ali, an Albanian officer who had taken over Egypt in the turbulent years following Napoleon's invasion. After landing at Alexandria with a Turkish expeditionary force transported there aboard English ships in order to fight the French, the young officer soon distinguished himself for his tactical skill and for his unquestioned gift for intrigue. Once Egypt had been abandoned, first by the French and then by the English, Mehemet Ali—at the head of a corps of ten thousand soldiers, almost all Albanians like him and all exceedingly loyal—had lured the Mamluks, former masters of Egypt, into a trap, massacring every last one. Even though he governed formally in the name of the sultan of Constantinople, to whom the country technically belonged, he was an empire builder, and he had set out to conquer the immense territory of the Sudan, to plunder it of its wealth (although he soon learned there was very little to plunder), but especially for slaves to impress in the huge army he hoped would fulfill his dreams of expansion. Once he felt sufficiently strong, he mutinied against the sultan's rule, capturing Crete and Syria. He would have marched on Constantinople itself had he not been halted by threats from the European powers, who warned they were ready to intervene. He did obtain one concession: the office of viceroy of Egypt was made hereditary. In 1862 his great-grandson Said reigned, and under the influence of European advisers, he was trying to impose a slightly less savage policy of exploitation in the provinces of Sudan. Still, the Khartoum that greeted the Bakers was decidedly the cesspit of the Egyptian empire. Cairo regularly shipped out to this sepulchre in the desert disgraced functionaries and undesirables of every sort; the lure of easy money attracted rogues and scoundrels from all over the Levant and Europe—Greeks, Turks, Maltese, Italians, Frenchmen, Englishmen, Austrians, Prussians. Ship pilots from the Nile and Nubian peasants came here in search of fortune. The great fleet of sailing vessels and steamships attracted carpenters and mechanics. The herds of horses, donkeys, and camels used by caravans and armies required foragers and tanners, and just as in any city in the vast network of African and Asiatic Islam, there were scribes, pipe makers, water bearers, and strolling vendors of all stripes and varieties. Along the riverbank, half-naked natives loaded and unloaded boats in a hurly-burly that never ceased, while merchants, stretched out on divans in the shade of rudimentary patios, negotiated deals and concluded affairs while smoking a hookah or sipping a tiny cup of coffee. The garrison lived on theft, Baker states dryly, while every government official was dishonest and given to thievery. The governor himself was the greatest cause of the ruin of the land, with his corruption and malfeasance.

Rubber, ostrich feathers, hides, ivory, and slaves were the merchandise that Khartoum shipped north, downriver. The most important merchandise of them all was slaves, a trade that was outlawed in theory, but was in fact the foundation of what little prosperity could be found in the Sudan at that time.

Baker explained briefly, in an account of his adventures, how the business worked. Anyone, even if they were penniless, could find a loan, though at a usurious interest rate of 100 percent. Once an adventurer had obtained the cash, he would join a band of cutthroats, always available in that wicked city, and toward December they would head south, upstream, toward the equatorial regions. Once beyond Gondokoro, the last Egyptian outpost, they would form an alliance with any African tribal chief they could find, and then encircle a village of the chief's enemies, torching huts, killing men, and carrying off women, children, livestock, ivory, and foodstuffs. The chief would be paid off with thirty or forty head of cattle; 30 percent of the cows and oxen were set aside to reward the native members of the expedition; the rest went to the slaver, who would then take advantage of a cunningly concocted dispute to murder his native ally and force his people into slavery as well. The livestock was then sold to neighboring tribes, in exchange for more slaves and ivory. After repeating these steps until a sizable booty had been amassed, the caravan would set out for Khartoum. To save appearances, the slaves were hurried back by alternate routes, and the cutthroats would return to town, ostensibly peaceable ivory-hunters returning home with their catch. Everyone, from the governor to the lowliest functionary, was in on the trade.

In "filthy and wicked" Khartoum, Baker found a message that filled him with joy. The famous Peterick who had been charged with rescuing Speke and Grant had vanished who-knew-where in the deep south and was probably dead. The Royal Geographical Society hoped that Baker would be willing to take over the mission. The most audacious couple of newlyweds in all Africa could not have asked for anything more, and they quickly set out organizing their expedition to the region of equatorial lakes.

It required, however, six months of exhausting negotiations, despite the small river of cash that was laid out, because all those who were involved in the slave trade—which is to say the entire city of Khartoum and surrounding areas—were reluctant to allow

European witnesses, possibly tinged with humanitarian feelings, to travel through their realm of violence and terror. Behind a mask of the most refined courtesy, the governor Musa Pasha cast up obstacles and delayed and sabotaged the Bakers' plans. In the end, however, tenacity and the British pound sterling won out, and on December 18, 1862, the Bakers spread the sails of their three vessels, loaded with about a hundred men, and set off southward against the current of the White Nile. Two months later came the meeting in Gondokoro with Grant and Speke and the information that they provided concerning a great lake still to be explored. The Bakers decided to continue on toward the Equator. They could not have chosen a worse time: drastically swollen by the winter rains, the Nile had flooded immense expanses of land, transforming them into impassable swamps. The unfavorable winter winds hindered upstream navigation. For nine interminable months, they lay at forced anchor, while horses and mules died off, one by one, until none was left. It was not until January 1864 that they resumed their march, on ox-back, with a broad sweep inland to the east of the river. They reached the Nile again on January 22, near the Karuma Falls, beyond which began the kingdom of Unyoro. On the opposite bank, however, stood the army of King Kamrasi, with intentions that were anything but friendly. A few months before a column of slave-raiders had devastated the land, and the people of Unyoro feared a new incursion. Baker resolved the impasse with a stroke of genius: claiming to be the brother of Speke, he climbed onto a high outcropping and showed off the long blond beard that made him resemble his friend, the explorer. An even greater impression was made when his wife climbed up and undid the long blond locks that reached to her waist. The warriors lowered their weapons and broke into a dance of welcome. Ten days later, carried on a litter because he was ill with a particularly bad case of malaria, Baker was set down at the feet of King Kamrasi. The monarch of Unyoro immediately listed for the feverish explorer the many gifts that he expected to receive as tribute. In return, the Englishman asked that he be taken immediately to the lake, about which he had heard in the meanwhile astonishing—and false—information. The natives had told him that the lake was much bigger than Victoria (in fact, it covers less than a tenth the area). The wily Kamrasi, who did not wish to lose so quickly an opportunity to strip his precious prey to the bone, told Baker that the lake was at least a six months' march away, and that it was necessary to pass through extremely difficult territory. Baker would need to rest and convalesce before undertaking so difficult a journey. The meeting ended with the king suggesting that they become blood brothers, an offer that no guest could refuse. Alleging religious impediments, the explorer forestalled by having one of his men substitute for him; the man licked blood from an incision in the sovereign's forearm, and the sovereign reciprocated.

Baker, as battered by fever as his wife, was in the throes of desperation. The lake was too far away to reach, they were out of quinine, and his men were beginning to desert. Suddenly, unexpectedly, things took a turn for the better. A kindly courtier from Kamrasi's court whispered into his ear that in reality Luta Nzige was quite close, perhaps ten days' march. The king, realizing that he had squeezed his guests dry, and having received gifts of a saber and a shotgun, decided he would allow the Bakers to leave. But he indulged in one final, supreme caprice at the last minute. Since they were already blood brothers, said Kamrasi, they could trade wives as well. Wouldn't he prefer a lovely young black wife, fresh and innocent, in place of his white wife, who was frankly starting to look a bit tired and worn out? Baker grew pale with fury, pulled out his pistol, and pointed it at the head of the "insolent monarch," threatening to blow his brains out again if he dared to repeat his proposal. At the same time Florence Baker launched into a violent invective in impeccable Arabic, a stream of insults and offenses that were promptly translated into Unyoro by Madame Florence's zealous black maid. The startled and insulted king responded that there was no reason to take offense. He had only meant to honor his guests with a traditional offer, in keeping with the local bon ton.

The touchy couple was finally allowed to depart, still seething with indignation; they promptly found themselves in an endless labyrinth of foul swamps in which it was impossible to make progress except on foot. Baker dismounted from his ox and splashed forward in water up to his waist. Shortly thereafter he watched in horror as his adored wife fell senseless and sank into the mud. She had suffered a sunstroke. She raved for a week, carried on a stretcher of braided branches under a relentless downpour. Her husband, who continued on driven only by desperation, finally collapsed in exhaustion after days and days of worry, fever, and rain, overwhelmed by nervous collapse. When he recovered consciousness many hours later, his Florence had made it through the crisis and was again able to recognize him.

That enervating march found its reward on the morning of March 14, when they finally glimpsed the waters of the lake, which seemed to be "a sea of quicksilver." Baker dove into it—actually, he fell into it, exhausted as he was—and drank deep gulps "from the source of the Nile," giddy at the thought that "no European foot had ever trod this sand." The Luta Nzige was named after Prince Albert, the recently deceased husband of Queen Victoria; but it was hardly "the great reservoir of the Nile" that Baker insisted on calling it: it was only a smaller body of water in a vast basin. They coasted along the northeast shore in a canoe, miraculously surviving a tremendous storm, and after thirteen days of paddling they reached the village of Magungu. There they found the point where the river enters the lake. They paddled upriver until they reached an imposing waterfall that they named Murchison Falls. Here their lives were in jeopardy once again when an enraged hippopotamus overturned their boat, tumbling them into crocodile-infested waters. Fortunately, the rushing current produced by the falls was so strong that it literally hurled them up onto the bank. Two months later they returned, exhausted but happy, to the rustic capital of Unyoro, where a surprise awaited them: the Kamrasi who had cast his eyes upon Mrs. Baker was not Kamrasi at all, but his brother

M'Gambi; the real Kamrasi had sent his brother to masquerade as him because he was deathly afraid of the spells and enchantments of those white sorcerers, especially of that woman with long yellow hair who had all the earmarks of a powerful witch. Now he was taking his rightful place, having determined to his own satisfaction that the couple was not dangerous. Baker, indignant at the "ignoble comedy," acted offended; and it was not until the king had been forced to beg at some length that he agreed to meet him. He took his revenge by appearing in the "costume of a Scottish mountain man from Athol, which won the admiration of the crowd"; he sat as an equal on a bench identical to that of Kamrasi, "a bronze statue with a sinister glare," before whom all his subjects crawled in the dust.

For six months more, the Bakers remained in Unyoro, trying to recover a bit of strength and health. They even saved the realm from a raiding party of 150 slavers who had come all the way from Khartoum (while the "feckless" and "cowardly" Kamrasi fled in terror). Baker had the Union Jack raised over his hut, and when the commander of the slavers appeared before him, Baker informed him that Unyoro was under British protection and that he would make sure that the slavers paid for every hostile action by hanging; the raiders withdrew meekly. Kamrasi asked the explorer to sell him that powerful cloth talisman, but Baker shot back that the flag worked "only in the hands of someone who knew how to defend it."

In the end a much more fearsome enemy, M'tesa, king of Uganda, decided to declare war on the unfortunate Kamrasi. As Kamrasi fled northward, he took the whites with him, finally abandoning them near the Karuma Falls. They managed to get a message to a caravan of ivory hunters that they had met on their journey south, who were still wandering in the area. With the column of ivory hunters they set off northward, toward home, but even in that last stretch they came within a hair's breadth of dying when the caravan was set upon by a tribe of Bari. Many of the hunters died under a hail of poisoned arrows. In February 1865, however, they finally entered triumphantly into Gondokoro after two years away, straddling oxen that lumbered along in something approximating a gallop, behind the Union Jack fluttering in the wind, amid festive gunshots and shouts of joy.

Even then, their odyssey was not over. The boat that carried them northward, back down the White Nile, was becalmed, trapped in the marshes of the Sudd when the wind died. The Sudd was a frightful expanse of muck, a desolate desert of endless canebrakes, where the great river piled up the detritus it dragged down from the mountains in an inextricable welter, until it would finally rot, exuding death-dealing miasmas. There, many of the men who had faithfully accompanied the Bakers through the entire long voyage died, practically within sight of home, of fever.

At last, in October 1865, at Port Suez, Baker was able to gulp down a flagon of Allsopp's beer, a desire that had tormented him for four long years.

12

The Man-Eaters

Terrifying stories circulated in corrupt Khartoum and languid Zanzibar concerning the unknown, impenetrable jungles that stretched mile after mile to the west of the Great Lakes of Africa, like a mantle of green shadow, where not even the rays of the sun could penetrate. In these forests, the trees themselves were evil. It was necessary to cut tunnels through the tangled liana vines in order to get anywhere. The air was unbreathable, so drenched with water that it seemed as if one were walking in a pouring rainstorm. These were vegetal barriers infested by spirits—and by beings worse than any spirits, half men and half dogs, with massive tusks and fanlike tails, who used human fat as their only condiment, who fed not only on their prisoners but on their own relatives, especially when those relatives were old or unwell (nothing was wasted in these lands of sharpened teeth).

Other black Africans—who often fell victim to their raids and wound up in their boiling kettles—called them the Nyam-Nyams, an onomatopoeic name that was meant to echo the sound of chomping jaws.

In November 1863, a white man entered the land of the Nyam-

Nyams, unconcerned by their terrifying reputation. He was a thirty-six-year-old Italian named Carlo Piaggia; he was not an ambitious explorer, but simply a poor émigré who had come to Africa seeking his fortune. In Tunis, Cairo, and places in between, he had worked in such humble trades as gardening, hat making, bookbinding, and painting; then he had wound up in the Sudan, where his infallible accuracy with a rifle allowed him to procure rare specimens of the local fauna for zoological museums and for collectors. Often, he went hungry; he was so skinny that he liked to boast no other white man had ever cast so little shadow on the soil of the Dark Continent. He penetrated into Zande—the native name for the land—in a large caravan of ivory traders that had come from Khartoum; the plan was that the caravan would leave him there, head south, and come back to pick him up a year later. In the meanwhile, the hunter would have piled up a cache of prey without competition in that unspoilt cannibal territory.

Tombo, the chief of the tribe among whom Piaggia decided to stay, welcomed him hospitably, amply persuaded by the European's generous gift of copper rings and colored beads, and perhaps by the unprecedented powers of that skinny visitor who could kill animals from a distance and who carried fire in his pocket (in the form of a box of matches).

Wherever he went, from village to village, instead of being viewed as dinner the white man was honored and almost worshiped. Pregnant women would follow him step by step gazing at him intensely, in the hopes of bearing a son as white as him.

One day Tombo, the courteous cannibal chief, invited him to dine in his hut. Piaggia had already eaten, but he could hardly refuse without offending the chief. "I took a bit of meat from a particularly large hunk that had been served to us. I could not tell what animal the meat came from. It was not at all stringy, and it was mixed with greens. The taste struck me as rather sweet, and I only ate as much as was needed to fulfill my obligations as a guest. But because Tombo insisted that I should eat more, I found myself obliged to have another mouthful. And once again I noted a new flavor, tasty and slightly sweet."

Piaggia thanked his host and withdrew, heading into the jungle to hunt. He walked for half an hour and then happened upon a group of warriors who stood motionless, leaning on their spears, around a corpse that dangled from a tree branch. From the corpse's posterior great chunks of meat had been removed.

"Tombo," the warriors explained, "caught this man with one of his wives right on this spot. He killed him with a spear, strung him up, and left him like this."

A sudden flash of horror filled Piaggia's mind. He rushed to Tombo's hut and began shouting at him, indignantly asking him why he had tricked him into eating the flesh of his people. The chief was playing a flute, and he unhurriedly finished his little concert before answering: "My people are your people; if you do not show them that you eat them when they are bad, then they will not respect your women. This is how all great men act."

The hunter stayed with Tombo's tribe for eighteen months longer, and his stay was troubled by no more culinary incidents. When Piaggia departed, he left behind him a fond memory and his long locks. The women took the cuttings of his hair and arranged them in little tufts to adorn their grass skirts.

Five years later, the eaters of human flesh received a second visit from a European traveler, Georg Schweinfurth. He was a Baltic German, a Russian subject, born in Riga in 1836. He was a botanist, and he had already "herbalized" in the Sudan and in Ethiopia; then, in 1868, he had begun to travel up the White Nile along with the inevitable company of ivory traders, who traveled through the most remote regions of central Africa, rudely indifferent to the fact that they were officially unexplored only because no white man had ever set foot there.

The scientist first traveled through the territory of the Scilluk, whose hair, smeared with raw rubber, a practice done from childhood on, resembled the crest of the guinea fowl. Then he traveled

This engraving of Ferdinand Magellan dates from about a quarter century after the great navigator's death. He is shown holding a chart and a compass, symbols of his skill, and gazing toward a constellation of the Southern Hemisphere. —Royal Geographical Society, London, UK/Bridgeman Art Library

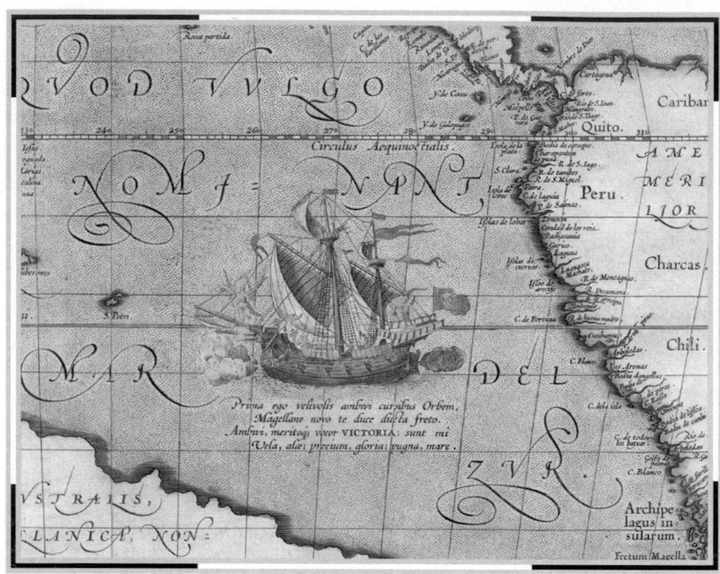

This map of the Pacific Ocean was drawn by Abrahamus Ortelius at the end of the sixteenth century. Noteworthy details: Magellan's flagship, the Victoria, *cannon blasting and sails billowing. Also, the great Magellanic continent, jutting alarmingly far north.* —Private Collection/Bridgeman Art Library

Henry Morton Stanley's hat. Stanley marched across Africa wearing this pith helmet, as he hurried to rescue other explorers who either didn't know they needed rescuing or who didn't want to be rescued. —Royal Geographical Society, London, UK/Bridgeman Art Library

Robert Louis Stevenson. Tusitala, the storyteller of the South Seas: that was how Stevenson was known to his island neighbors in his last years on Samoa. —Stapleton Collection, UK/Bridgeman Art Library

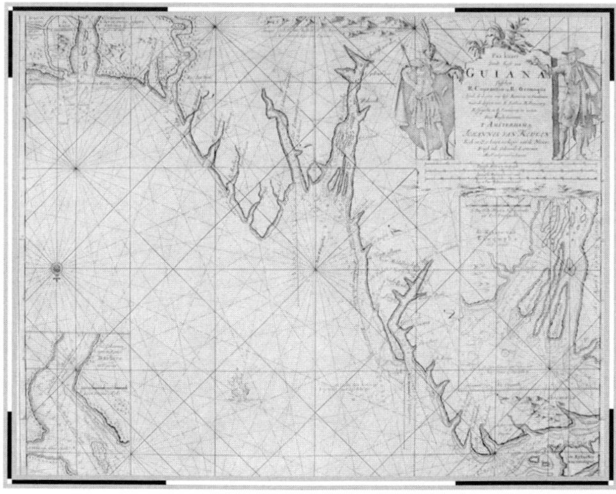

Van Keulen, Guiana. This map shows the intricate coastline of Guiana and the mountains, inland, where it was thought El Dorado ruled over a kingdom of golden palaces and silver furniture. —Courtesy of Thomas Suarez

Henry Morton Stanley in his comfortable older years.—Stapleton Collection, UK, and the Bridgeman Art Library

This lithograph was based on a photograph of Krakatoa taken in 1883, during the earlier stage of the eruption, when the volcanic island was still a popular tourist attraction. —Natural History Museum, London,UK/Bridgeman Art Library,

This Portuguese map of equatorial Africa shows Lake Victoria as little more than a wide spot along the course of the Nile. —Courtesy of Thomas Suarez

This relatively early world map by Grynaeus shows a fanciful Nile River, a truncated South America, and a tiny slice of land where North America ought to be. —Courtesy of Thomas Suarez

Portrait of Sir Walter Raleigh (c. 1552-1618) from Memoirs of the Court of Queen Elizabeth, *published in 1825.* —Stapleton Collection, UK/Bridgeman Art Library

This map by Hondius shows the East Indies in great detail, but perhaps with not enough ocean. —Courtesy of Thomas Suarez

This map of the Americas, done by Ortelius in the late sixteenth century, shows a strangely distorted South America bordering a huge and ill-defined Great Southern Land. —Courtesy of Thomas Suarez

through the territory of the imposing and bronzed Dinkas, their skin dusted with ash, their hair twisted like corkscrews, arms and legs covered with a tinkling array of metal gewgaws, exceedingly long pipes in their mouths. Lastly he marched across the territory of the Bongos, nearly wiped out by slavers, through dense forests of giant bamboo plants where it was almost impossible to move an inch. Finally he wound up in that botanist's paradise, the land of the "tunnel-forests," as Piaggia had so aptly described them.

In January 1869, Schweinfurth—like his Italian predecessor—was warmly welcomed by the notorious devourers of their fellow men. Schweinfurth described them as imposing warriors with teeth filed to razor tips, the better to bite with, hair done in spirals or crests, dressed in civet skins, armed with spears and scimitars.

Beneath their fierce appearance, however, they must have concealed delicate souls, because like Tombo they were all passionate lovers of music; they would break into tears as they listened to endless concerts for harp and mandolin, held in the clearings between their huts, whose roofs were adorned by great numbers of human skulls. Nearby, wooden frames held up choice hunks of flesh, set out to tenderize: arms, legs, and other anatomical specimens.

In no wise frightened by these charnel racks, indeed, delighted at the music of the countless strolling songsters, the Baltic explorer and botanist continued on his way toward the Equator, leaving the land of the Nyam-Nyams and entering the territory of the Mombuttu, who were also reputed to be cannibals. Their king, Munza, awaited the arrival of the expedition impatiently, because he had already been visited once in previous years by ivory traders, and in the intervening time he had accumulated a huge quantity of ivory tusks, which he was anxious to exchange for piles of copper bracelets.

As the guest of honor, Schweinfurth was received in a private audience with King Munza in his palace, an immense pavilion 150 feet in length and 50 feet tall, to the sound of a trumpet fanfare followed by a solo played on an ivory cornet. The king beat time with a little straw basket full of stones. "With all of the copper decorating his arms, legs, neck, chest, and head—bracelets, chains, rings, and brooches—he glittered and gleamed like a *batterie de cuisine,*" recalled the Baltic German. In Schweinfurth's descriptions of Africans, he always poured on the irony. "Munza was a man of about forty, well built, slender yet powerful, who stood straight and stiff as if he had a metal ribbing. Though he had handsome features, his face was anything but winning: a Neroesque visage, jaded and bored. Around his mouth there lurked an expression which I had not seen in any other Mombuttu: a mixture of greed, violence, and refined cruelty."

These penetrating psychological observations certainly laid the foundations for the stereotypes that were reinforced in the Western imagination by travelers who followed in Schweinfurth's footsteps: an Africa inhabited by barbarous chiefs, with alarm clocks hanging on chains around their necks. Later in his account, Schweinfurth went so far as to state that Munza was tremendously impressed with his boots, and that the chief believed that they were part of his legs, like a horse's hooves.

All the same, Schweinfurth was extremely irritated by the fact that the chief had received the European's gifts in absolute indifference: a swatch of black cloth, a spyglass, a silver dish, a porcelain vase, a book with "gilt tooling." In exchange for the gift of a book that was illegible to him, but glittering with gold, the sovereign showed extreme generosity (or a subtle sense of humor) by sending a royal tribute the next day. Schweinfurth was awakened early in the morning by the panting breaths of some twenty huge and muscular porters bearing on their shoulders the four walls of a hut, while other porters followed with the roof. They rapidly erected the hut next to the explorer's hut, and the king's emissaries announced that now Schweinfurth could put his inestimable treasures in safekeeping, since they might be damaged if left out in the open air.

In the weeks that followed, Schweinfurth's main activity was the defense of his double residence from the overbearing curiosity of the natives, who gathered in huge crowds to admire the white visitor. To ward them off, Schweinfurth surrounded the huts with a hedge of thorns, tossed bucketfuls of water onto the crowd, lit trails of black powder among them, and tossed loud firecrackers in their midst. All of these efforts to disperse the crowd only made it grow; he became as popular as a Punch-and-Judy show.

He became particularly upset when he went out to search for herbs, because the rubberneckers—women for the most part—followed closely on his heels, often trampling the rare plants that he was trying to gather. "A hundred of them trailed along behind me: with every hut and every village that I passed, the throng increased. I was in a pit of despair." If he tried to sneak out early to wash in a stream, he would inevitably be spied upon by "some horrendous woman, peering through the foliage."

That torture lasted for five weeks, the entire time that the explorer spent in the territory of the Mombuttu. But finally, one morning, Schweinfurth had a pleasant surprise: a message from the king was delivered by his royal pages, two Akka Pygmies. When he saw them, Schweinfurth's joy rose to the stars: he had suggested that the king should sell him one of these specimens of Lilliputian humanity. Now, after extensive bargaining, the king traded the Pygmy for a dog. Of course, Schweinfurth chose the smaller of the two and when he set out for the coast, a few days later, he took the little creature with him.

The poor Pygmy was distraught, convinced that he was the food supply for the journey ahead, and at last died of malaria after they reached Egypt. Schweinfurth—who had created the myth of savage and murderous Africans, but himself seemed fairly indifferent to the fate of his fellow human beings—had named him Tikkitikki.

13
The Front Page

The discoveries made in the Great Lakes region by the Speke-Grant expedition, and later by the Bakers, left unsolved many problems concerning the source of the Nile. In 1866 the Royal Geographical Society, in the person of the immortal Sir Roderick Murchison, had given the responsibility of pronouncing the final word on the intricate question to the man whom everyone considered the prince of African explorers, the first man to cross Africa from one ocean to the other, the man who had discovered Lake Ngami and Lake Nyasa, the man who had traced the course of the Zambesi all the way to the river's mouth: David Livingstone.

Livingstone was fifty-three by this time, and he truly was the greatest explorer then alive. He was also—and above all—a solitary explorer. Now that he had been put in charge of a numerous and undisciplined expedition, he proved incapable of, and uninterested in, organizing and commanding it. And so, shortly after the caravan set out inland from the coast toward the region of the lakes, it was already breaking up, with stragglers stringing out behind. The leader preferred to push ahead, as the column followed lazily behind, arrogantly stripping the natives of food and possessions, and mistreating the livestock, which died wholesale. Disgusted by the behavior of his low-life horde, Livingstone sent most of his men back to the coast. In the end, he had a column of just five young black Africans with whom he vanished into the interior, beyond Lake Tanganyika. From Zanzibar, the sounding board of everything that happened in Africa—as well as many things that never did—alarming reports bounced back to Europe. Some of Livingstone's native bearers, in an attempt to conceal their disgraceful behavior and their embarrassing return to the coast, announced that the explorer had been killed.

Once their feverish reports had been closely and critically examined by those who knew the African interior well, they were shown to be contradictory and scarcely credible; still, there was no news at all of Livingstone, and the silence began to be worrisome. Plans were drawn up for a rescue expedition. To the extreme indignation of the professionals (indignation that soon translated into venomous attacks), it was a mere dilettante who actually rescued Livingstone. The explorer was saved by a journalist. The most famous phrase in African exploration ("Dr. Livingstone, I presume?") was pronounced on the morning of November 10, 1871, at Ujiji, the Arab station on Lake Tanganyika. There the supposedly lost explorer was surviving nicely, and had been for months, thanks to the benevolent generosity of the courteous slavers. Livingstone would send hair-raising accounts of the slavers' cruelty back to Europe; the slavers in turn would patiently arrange to intercept those reports and destroy them before they could reach the coast.

A new arrival on the African stage, the rescuer would play a starring role on that stage for the next twenty years. His overwhelming personality would cast a long shadow over his various rivals, arousing equal degrees of admiration and execration. His pen name was Henry Morton Stanley, but he had been born John Rowlands, in Denbigh, Wales, in 1841. The early years of his life seemed taken from a novel by Dickens: a miserable childhood, full of hunger, strife, humiliation; emigration to the United States at age fifteen, working as a cabin boy to pay his passage; a chance encounter in New Orleans with a generous American named Henry Stanley, who decided to adopt him. He went on to fight in the American Civil War and then wrote his first few articles for the New York *Herald,* which sent him as a correspondent to Abyssinia to report on the English expedition against the king, Theodore, who was holding a number of white Europeans hostage. In 1869, the editor of the *Herald,* James Gordon Bennett, happened to be passing through Paris and he invited Stanley to join him. He gave him a substantial series of assignments. He was to travel to Egypt to witness the inauguration of the Suez Canal, then he was to travel up the Nile, describing anything and everything that might be of interest to American tourists. He would then go to Jerusalem, Constantinople, the Crimea, and then the Caucasus. On to Persia, and finally India, sending reports back as he went. Once he reached Bombay, he was to take ship for Zanzibar, and from there he would trek inland to Central Africa, where he was to find Livingstone, if he was still alive; otherwise he was to find proof of Livingstone's death.

When Stanley finally reached Zanzibar in January 1871, after traveling to each and every place on the list given him by James Gordon Bennett, he went to see Dr. Kirk, who had accompanied Livingstone in his exploration of the Zambesi. Kirk told Stanley that the last reports of Livingstone had come from Ujiji, but that had been some time ago. Since then, there had been no news at all.

Stanley did not have much hope of finding Livingstone, but he did have plenty of money (supplied by the *Herald*), so he hired a caravan of native bearers, many of whom had taken part in Speke's expedition. He set out quite promptly, hoping to avoid being caught midway by the rainy season. He had been forced to take a lengthy detour, because a native chief, Mirambo, was waging a fierce war against the Arab slavers, and the entire region was in chaos. It took him eight months to reach Lake Tanganyika. He had lost the two white men who had set out with him, the English sailors Furquhar and Shaw, both killed by tropical fevers. All the same, as he traveled, he had gathered more and more persuasive evidence and more and more persistent rumors concerning the presence of a "white man with a long beard" at Ujiji. Most important, he had discovered his own calling as a commander, capable of overcoming—perhaps we should say, overwhelming—all obstacles. At last, he had reached his destination and had found the needle in the haystack, a single lost white man in the vastness of the African continent. The man with the long beard at Ujiji was none other than Livingstone.

An immediate friendship was sparked between the young journalist and the explorer almost thirty years older than he. Stanley felt an almost filial respect and fondness toward Livingstone. With improved care and nourishment, Livingstone regained his health. He was now eager to resume exploring; Livingstone still believed that Lake Tanganyika was part of the Nile basin. The two men set out together to sail around the northern part of the lake, and they discovered that Livingstone had been wrong. Lake Tanganyika had nothing to do with the Nile. At that point, Stanley decided to head back to the coast, but Livingstone despite the younger man's entreaties, refused to accompany him. He said that his mission was to finish the task he had begun, and he was determined to explore the region to the west of Lake Tanganyika.

The two men parted ways at Tabora, where Livingstone remained to await supplies. Stanley hastened east to Zanzibar—reaching the island in just fifty-four days—carrying with him his sensational scoop, the Discovery of the Lost Explorer, along with Livingstone's invaluable diaries, and an article written exclusively for the *Herald.* At Bagamoyo, on the coast, he crossed paths with a rescue expedition organized by the Royal Geographical Society. One member of the expedition was one of Livingstone's sons, Oswell Livingstone. When he learned that his father was alive, and that he had come too late to rescue him, he simply turned on his heel and returned to England.

The triumph of Stanley as a journalist—his book, *How I Found Livingstone,* was translated into all the major languages of Europe and became an instant best-seller—was clouded by the envy of those he had bested. Rival newspapers insinuated that Stanley was a con artist, that he had invented everything. Veteran African explorers were extremely put out by the exploit of that previously unknown but all-too-lucky traveling correspondent. And not only did he write for a living, but he had given up his British citizenship to become an American.

In the final analysis, the attacks on Stanley were manifestations of a guilty national conscience: England was actually ashamed of having ignored for years its greatest explorer, who had vanished amid a welter of tragic rumors and had then been rescued by an American newspaper instead of a national expedition.

Unaware of these intricate maneuvers, Livingstone waited patiently in Tabora for the supplies he had been promised. When they arrived, five months later, he immediately set out with feverish haste: he was fifty-nine years old; his body was wracked by the diseases he had contracted in Africa and the hardships he had undergone; perhaps he sensed that he did not have long to live, and he was determined to solve the mystery of the true source of the Nile before leaving this life.

He died ten months after leaving Tabora, on May 1, 1873, in a village not far from Lake Bangweolo, the lake he had discovered four years before. His body was carried to the coast on a stretcher by two loyal natives, Susi and Chima. It took them almost ten months to cover the thousand miles.

Livingstone was buried with official pomp and circumstance in Westminster Abbey on April 18, 1874, nearly a year after his death.

In the meantime, Stanley had traveled as a war correspondent with the British expedition against the Ashantis, in present-day Ghana (between five and ten degrees north latitude). When he learned of Livingstone's death he decided that he would complete the explorer's lifework. His enormous renown made it easy for him to obtain the needed funds from two newspapers: his own New York *Herald* and the English newspaper, the *Daily Telegraph.*

On September 21, 1874, he reached Zanzibar and set about organizing the largest caravan that the Dark Continent had ever seen. Drawn up in quasi-military precision, the column stretched for more than half a mile. There were four white men: besides Stanley, there was Frederick Barker and two brothers, Edward and Frank Pocock, chosen for their qualities of determination and discipline. There were 356 black Africans, including bearers and soldiers. Tall, strong men each carried a bale of cloth weighing sixty pounds. Shorter men carried bags of beads weighing fifty pounds. Young men carried forty-five-pound crates of ammunition or preserved foodstuffs. Older or more trusted bearers carried precious, fragile instruments, such as thermometers, barometers, and cameras. The bearers who were known for their smooth, regular gait were entrusted with the three chronometers, wrapped in cotton and enclosed in a crate that weighed no more than twenty-five pounds. Twelve native guides, splendidly adorned in scarlet mantles that bespoke their rank, supervised the column. Bringing up the rear of the procession were two dozen fantastically strong men who carried a forty-foot wooden boat, the *Lady Alice,* dismantled into six sections, each one carried by four men. Each of these boat-bearers received higher pay, was given double rations, and enjoyed the privilege of bringing their wives. And so there were also thirty-six women, who carried kitchen implements, and six children. Other children were born over the course of the long journey.

The expedition's goal was Lake Victoria. To reach the lake, however, the column would have to make its way through a land torn by unrest and blighted by tropical fevers. On January 17, 1875, exactly two months after the departure from Bagamoyo, the fevers took their first white victim: Edward Pocock.

A few days later, after entering Ituri, Stanley met for the first time with hostile natives and decided to force his way through in a furious battle that lasted three days and cost the lives of fifty-three men. This was the first in a long series of battles that marked all of Stanley's journeys of exploration, with the unfailing corollary of villages sacked and burned. This was the one unquestionable accusation leveled against Stanley by his critics: he was arrogant and impatient, he would stop at nothing to attain his goals, and all too often he would cut short the enervating delays of tribal diplomacy with the use of force, caring little for the lives of his adversaries and caring little more for the lives of his own men. He was also indifferent to the less immediate effects: many of those who traveled later through the areas that he first explored paid the consequences of his aggression toward the natives who failed to submit immediately to his demands. He had the mentality of a sixteenth-century Spanish conquistador, and Stanley definitely did not follow in the footsteps of his idol Livingstone, who wandered unharmed through half of Africa, winning the hearts of blacks and Arabs with his mild determination.

On February 26, the survivors reached the shores of Lake Victoria. They were welcomed warmly by the local chief, Kaduma, a prodigious drinker of foamy beer, which was served to him by a fifteen-year-old black Ganymede in Kaduma's favorite goblet, a hollowed-out gourd with a quart capacity. Kaduma was accustomed to alternating two or three hours of drinking with an equivalent period of sleep. It took all of Stanley's skimpy supply of patience to gain any advantage from the chief's short intervals of lucidity. In the end, however, Stanley was given a piece of ground on which to make camp, and the chief's cooperation in the daunting project of sailing all the way around the lake. Once the *Lady Alice* had been assembled, the explorer set out with a crew of eleven black sailors, all pressed unwillingly into service, reluctant as they were to challenge the wrath of the God of the Great Water. And that wrath was in full evidence over the following weeks of navigation. Furious tempests; lines of hostile warriors along the lakeshore, preventing them from landing; canoe-loads of lake pirates that tried to surround the strange embarkation; and elderly fishermen who cackled in glee at the sight of the bumbling progress of those unskilled mariners. Poor gods of Africa! They could do little to halt the relentless progress of

Stanley (and his rifles). In the end, the gods of Africa decided to join the powerful white sorcerer and interloper, and their intervention may be credited in part with his surprisingly triumphant welcome in the lakeside port of Usavara: drum rolls, fluttering colorful banners, salvos of rifle fire, and cries of greeting from a crowd clothed in handsome red, white, and black robes. Stanley, the Columbus of Lake Victoria, had entered the vast, wealthy, and powerful empire of Uganda.

The instant that the explorer set foot on Ugandan soil, a messenger from the sovereign kneeled before him, bringing an invitation to be received at the imperial court, but only once he had rested and taken refreshments. As the messenger spoke, he indicated with a sweeping gesture the abundant welcoming gift that the king had sent to the explorer. Lined up on the shore were fourteen fatted head of cattle, eight goats, eight rams, one hundred bunches of bananas, three dozen chickens, four jars of milk, four bushels of sweet potatoes, five hundred cobs of maize, a basket of rice, twenty fresh eggs, and ten carafes of palm wine.

Well fed thanks to the emperor's generosity, Stanley and his men washed, redressed, did their best to brush and scrub their ragged clothing, and then followed two pages who led them up a hillside to the residence of the kabaka, the monarch, the highest ruler, the emperor of Uganda: M'tesa.

After making their way through a dozen vast courtyards—in each of which the visitors were greeted with an overwhelming clatter and roar of musical instruments, each one stranger and more deafening than the last—Stanley and his men were met at the threshold of the audience hall by the king in person. M'tesa warmly shook Stanley's hand and led him between two throngs of courtiers toward the chair reserved for the European explorer. The great hall was divided into three aisles by rows of wooden columns. Before each column stood a royal guard, stiffly at attention, dressed in an impeccable uniform: red cape, black shirt, white trousers with a red stripe, white turban adorned with a chimpanzee skin. All of the guards were armed with a rifle. From the times of Speke, civilization had made giant strides in Uganda. Sitting in his throne—"a wooden office chair"—M'tesa invited his white guest to sit at his right on an iron stool, while the various court dignitaries sat on straw mats. The sovereign's naked feet rested on a white cushion lying on a leopard skin, which in turn lay atop a carpet from Smyrna; before the king stood an elephant tusk, polished to a satiny gleam; behind him were an iron spear and a copper spear, insignia of Ugandan royalty, held by two guards. Two embroidered Turkish slippers awaited the imperial feet. The king wore an exceedingly elegant caftan over his white Ugandan robe, and on his shaved head was perched a red fez. He was about thirty years old.

The surprising transformation of the conceited, frivolous, and blood-thirsty tyrant depicted by Speke into the "prince worthy of the sympathies of Europe" described by Stanley had been the work of a Muslim preacher, Muley bin Salim, who had ameliorated and Arabized the customs of M'tesa's court over the course of the last few years, putting it "on a par with the courts of Zanzibar or Oman." Impressed by the rapidity with which civilization had progressed, Stanley immediately aspired to push the process even farther, by teaching the emperor and his subjects "the doctrines of Jesus of Nazareth."

In the meanwhile, the explorer was resting and enjoying the pleasures of life at court: a presentation of the two hundred beauties who comprised the royal harem, a procession of war canoes, crocodile hunting, a reception of ambassadors from realms near and distant, including—surprise!—a white man, the Frenchman Linant de Bellefonds, who had come from Khartoum to propose an alliance between Egypt and Uganda, and who brought with him gastronomical gifts: pâté de foie gras, sausages, and sardines.

Stanley's mission, however, was to complete his circumnavigation of the lake and return to his men, at the far end of the huge body of water. He asked M'tesa for an escort of dugouts and for supplies, and his wishes were granted by the amiable sovereign. But once the admiral of the Ugandan navy, Magassa, had traveled far away from the court with his charges, he failed to deliver the supplies or the escort, and the return to the base camp of Stanley and his crew was a latter-day odyssey, with lingering hunger and native attacks held at bay only by the accurate rifleshots of the commander. And once they reached the camp, only bad news awaited them: Barker had died of typhus, and the local native chiefs were conspiring to wipe the camp out. Stanley's return was providential: with equal parts of wheedling and threats, he persuaded Lukundje, king of Ukerewe, to give him fifty dugouts with which he was able to ferry all his men to Uganda.

In the meanwhile, M'tesa had declared war against his neighboring chief, Uvuma, thus making it impossible for Stanley to reach Lake Albert as he had hoped. With his customary energy, Stanley decided to work around the obstacle by helping M'tesa to defeat his enemies. It was not as easy as Stanley had expected: Uvuma's people were genuinely amphibious, diabolically skilled in lakewater combat. The Ugandan war fleet, in contrast, was manned by landlubbers. They outnumbered their enemy but they could not swim and manuevered awkwardly at best. They suffered numerous defeats.

Stanley considered the vast numbers of the imperial army—150,000 men, 100,000 women and children followers—and had an idea worthy of a Persian satrap: if each one of those swarming subjects were to toss rocks into the lake for several days, the channel between the lakeshore and the island of Inghira, Uvuma's chief citadel, would soon be filled in, and the Ugandans could comfortably invade the island, without wetting their feet. Work duly began, amid much singing and dancing, but it took longer than expected. The channel was only half filled-in when the sovereign lost patience and ordered new naval engagements, which resulted in crushing new naval defeats, despite the tireless efforts of the court magicians. Things looked bad, but Stanley came up with an ingenious new idea. He ordered three great war canoes, each more than sixty-five feet long, bound together to make a great platform. Atop that platform, he had a little fortress built out of cane. There was room in the fortress for more than 150 sharpshooters. It was something more than a floating barricade, something less than a modern battleship. The platform was launched, bedecked with parti-colored banners; crowned with the American flag and bristling with rifle barrels, the platform appeared, majestic and dangerous, just off the impregnable island. From this unprecedented vessel of war thundered a powerful voice, demanding Uvuma's surrender to the forces of the emperor. A spirit, thought Uvuma, a spirit of the lake summoned up by the sorcery of the white wizard. Uvuma surrendered to M'tesa the invincible.

Thus ended the war, and M'tesa rewarded Stanley with an escort of two thousand warriors to see him across the hostile territory of Unyoro, where Kabba Rega still ruled. After the king's misadventures with the Bakers, he wanted nothing more to do with whites or Egyptians.

After charting the course of the Alexandra Nile, the present-day Kagera River, the most important tributary of the great river, and having determined that Speke's hypotheses were substantially accurate, Stanley returned briefly to Uganda and then headed south toward Lake Tanganyika. In the course of that trip, he made the acquaintance of another great African personality of those days, the much-feared Mirambo, chief of the Ruga-Ruga. Mirambo was fighting against the Arab slavers, and had been depicted by them as a ferocious bandit. Instead, Stanley saw in him "a patriot, an African gentleman dressed like a wealthy Arab, right down to the slippers. . . . His demeanor is dignified and free of arrogance; only the calmness and authority of his gaze betray in him the Napoleonic genius that he has shown in this region over the past five years." The two commanders, one white and one black, became blood brothers (Stanley did not actually give blood, but participated only through a stand-in) and exchanged gifts.

At the end of May 1876 the caravan, preceded by the American flag, entered the rich town of Ujiji (five degrees south latitude, in present-day western Tanzania, on Lake Tanganyika), and a few days later Stanley gave the order for the *Lady Alice* to be reassembled and launched in the largely unexplored waters of Lake Tanganyika. When his Arab friends bade him farewell, they did so in the spirit with which one sends a man off to an inevitable shipwreck. No one thought that the fragile wooden shell could survive the lake's fierce tempests. But the gods of Lake Tanganyika were kind to the daring navigators (who had gained some practice in their travels across Lake Victoria), and fifty-one days later Stanley was back. He had sailed completely around the lake and proved that Livingstone was wrong; Lake Tanganyika had nothing at all to do with the Nile basin. It still remained to be seen where the great river known as Lualaba flowed. The river flowed north to the west of Lake Tanganyika. Livingstone had theorized that this was the true upper course of the Nile. (It is in fact the headwater of the Congo.)

Stanley left Ujiji for good in mid-August, and in October he reached Muana Mamba, an Arab trading station not far from the Lualaba, where he made another memorable acquaintance. This vast region was ruled by Tippu Tib, monicker of an Arab slave trader named Ahmed ben Mohammed, without whose permission not a leaf moved between the Lualaba and Lake Tanganyika. Tippu Tib (whose name was onomatopoeic in origin, echoing the crackle of rifle fire that always announced the arrival of this warlord of Central Africa in villages that he planned to plunder) made an enormous impression on the explorer. Stanley described him as a tall man with a black beard, with Negro features, in the prime of his life. He had a handsome, intelligent face, with a nervous tic in his eyes and exceedingly white teeth. His white robes were immaculate, his red fez was bright and new, his belt was finely worked, and his dagger was decorated with silver filigree. This wealthy gentleman had already escorted the English explorer Cameron along a stretch of the Lualaba in 1874, but the expedition had been halted by the hostility of the natives. Delighted to learn that his predecessor in that region had failed, Stanley invited Tippu Tib to travel with him down the river and to bring his four hundred armed men along as well. Tippu Tib showed his exceedingly white teeth in a charming smile and named a figure. After a few days of negotiations, the contract was written up and signed, in English and in Arabic. Tippu Tib agreed to accompany Stanley for sixty marches (about six hundred miles) in exchange for five thousand dollars. Then he would be free to return home. The night before their departure, the commander of the expedition had discussed at length the best route to follow with the only other surviving white explorer, Frank Pocock: should they follow the river or explore the surrounding regions, still a complete mystery? In the end, they decided to resolve the matter by tossing a coin. But the coin came up tails six times in a row, while Stanley had chosen heads. As a result, Stanley ignored the results of the coin toss and chose to follow the river, which he renamed after Livingstone.

From Nyangwé, the very last Arab station on the threshold of the unknown, Stanley's 146 native porters and Tippu Tib's four hundred marauders pushed north and soon found themselves amid the unexpected horrors of the rain forest. Forced to make their way—rather, to slash and cut their way—through the tangled shrubs and hanging vines, in an unchanging half-light, dripping with the water that poured off the foliage, the porters could advance no more than a few miles a day. Moreover, they were marching toward the lands of cannibals, a prospect that was hardly likely to raise the spirits of the men. After a dozen or so days of excruciating progress, Tippu Tib (who'd had no idea of the bramble patch into which Stanley was going to lead him) was ready to break their contract. At that rate, he said, it would take a year to travel the six hundred miles they had agreed upon, and another year to return. Stanley promised him twenty-six hundred dollars if he would accompany him for twenty marches along the opposite shore of the Lualaba, which was said to be less daunting. The Arab agreed reluctantly, cursing that jungle, suitable for "apes, savages, and wild beasts."

When they reached the village of Kampunzu, where the river was almost a mile across, Stanley ordered the men to assemble and launch the *Lady Alice*—whose six segments had been an enormous burden in the forest—and the expedition proceeded partly down the current and partly along the riverbank. The expedition was plagued by hunger because the natives, instead of supplying the caravan with food, would flee at the approach of strangers, or would even attack the outsiders with poisoned darts. "Food, food, food—we must have food today!" the cannibals would chant in chorus amid the trees; and the already difficult journey was transformed into an endless series of clashes, to eat and to avoid being eaten.

After twelve of the twenty days of marching that had been agreed upon, the Arabs decided that they had had enough. Stanley could see that they were so exhausted and demoralized that he decided he could insist no further. He decided to pay Tippu Tib the entire amount agreed upon and lavished gifts upon him and his lieutenants. The next day, to the "sweet, sad" chant of farewell sung by Tippu Tib's black raiders, the expedition took to the river aboard canoes that they had pilfered from the abandoned native villages and continued their journey by water, along that river "that would take them to Zanzibar," as Stanley would say to console his men, who were by now openly weeping at the destiny that awaited them.

And there was good reason to weep. Day after day, from both banks of the river, war cries and thumping drumbeats echoed, little fleets of canoes sallied out, showers of arrows and spear came whistling down. And the current of the great river, instead of sweeping them smoothly and safely down to the sea, to the Zanzibar they so yearned after, began to tumble and roar over a series of cataracts and rapids. Whenever the rapids became sufficiently swift, it was necessary to land on the treacherous shore and venture into the dangerous forest, unload all their baggage, and cut a path; they would drag their boats, and baggage, by main force uphill and downhill until they reached navigable water once again, all the while under a rain of spears and arrows. It took them twenty-two full days to portage around the seventh cataract—still known as

Stanley Falls—under relentless attack from enthusiastic cannibals who had never seen so much human flesh. Many of those cannibals, indeed, never knew what hit them. Just as they were making a mental menu, a sound of thunder roared out and they would fall, cut down by rifle fire. At the confluence with the Aruwimi River (about a hundred miles downstream from present-day Kisangani, once Stanleyville, and about one degree north latitude from the Equator), a full battle was fought. About fifty giant canoes pushed out from the riverbank; each canoe was paddled by about forty oarsmen who bent over, pushing their craft forward to the rhythm of a war chant. At the prow stood a dozen young warriors bedecked in parrot plumes; astern, eight helmsmen worked to steer the craft; in the middle, rushing back and forth, were the chiefs. Trumpets, horns, and chants made a terrifying din. Stanley ordered all his canoes moored in a single line, and ten unbroken minutes of rifle fire overwhelmed the attackers, who fled. They were chased down by Stanley's men to the riverbank, to the lanes of their villages, and beyond, into the forest where they had scattered and where they were ruthlessly cut down.

At last, at Chumbiri, by now fairly close to the mouth of the river, they met with a much more agreeable welcome. The king received them personally, with the full contingent of all his wives; the travelers were regaled with delicacies. The wives in particular were a sight to behold: they were beautiful, and the fashion of their tribe demanded that they wear heavy copper collars, the greater the king's favor, the heavier the collar. The king's favorites wore some forty pounds of copper around their necks. Examining the lovely ladies of the king's harem with a sharp eye, Stanley calculated that the chief possessed a walking treasure house of some fourteen hundred pounds of copper. When Stanley asked the king what happened to the unremovable collars when any of his consorts died, the happy husband smiled and looked at Stanley fondly, as if the question pleased him particularly. He then drew his finger across his throat with a meaningful expression.

The descent to the river mouth continued fairly peacefully, though it was all still tremendously hard work. Trouble, however, continued to dog the caravan. At Zinga Falls, beyond the Stanley Pool, Frank Pocock was drowned, beside Stanley, the last surviving European. On July 31, 1877, at the cataract of Isangila (around five degrees south latitude), the *Lady Alice* was abandoned, after seven thousand miles of honorable service, and the caravan continued on foot. By now, the Atlantic was not far off, but in the final leg of the march it became impossible to procure foodstuffs. They were among civilized Africans now, who were not about to trade for copper wire or scraps of cloth. Did Stanley take them for savages? Did they happen to have any rum with them? No, they had no rum, and in exasperation Stanley decided to halt with the main part of the column and send five of his men who knew a few words of English to the nearby Portuguese trading station of Boma. They carried a message directed to "any gentleman" who happened to be living in Boma, requesting supplies and promising to repay their expenses. On August 6, the emissaries returned with a caravan of food, and on August 9, exactly 999 days after leaving Zanzibar, reduced to living skeletons, the survivors entered Boma (six degrees south latitude). There were 114 out of the original 356 native bearers. They had followed the entire course of the Congo, in all its extension. Stanley had solved another great mystery of African hydrography, and no one could any longer question his status as Livingstone's successor.

14
The Conquest of Equatoria

In the 1860s, Egypt seemed determined to recapture the magnificence of Pharaonic times. The viceroy Ismail, who had taken the throne in 1863 and assumed the Persian title of khedive, or "master," was a man of boundless ambitions and broad views. Learned, intelligent, astute, tightfisted in small matters and generous in large ones, he dreamed of modernizing his country and extending its dominion as far as the Horn of Africa. International economic developments seemed to favor his plans: the American Civil War had driven the price of cotton sky-high, and the Egyptian harvest was worth five times as much as before. That income allowed Ismail to undertake a vast program of public works: irrigation canals, railroads, telegraph lines, and steamboats made the Nile Valley an ambitious Levantine imitation of the Rhineland, with Egyptian indolence conferring a touch of amiable exoticism.

This latter-day North African industrial revolution attained its culmination in November 1869, when ten years of digging came to an end with the inauguration of one of the nineteenth century's most impressive pieces of engineering, the Suez Canal. The celebrations were worthy of a government with its eyes on a future of progress, prosperity, and glory. In Cairo and Alexandria the most decrepit neighborhoods had been razed to the ground, replaced by broad boulevards lined with European-style apartment buildings. In Cairo, an opera house had been built and the greatest living composer, Giuseppe Verdi, was commissioned to create an opera on an Egyptian subject: *Aida.* At Port Said, three sumptuous pavilions were built: one for illustrious guests from Islamic countries, another for the crowned heads of Europe, and a third for European commoners. The Austro-Hungarian emperor Franz-Josef attended, as did the Empress Eugénie of France (who telegraphed to her husband Napoleon III, who had stayed in Paris: "Magical reception. I have never seen anything like it in my life"). Other attendees included the hereditary prince of Prussia, Friedrich Wilhelm, as well as Russian grand dukes and German princes.

Blessed by priests of every religion, on the morning of November 17 the canal was plied by a fleet of ships and vessels, powered by wind and steam and flying the flags of every nation; in the sparkling new city of Ismailia, the fleet of ships landed a crowd of sovereigns, ambassadors, scientists, aristocrats, and magnates, honored by a gala banquet, endless displays of fireworks, and a ball illuminated by ten thousand flaming lanterns.

As Europe's crème de la crème danced and dined in celebration of "the transformation of Africa into an island" (as the more rhetorically minded journalists wrote in those weeks), there was one notable absence: the English royal family. Great Britain, which had opposed the construction of the canal, a French-controlled enterprise, took the opportunity to signal its disapproval.

But a few months earlier, the heir to the British throne, Edward, Prince of Wales, had taken a cruise on the Nile with his wife, Alexandra. Among those in his entourage was Samuel Baker, chosen as an interpreter for his skill in Arabic and honored by Queen Victoria with the title of baronet in recognition of his equatorial discoveries.

In Cairo, Ismail had held a masked ball to celebrate the arrival of the princely couple; during the ball, as in the finest feuilleton novel, Sir Samuel Baker was summoned to a private audience with the khedive, who offered him a thorny but flattering task.

The job was this: to put an end, once and for all, to the slave trade in the Sudan. Though Ismail had already abolished it by decree, it was in fact still a flourishing business. Indeed, it was flourishing as never before. In the vast anarchic territories to the south and the west of Khartoum, the leading slavers had carved out full-fledged independent principalities, where they lived like kings. They were the "sultans of black ivory"—as the slave trade had been dubbed, with a reference to the other murderous commerce of the region—and they were all Sudanese Arabs. One of them had over twenty-five hundred armed men on his payroll. Another, Agad, held sway over a region of ninety thousand square miles. But the richest and most famous was Zobeir, who had once been a scribe for an ivory trader. He was now the master of thirty *zeribes* (Arabic for the fortified tent-villages established in the lands to be plundered). Zobeir had been given the title of pasha by a governor of Khartoum who wanted to win his favor. He ruled in the Bahr al-Ghazal, a province in the extreme south of what is now Sudan. His palace contained dozens of rooms; each room was papered with French wallpaper and filled with sofas brought all the way up the Nile. There were dozens of silk-clad slaves, serving the guests coffee, pipes, and sorbets amid the roaring of lions chained to the walls. At his banquets, arrack and beer brewed from millet flowed freely, in open contravention of the precepts of the Koran. There was even champagne, though lukewarm, and the pleasures of the table were made even more enjoyable by the songs and gyrations of nude black dancing girls.

Till then, the only effect of Ismail's decree abolishing the slave trade had been to drive up the price of slaves and enrich the traffickers even more. But now the khedive, who wanted to bring his nation into the community of great powers and therefore wished to present it as truly civilized, had decided to act boldly. Baker was offered the rank of general and the title of pasha, ten thousand pounds sterling a year for the four years that the job was expected to take, and an army of seventeen hundred men whom he could equip as he saw best.

Baker accepted the position and set to work immediately, feverishly overseeing even the smallest details in what would be a complex military expedition lacking nothing, "from needles to iron crowbars, from handkerchiefs to sails." He summoned ten Europeans to serve as joint chiefs of staff: his nephew Julian, a lieutenant in the Royal Navy; a physician; two engineers; five carpenters; and a warehouseman to keep the overwhelming flow of equipment in order. The material even included prefabricated sheds made of zinc-plated sheet metal and an entire fleet of boats broken up into sections, which would be transported by camels to the south of the cataracts. The largest of these vessels was a side-wheeler and measured more than a hundred feet in length. As for the army itself, it was organized into two regiments of riflemen—one Sudanese, one Egyptian—(largely composed of jailbirds, as was inevitable in Egypt under the khedive, where prison labor was a staple of all public works), a squadron of cavalry, and two batteries of cannon. Taking a page from Napoleon and another from Ali Baba, Baker created a personal bodyguard made up of forty sharpshooters, called the Forty Thieves.

Red banners emblazoned with the crescent moon of Islam fluttered in the breeze, as ninety steamboats and fifty-five sailboats, all loaded well beyond their gunwales, steamed and sailed up the Nile, while troops marched in columns along the riverbanks. In February 1870, they unloaded just outside the astonished city of Khartoum: a flood of bales, crates, tents, quadrupeds, and bipeds. From the governor to the most miserable mendicant, the entire city stood and gaped, blinked and cursed. The end of the slave trade would also spell the end of the city, or at least of Khartoum as the cesspool of the Egyptian empire. Red fez on his head and wearing the garish uniform of general of the khedive, studded with decorations under his long beard, Pasha Baker paid a visit to the hostile governor, ostensibly as a courtesy but actually to intimidate him. Baker then decided to set out as soon as possible, in order to avoid delays or sabotage. He set sail up the current of the White Nile with a thousand men and, of course, Florence, his beloved, daring, and loyal wife.

But the first enemy he would have to beat in that land was nature. When the boats reached the immense marsh of the Sudd, it was discovered that all of the channels that had once been navigable were now blocked by masses of vegetation swept downriver, accumulating to create a weltering tangle that extended for miles. Every fit man climbed down into the muck, and with water up to their belts, they chopped at reed banks for two months. They made some progress, but it was laughable: just a mile or two had been gained. Now the water was draining away because the dry season had arrived. There was nothing left to do but withdraw and wait for the flood at the end of the year. So the fleet retreated north to Malakal, where it made good use of the seven months of forced idleness by chasing down and impounding the boats that came downriver, and freeing the slaves that were being transported to the market at Khartoum. The slavers were unaware that things had changed or were hopeful that Baker, like all the pashas in Egypt, would in the end succumb to corruption.

At the end of December the blessed flood finally arrived, and fifty-nine vessels with sixteen hundred persons aboard, men and women, sailed south, only to be trapped anew in the amphibian inferno of the Sudd. Once again the soldiers splashed down into the muck, chopping at plants and pulling the boats along with cables. Once again they died by the dozen, victims of malarial fever and sunstroke. In March 1871, when the waters began to recede, the reeds were still there, and Baker almost lost hope of making it through. He felt obliged to make one last effort. He ventured a little farther along and found that they were tantalizingly close to open water. The short distance that remained, however, was impossible to get through, given the draught of his larger boats.

Still, the Englishman was tenacious and resourceful, and he was at his best in desperate situations. He rapidly came up with a plan that might not have occurred to anyone else: he decided to build a rough temporary dam to raise the level of the Nile, floating free his grounded ships. The carpenters planted poles and beams, the soldiers filled sandbags and tied together bundles of reeds for days and days. Finally the fatal hour of the last attempt arrived. Baker later recalled:

> I stood on one of the stranded boats only a few yards from the row of piles. The men were all in their places. The buglers and drummers stood upon another vessel ready to give the signal. At the first bugle, every two men lifted the sacks of sand and clay. At once all the drums and bugles then sounded the advance, and 500 heavy sacks were dropped into the row of piles, and firmly stamped down by the men. The troops now worked with intense energy. It was a race between the Soudanis and the Egyptians; this was a work to which the latter were accustomed in their own country. The sailors worked as vigorously as the troops; piles of fascines and clay balls were laid with extraordinary rapidity, while some stamped frantically and danced upon the entangled mass, all screaming and shouting in great excitement, and the bugles and drums kept up an incessant din. A long double line of men formed a transport corps, and passed a never-failing supply of fascines to the workers who stood in the water and kneaded firmly the adhesive mass.
>
> At 2.15 P.M. the river was completely shut in, and the people with increased energy worked at the superstructure of the dam, which now rose like a causeway for about one hundred and ten yards from shore to shore.
>
> At 3.30 the water had risen to an extent that obliged the men in some places to swim. The steamer that had been hopelessly stranded, and the entire fleet, were floating merrily in the pond.

Having beaten the Nile, Baker could now take on the slavers. One month later, the expedition reached Gondokoro, which had been abandoned for years; nothing remained of the Austrian mission but desolate ruins. The English pasha decided to make this abandoned site the nerve center of all his future conquests. He had a village built, defended by a small fortress, and ordered the fields plowed and sown. When work was finished, his men were ordered to wash in the Nile's waters the tattered rags that their uniforms had become and to patch them up as best they could. The next morning, May 26, 1871, he ordered his men into parade ranks and ran a fluttering Egyptian flag up the flagstaff. Pasha Baker, on horseback, proclaimed that Egypt had just annexed a new province, to be known as Equatoria, in Arabic Hatalastiva, with a capital named Ismailia on the site of the vanished Gondokoro. His chiefs of staff dined that evening on roast gazelle and a Christmas pudding carefully saved for such an occasion, generously doused with rum. It was all very nice, but also very theoretical. The African tribes that lived in the area did not yet know that in the name of the khedive they had been liberated from the barbaric practice of slave raiding. Indeed, they failed to see the difference between their present-day liberators and the previous predators. The stockade that surrounded the newly founded Ismailia was the target of a daily hail of poisoned arrows. Even the least hostile of the natives refused to provide food for those hundreds of hungry mouths that had come downriver, and to keep from starving to death the soldiers were forced to plunder just as the slavers had done. No supplies arrived from the resentful city of Khartoum, both because of the ill will of the authorities there and because the Nile had once again clogged up with the impenetrable Sudd, providing an excellent alibi for those who secretly hoped that the expedition might wind up simply vanishing silently in the mystery of the equatorial wasteland.

Soldiers began to desert one by one, and soon the trickle turned into a flood. One day, after returning from a raid for foodstuffs in one of the neighboring villages, Baker discovered that his grand army had simply evaporated in the sun of Equatoria: a thousand men, making off with thirty boats, had fled down the Nile. But the indomitable English explorer—who could not have retreated had he wanted to because he would have simply been trapped in the bogs of the Sudd—decided to leave a garrison at Ismailia and to push forward with a column of troops to make a sweep through the country. He reached Fatiko so quickly that the slave merchants camped there could not escape, and they surrendered, obeying his orders to stop their slaving and return at once to Khartoum. Then he pushed even farther south, entering the kingdom of Unyoro where he had been greeted back in 1864 by two Kamrasis, one real and one a pretender. Both were now dead, and now Kabba Rega, son of the real Kamrasi, ruled in his capital at Masindi. His throne was contested by other pretenders, however, and a civil war was raging. The war made excellent business for the slavers, because merchandise was abundant and cheap.

Like an African Cortés, Baker felt certain that a bold attack was the only winning card. He entered Masindi like a conqueror, wasted no time in arresting every slaver he could lay hands on, and raised the Egyptian flag over the town. The bewildered and humiliated Kabba Rega immediately presented himself, beseeching the Englishman for clemency. Ismail's empire had extended to the heart of the Dark Continent, just a hundred miles north of the Equator.

In Masindi (two degrees north latitude), however, just as in Ismailia, appearances were deceptive. The wily Kabba Rega had not the slightest intention of becoming a subject of the khedive, and he was already spinning webs of intrigue. One day, a gracious gift arrived for the Egyptian troops: seven huge jars filled with palm wine. Many of the soldiers gladly drank, and deeply. They would have been wiser to obey the precepts of the Koran. A few minutes later forty men lay writhing in atrocious agony.

Fortunately, the officers had not tasted the poisoned drink, and after administering emetics to the victims, they prepared for the inevitable onslaught to follow.

The attack came the following morning. Even though there were several thousand warriors of Unyoro, Baker's soldiers possessed grim discipline and numerous rifles. The rifles proved superior. It was a battle with no quarter given: Masindi was burned to the ground, the eight thousand inhabitants panicking and fleeing into the forest. Left alone in a sea of rubble and smoking embers, the victors also decided to abandon the field. Baker ordered his men to put even the last house left standing to the torch—this was the newly built khedivial governor's residence, a hut whose imperial furnishings consisted of fashion drawings torn from a magazine and pinned to the walls.

Leaving behind them a trail of dead men—their own and the enemy's, killed by rifle shot and by the hail of poisoned arrows unleashed by enemy soldiers skulking amid the tall grass—the column reached the Victoria Nile, the stretch of river that flows from Lake Victoria into Lake Albert. There Baker established an alliance with a chief who was an enemy of Kabba Rega, promising him an illusory chance to take the place of the would-be poisoner on the throne of Unyoro. Then Baker set off with some of his troops to Fatiko in search of reinforcements. He certainly was going to need them, because in the meanwhile word had spread that Baker was dead, and the entire country was riven with internecine combat, armed bands slaughtering and pillaging. Samuel Baker, however, was quite alive, and he fell upon his enemy like a wolf upon the fold. He attacked a slaving chief, Mohammed Uat el-Mek, and defeated him so thoroughly that he swore obedience on the Koran and even helped him to recruit more men. Other slave drivers left the country, so the Englishman was finally able to turn against Kabba Rega, hounding him out onto an island on Lake Albert, where the former king took miserable refuge.

The worst now seemed over, and from August 1872 until March 1873 Baker operated out of Fatiko, organizing the equatorial province, at least half of which was still entirely unexplored. Five months later, Baker returned to Cairo with his beloved Florence.

The khedive Ismail grew pale when he received the bill for the enterprise: half a million piastres. But Egypt now had its empire, and it could hold its head up high among other powers, asking in the name of enlightened civilization for the loans that would, in the fullness of time, lead it to a great national bankruptcy.

15
The Calamities of Equatoria

In 1873, when Sir Samuel Baker left the court of the khedive Ismail, covered with great honors and pocketing the considerable sum of forty-thousand pounds sterling, he sailed from the port of Alexandria back to England, feeling pretty pleased with the work he had done and certain that he had dealt a mortal blow to the slave trade in the Egyptian Sudan. Things were quite different in reality. According to numerous witnesses, the effects of that sudden crusade against slavery, the foundation of the Sudanese economy, were much worse than the evil the crusade had been meant to cure. First of all, the Koran continued to sanction the right to own slaves, and to the ears of any good Muslim the abolition of slavery sounded like heresy. Moreover, none of those who had made small fortunes out of the slave trade were willing to give up a chance to add to those fortunes, and certainly not in the name of some abstract principle imposed by European infidels, in glaring contrast with profound religious convictions and ways of life that stretched back for centuries. The slave trade was not likely to vanish all at once, and indeed it did not vanish at all: it only went into hiding, abandoning the easier and more convenient water routes that had been used until then with the approval and participation of the Egyptian authorities. The trade found new routes to use. From Khartoum, where boats loaded with "black ivory" no longer descended the Nile, European consuls wrote back to their capitals that the traffic had been stopped. In truth, when river transport was eliminated, the torments of black Africans captured by slavers became much, much worse. Previously, some 10 percent of the human merchandise crammed into the holds of the slave ships—deprived of water or air—had died. Now the death rate climbed to 30 percent, and in some cases 50 percent, as the captives were obliged to march for hundreds of miles, leaving the Nile behind and heading for Kordofan, across the Sahara Desert, and finally reaching distant Tripoli, where they were sold into slavery. The slavers cared little about the dizzying increase in losses, because once the slave trade became illegal prices for slaves increased more than tenfold. The lot of the surviving slave improved with his or her sale; the precepts of the Koran ensured that slaves were treated in a reasonably humane manner in Islamic countries, like a sort of second-class family member with some limited rights. The horrors described in *Uncle Tom's Cabin* were specialties of Christian masters.

Ismail was perfectly well aware of the difficulties of ridding the Sudan of the slave trade. He decided that he needed to call on the assistance of a man renowned for his enormous energy. The choice fell on Charles George Gordon. Gordon's name had been mentioned by Nubar Pasha, an Egyptian minister who had made the acquaintance of the English officer a few years before in Constantinople. China Gordon, as he was known, was born in 1833 and had won his nickname by fighting in the Celestial Empire against the Taiping rebels who were threatening to overthrow the Manchu Dynasty. He had become legendary for his military prowess, his disregard for danger, and above all for his Christian sense of charity and sense of honor. More than once, he had harsh words with the Chinese authorities who wanted to violate terms of surrender by simply executing inconvenient prisoners. An idealist who aspired to achieve great deeds, just then Gordon was whiling away his time unhappily in the gloomy port city of Galatz, on the Black Sea, where he had been sent as a British member of the International Commission for the Danube. He welcomed the Egyptian proposal enthusiastically; this opportunity would finally free him from a bureaucratic backwater, unworthy of his vast ambitions. In February 1874 he was in Cairo, and Ismail conferred upon him the title of governor general of Equatoria, independent of Khartoum, answerable only to the khedive himself. He had been given only "delightfully vague" instructions: he was to expand Egyptian rule and eliminate slavery.

In mid-April, Gordon Pasha was entering his capital on the Upper White Nile, the village of huts and hovels that Baker had renamed Ismailia, but which everyone continued to call Gondokoro. Gordon found the little settlement desolate and unhealthy, and he ordered a new town built at Lado, not far away, on the opposite bank of the river. He also found that Egyptian rule over Equatoria was nominal at best: there were only two garrisons, one at Gondokoro and another at Fatiko. Everywhere else in Equatoria, columns of slavers roamed freely, capturing slaves with impunity.

Unleashing a level of energy that over the next few months "almost killed him," the governor general gradually extended control over the territory, with the assistance of his European lieutenants, establishing fortified outposts along the course of the Nile and its principal tributaries. Gordon destroyed slaving camps, ruthlessly ousted corrupt Egyptian functionaries, and conceived grandiose plans for expansion that could hardly help but please Ismail, with his pharaonic ambitions. His American lieutenant, Chaillé-Long, was sent to Uganda, where he received a warm welcome from King M'tesa who appeared willing to accept a vague form of Egyptian protectorate; later, the Ugandan imperial court saw a second emissary arrive from the north, the same Linant de Bellefonds who had shared French pâté and sausages with M'tesa and Stanley. In the meanwhile, Chaillé-Long was exploring the cannibal-ridden area of Mombuttu, which the climate seemed to make ideal for colonizing. And so, the Egyptian flag was raised and a small garrison was established. Farther south, Gordon's Italian lieutenant, Romolo Gessi, managed to haul iron-hulled boats as far as Lake Albert, circumnavigating the huge body of water despite torrential rains, towering waves, native attacks, and mutinous revolts on the part of his terrified Sudanese crews, unaccustomed to any water other than that of the tranquil Nile. Thus, Unyoro also entered, theoretically, the Egyptian sphere of influence. But Gordon's ambitions aimed much farther: he dreamed of annexing the entire Horn of Africa for the khedive's Egypt. Ismail already possessed Massawa, governed by his Swiss hireling Munzinger; Munzinger then went on to occupy Zeila in northern Somalia, and from there sent out an Egyptian column that took possession of the emirate of Harar. In great secrecy, Gordon suggested to the khedive a daring exploit. From Cairo to Uganda was an overland trek of thirty-one hundred miles, over exceedingly rough terrain, often completely impassable for most of the year. From Suez to Uganda, on the other hand, was farther, thirty-three hundred miles, but only three hundred miles of that was overland, and it was much easier going. The rest was by sea. The logical thing to do, then, suggested Gordon, was to occupy a base, for instance, at Mombasa, on the coast of modern-day Kenya, and from there establish communications with the interior. With such an outlet on the Indian Ocean, the Egyptian empire could finally become a vital reality.

Ismail did not require much convincing. In September 1875 thirteen hundred men under the command of Chaillé-Long landed from four Egyptian steamships, commanded by a Scottish sea captain called MacKilleb, at the mouth of the river Jubba, or Webi Jubba, at Chisimayu (Kismaayo, in modern-day Somalia, just twenty miles south of the Equator on the Indian Ocean); this expedition marked the only moment in history when Equatoria actually extended to the Equator.

Mombasa, farther south and much more convenient, had been rejected to avoid arousing the wrath of the sultan of Zanzibar, who controlled Mombasa along with the entire coast. But, poverty-stricken and desolate though Chisimayu may have been, it too was the property of the sultan, and he was unwilling to be deprived of it. The sultan reached out to his English friends, who were none too eager to see the Egyptians expanding into territory that was uncomfortably close to India. And so, a few weeks later, as Chaillé-Long waited impatiently in the muggy heat to begin his march inland toward Uganda, raising a red flag with a crescent moon in every village he passed through, he was surprised to see a British gunship enter the port of Chisimayu. He received new and decidedly different orders from the captain of the gunship, and under the threat of British cannon he ordered his men back aboard the Egyptian steamships and sailed away.

This was a bad period for the Egyptians. In November, Munzinger—who had marched into Abyssinia to overthrow the negus Johannes and replace him on the throne with the far more pliable Menelik—fell into an ambush laid by Danakil bandits. He was slaughtered, with all his men. In March, a punitive expedition sent out by the indignant khedive under the command of his son Hassan (who had been sent to study military tactics in Germany) fared even worse. When the Egyptian forces, some ten thousand in number, reached the Eritrean highlands, they dug in and waited in their trenches for the inevitable Abyssinian attack. The Abyssinians surrounded them like a cloud of locusts, numbering at least seventy thousand. The more experienced Egyptian officers advised waiting patiently in the strong fortifications, well defended by cannon and Remington rifles. Within a few days, the enemy would be forced to scatter as they began to run out of food. But Hassan scorned what he considered a horde of black savages. He was in search of military glory, and he ventured out into the open field. All day long the Egyptians, with their superior weaponry, mowed down row after row of Abyssinians as they advanced in compact formation. Finally, however, as ammunition began to become scarce, Hassan found himself obliged to order a retreat back into the fortified perimeter.

Retreats are never easy, and this one was infinitely more complex because of a general awareness among the Egyptian troops that Abyssinian practice was to castrate prisoners. No one was eager to be the last man back; what should have been an orderly withdrawal turned into a panicky stampede. The combatants mingled so thoroughly that the Egyptian captain of artillery did not have the nerve to shell the enemy; he was afraid of killing as many Egyptians as Abyssinians. In time, the Abyssinians penetrated into the fortifications along with the fleeing Egyptians. Only a single redoubt managed to resist, and behind the walls the surviving Egyptians spent a terrible night, listening to the screams of their less fortunate companions as they were castrated.

The following day, parleys began to establish terms, but the negus demanded unconditional surrender. The besieged soldiers were able to escape only because one of the Abyssinian chiefs, Ras Bariù, accepted a bribe. In exchange for the entire treasure of the expedition—twenty thousand pounds sterling and thirty thousand silver thalers—Ras Bariù left unguarded the road to Massawa. Hassan arrived there the next day, alone, on horseback, after galloping all night long. A few survivors followed, a day later, exhausted and crazed with terror. No Egyptian army ever tried to conquer Abyssinia again. Ras Bariù met a bad end as well; the negus suspected his treachery and had him blinded.

In the meanwhile Gordon had tendered his resignation because he felt that he was not receiving adequate support against the sabotage of the Egyptian authorities implicated in the slave trade. The khedive persuaded him to continue the work he had undertaken. He also named Gordon governor general of the Sudan, the Darfur, and the Egyptian equatorial provinces. This finally gave Gordon absolute power over an immense territory, more than half the size of all Europe.

For the slave traders, hard times finally arrived. Gessi, who won the sobriquet of the Garibaldi of Africa in this campaign, swept through the Bahr al-Ghazal, chasing down, capturing, and executing by firing squad—following an "attempted escape"—Suleiman, son of the biggest slave merchant in the region, Zobeir Pasha. In turn, Zobeir Pasha was lured to Cairo on some pretext, where he was captured and held prisoner.

After three years of exhausting expeditions, tired and in poor health but positive that he had "crushed the slavers in their lairs," Gordon decided to allow himself a well-deserved rest. He left his office in the Sudan and took ship for England in January 1880. Six months earlier, his patron Ismail had been deposed by the sultan in Constantinople—still formally Egypt's supreme sovereign—at the behest of the European powers with whom the khedive had run up enormous debts that he now could not honor. In the khedive's place ruled his son, Tawfiq. Gordon was leaving Tawfiq the Sudan with an equatorial appendage extending all the way to Lake Albert, a territory that he thought was now peaceful and embarking on a better, brighter future. In fact, this territory was about to experience the darkest days of its entire history.

The Sudan was in reality a powder keg, ready to blow at the slightest jostle. Over the course of decades of occupation, the Egyptians had piled one mistake on top of another, one outrage atop the next, and oppression upon oppression. Gordon had summoned a group of Europeans to run the governorships into which the region was divided: the Germans Giegler and Emin, the Austrian Slatin, the Englishman Lupton, all of them honest, all of them well-meaning in their fight against slavery and the slave trade. But it was too little and far too late. The hatred of the Sudanese against those they called "Turks"—that is, anyone who had come from the north to batten off the spoils of that El Dorado of the poor—was by now implacable. The "Turks" included the Maltese and the Greeks who swarmed down to the Sudan to trade, to open taverns, to set up little shops; the "Turks" included the Catholic and Protestant missionaries who had the khedive's permission to sneak into a Muslim land and purvey the teachings of an alien faith; above all, the "Turks" included the Egyptian functionaries and soldiers, scorned and detested more intensely than all the other "Turks" because they were considered traitors to Islam, false, corrupt, cruel, lazy, and incompetent, capable only of robbing, of demanding service without pay, of levying taxes enforced by the gun. And now the worst "Turks" of them all had declared war on the slave trade! Discontent boiled over into open rage. That intolerable band of heretics from Cairo and their white lackeys wanted to free the blacks, and this struck directly at the vital interests of the Sudan. And so, when a man rose up and proclaimed himself a messenger of God, sent to free the whole world and to restore the purity of the true faith, the entire Sudan welcomed him as the Mahdi, "he who is awaited."

The new prophet, Mohammed Ahmed, thirty-two years old, the son of a camel driver from Dongola, had won a reputation as an exceedingly holy man with a life of praying, meditating, and penitence. He preached the advent of a new era in his hermitage on an island in the White Nile, and more and more pilgrims came to listen to his sermons. The pilgrims saw him, recognized him, and proclaimed that his face had the signs that the Awaited One, or Messiah, was said to bear: a mole on the left cheek, a space between his upper incisors. The chief of a warrior tribe of the Kordofan, the Baggaras, great slave merchants, recognized him as the Mahdi. That spark set fire to all the Sudan. Holy war would sweep away the hated "Turks," the Egyptian oppressors. One after another, the armies sent out to conquer the rebels were destroyed, even the armies led by European commanders. And the modern European weapons of those armies wound up arming the followers of this heir to Mohammed. At the end of 1883, the very capital, Khartoum, was threatened. The British government, which had occupied Egypt the year before following anti-European rioting, decided that Khartoum was no longer defendable and asked Gordon to organize the evacuation of Europeans and Egyptians. Gordon accepted the assignment, but he intended to defend the city, not abandon it. He reached Khartoum on February 18, 1884, fortified it, reorganized the demoralized garrison, and stocked up on supplies and foodstuffs just in the nick of time. On March 12 began a siege that was to last for eleven months, ending only on January 26, 1885, when the followers of the Mahdi succeeded in taking one bastion by surprise and entering Khartoum. Gordon was run through by a spearpoint on the steps of his residence and was then decapitated. The head, wrapped in a cloth, was laid shortly thereafter at the feet of the Mahdi.

All of the Sudan was lost. The governors of the Darfur and the Bahr al-Ghazal, Slatin and Lupton, had been forced to surrender and were now slaves in the rebel camp. All that remained of the entire Egyptian empire was Equatoria, the southernmost province, governed by Emin Bey. Equatoria was an isolated, unreachable province, a phantom province. But it was a province that Emin Bey was resolved to defend.

Emin Bey's given name was Eduard Schnitzler. He was a German Jew, born in Prussia in 1840. He had taken a degree in medicine and had also studied natural history. Then he had decided to seek his fortune in the Ottoman empire. He had, indeed, found his fortune—relatively speaking—when he entered the service of a pasha. When his patron died, he returned briefly to Prussia, and then headed for Egypt and the Sudan, where Gordon hired him as a physician. From that time on, he called himself Emin Effendi Hakim, "the trusted doctor." He had earned the title of bey and the position of governor of Equatoria by carrying out sensitive diplomatic missions for Gordon to the courts of Uganda and Unyoro. When the Mahdi's revolt broke out, he had remained in isolation in his residence in Lado. No more steamboats carrying supplies arrived from Khartoum. All that arrived from the north now were rumors, some of them terrifying, some of them wonderful—such as the news that Gordon would be arriving any day with a huge army and dozens of Indian elephants. Instead, what did arrive were the vanguards of the Mahdi's army, beginning to attack the northernmost garrisons of Equatoria.

Emin Bey did not succumb to the temptation of challenging his enemy in open battle, in which he would certainly be outnumbered. Instead he chose a more elastic strategy, guerrilla warfare made up of many small hit-and-run battles, luring the army of the Mahdi into the heart of his territory, where it no longer enjoyed support from the natives. He inflicted countless tiny losses. Thus, the Mahdi's initial impetus was blunted; Emin Bey and Equatoria were left in peace.

His province, it is true, had been reduced to a small part of its original expanse, and the capital had been moved from Lado to Vadelai, two hundred miles farther south, for greater safety. But in that governorship where total isolation made him a total monarch, Emin lived peacefully with two other Europeans, an Italian captain named Gaetano Casati and a Russian-German explorer named Vassily Junker. Emin spent his time pursuing his beloved studies of entomology and botany. He was a first-rate administrator; he accumulated the wealth of the country with which he had been entrusted, biding his time until he could begin to send it northward to Cairo once again. He piled up rubber, coffee, ivory, cotton. He had plenty of supplies, a few thousand well-armed soldiers, cannons, two steamships, Egyptian and Sudanese officers with whom he was on excellent terms, in part because he had formally converted to Islam. Perhaps he was even secretly pleased to be receiving orders from no one; perhaps he rejoiced at the thought of having a little world all his own to shape as he thought best. But after many months of quiet, the long hand of the khedive Tawfiq managed to reach him. And that was when the trouble began.

In 1886, Cairo succeeded in conveying news and advice to the governor of Equatoria (via Zanzibar): the death of Gordon, the fall of Khartoum, the triumph of the Mahdi throughout Sudan, the impossibility of sending him help. All the same, Emin could organize an evacuation of the province by marching toward the Indian Ocean with all his people. It was a daring suggestion, to say the least, and it could easily have culminated in complete disaster: it meant undertaking a journey of thousands of miles through hostile territory, with an unprecedentedly huge caravan, comprising ten thousand people, half of them women and children. The governor, who saw absolutely no reason to leave a territory solidly under his control, where life was better than ever before, made the error of submitting the idea to the consideration of his officers and soldiers.

Discussions, disagreements, even violent disputes ensued; Emin began to lose control of his men. In any case, to determine whether the mass exodus was a practicable option, he decided to send Casati to the court of the king of Unyoro to establish an alliance and to obtain permission to pass through his realm. He sent Junker to Zanzibar to report on the true situation of Equatoria. Casati was welcomed in Unyoro with a smothering hospitality that began to seem like honeyed imprisonment after a while; in the end Casati escaped. Junker made it successfully to Zanzibar, and by December 1886 he was safe and sound in Cairo, where his excessive zeal set in motion the vast machinery of a rescue attempt that would prove fatal to the unsuspecting Emin.

Suddenly, Emin Bey, happily ignored by the world at large until now, was transformed by the press and the overemphatic statements of Junker into the hero of the day: a military commander and scientist who wielded a saber with one hand and an entomologist's magnifying glass with the other, an intrepid European alone in the heart of the Dark Continent, alone, abandoned, isolated, and surrounded by teeming hordes of fanatical savages. He was Livingstone and Gordon in one, in deeper trouble than either of the two ever had been, a symbol of civilization that needed to be rescued, cost what it may. And who could be trusted to undertake this rescue but the rescuer par excellence? As one, the newspapers of the world trumpeted the name of Henry Morton Stanley.

This may well have been a great collective humanitarian impulse, but another piece of news from far-off Equatoria may have contributed to the chorus: while Emin Bey remained in isolation, he had slowly built up a cache of ivory in the ramshackle huts of Vadelai that was now worth 100,000 pounds sterling, a treasure that also needed to be rescued from the barbarians and saved for the benefit of Civilization. A committee was established in England to organize the rescue party. Contributions poured in; volunteers flocked to the fore. Stanley, of course, accepted command of the expedition, and—overruling all dissent—he succeeded in imposing his own plan for the rescue. Stanley intended to reach Equatoria from the west coast of Africa, not the east, and he would do so by traveling up his beloved Congo. It may have been the long way, but he maintained that it was the safer and easier way, abounding in water and foodstuffs.

In January 1887, the American explorer set out for Zanzibar, where he procured the experienced porters and the goods with which to barter with the natives. Most important, he picked up Tippu Tib, the Arab merchant who ruled the region east of Stanley Falls and would be counted upon to provide all the porters needed to load the ivory when the time came. On January 18, the expedition landed at the mouth of the Congo. It comprised eight hundred men, including eleven English officers, armed with 524 rifles. From Léopoldville to Yambuya, at the confluence of the Aruwimi River with the Congo, the trip was safe and easy, on the steamboats that by now regularly plied the waters of the great river of the Congo Free State. In Yambuya, Stanley established a large fortified camp, and he assembled the provisions needed for his return, because he intended to come back the same way. He entrusted the camp to Major Barttelot and the naturalist Jameson. They were to wait there for the porters promised by Tippu Tib. On June 28, Stanley and the 380 men of his vanguard column entered the dripping shadows of the great Congo rain forest.

"We marched out of the gate, company after company in single file. Each with its flag, its trumpeter or drummer, each with its detail of supernumeraries, with fifty picked men as advance guard to handle the billhook and axe, to cut saplings, 'blaze,' or peel a portion of the bark of a tree a hand's-breadth, to sever the leaves and slash at the rattan, to remove all obtrusive branches that might interfere with the free passage of loaded porters, to cut trees to lay across streams for their passage, to form zeribas or bomas of bush and branch around the hutted camp at the end of the day's travel. The advance guard are to find a path, or, if none can be found, to choose the thinnest portions of the jungle and tunnel through without delay, for it is most fatiguing to stand in a heated atmosphere with a weighty load on the head."

After 155 days, they finally glimpsed the first glimmers of light, bellwethers of open country; after 166 days, on December 4, 1887, they emerged from the jungle and advanced toward Lake Albert, in the hope of soon seeing its waters. They actually reached the long-sought lakeshore on December 13, and they immediately set about anxiously questioning the natives: Where are the white men? Where is the great canoe that spits smoke? And the natives answered: You are the first white men that we have ever seen, and around here the only time that we see a canoe spit smoke is if we set it on fire. Moreover, all of the surrounding tribes had soon taken up arms against these unannounced intruders. Stanley decided to retrace his steps for a short distance to a less fraught region, around two hundred miles from the lake. There he built fortifications and waited for the rear guard, commanded by Barttelot, which would have begun its march in the meanwhile with the porters sent by Tippu Tib. And he sent his lieutenant Stairs even farther back, to pick up the disassembled steamer *Advance,* abandoned because of the difficulties with transporting it. With *Advance,* he would be able to reach the northernmost shore of Lake Albert, in the territory of Equatoria.

In the meanwhile, strange rumors began to circulate in Vadelai, paradise of entomologists. The talking drums began to tell of white men who emerged from the great forest and then immediately vanished back into it. In February 1888, Emin made a circuit of the lake with his steamboat, but the shore dwellers gave him only vague or contradictory information. And so Emin left letters with the tribal chiefs for those phantom visitors and returned to Vadelai to study insects. No piece of paper was ever lost in the immense and impenetrable African labyrinth. In April, when Stanley returned with the indispensable steamboat, he was immediately handed a letter from the governor, wrapped in wax-coated cloth. Finally, on April 29, on the western shore of the lake, near the station of Msua, the southernmost station in Equatoria, the long-awaited meeting finally took place. Stanley saw a shape emerging from the lake waters, amid whistles and puffs of steam: it was the steamship *Khedive,* and from it stepped down Emin and Casati, surrounded by numerous Egyptian officers. These men did not look in the slightest as if they needed rescuing, the explorer noted in his book, without managing to conceal his irritation. They all wore red fezzes and impeccable white uniforms, freshly laundered and ironed; they were all clean-shaven and scented, the very picture of health and well-being, while Stanley and his men looked like—well, they looked like men who had just walked through an equatorial jungle for the past six months. The meeting was followed by a refined and abundant banquet offered by the rescuees to the rescuers; over the meal, elevated conversation flowed in perfect English. Emin spoke a dozen languages fluently.

The American was disconcerted, to say the least, but he had traveled this far to rescue, and rescue—by God—he would. He did his best to explain to the newly named pasha (the khedive had promoted him, and Stanley himself had brought the decree of elevation) the exceedingly terrible situation in which Emin now found himself, conjuring up the specters of the Mahdi, the kings of Uganda and Unyoro, ready to attack him at any moment. Emin and Casati, however, found it difficult to recognize themselves or Equatoria in Stanley's exaggerations.

Both men loved Africa and the Africans—the governor had married an Abyssinian who, sadly, died, and they had had a daughter, who still lived with him in Vadelai—and both men were perfectly happy right where they were. So were most of the Egyptians and Sudanese, for that matter, who had wives, children, fields, and houses all right there. They had found a situation for themselves in

Equatoria such as they could never have hoped for in Cairo or Khartoum. For Equatoria, those had been years of great prosperity. The only things that were beginning to run short were ammunition and European medicines, but there were plenty of substitutes, based on native ingenuity and local herbs.

Stanley, however, insisted. He made peremptory threats; he issued ultimatums. It was his job to lead them all back to the "civilized world." He was also playing a double, even a triple game. If, for instance, Emin wished to enter the service of the king of the Belgians, then perhaps Emin could remain there as the representative of the Congo Free State, to which Equatoria could be annexed provisionally. Or else he and his men could march to Lake Victoria and raise the British flag there—in fact, an English company was working in that area to take control of Kenya and Uganda. Emin Effendi Hakim, "the trusted doctor," refused to betray those he had served, refused to betray his sovereign, the khedive of Egypt. Still, he was a mild-mannered man, indecisive by nature, and Stanley succeeded in spreading discord among his men. They began to argue and fight over whether they should stay or go.

In the meanwhile, Stanley was increasingly concerned about the fate of his rear guard, which should have caught up with him some time ago. Instead, days, weeks, and months passed, without any news. What had become of Barttelot's column? Could it have been wiped out in the deep jungle? In February, he had sent messengers to meet the column, but he had heard nothing from them, either. They seemed to have vanished, all swallowed up by the jungle. On June 16, the American decided to turn back with a few companions to find out for himself what had happened. At every twist and turn in the trail, he peered anxiously into the vegetable corridors, hoping to catch sight of Barttelot. But it was not until two months later, after nearly six hundred miles of trails, on the morning of August 17, in a place called Banalya, just ninety miles outside of Yambuya, that a camp was finally sighted in a clearing: finally, the rear guard, or we should say, what remained of it. Once Stanley passed through the wooden palisades, he came face-to-face with the horrible spectacle of a charnel house. The air reeked of dead flesh; bodies lay scattered, unburied, on the ground. Dying men lay on filthy straw, their faces ravaged and scarred by smallpox.

Out of the 271 original members of the rear guard, only 102 now survived; of the five white officers, only one—Bonny—presented himself to the commander. Bonny told Stanley that Barttelot, after beginning to show clear signs of an unhinged mind, had been killed a month previous during a dispute with a black man; that Jameson had set out in search of Tippu Tib in order to obtain more porters (it would later be learned that he too was dead); that Troup, seriously ill, had been sent back to England; and that Ward had marched back to the mouth of the Congo to telegraph back to London, seeking further instructions. The men had already begun to die like flies at Yambuya, of fevers, typhus, pernicious anemia, starvation, and smallpox. Tippu Tib had provided a much smaller number of porters—and eleven months later—than had been agreed. Finally, having heard nothing more from Stanley, Barttelot and the others were convinced that he had died in the forest because rumors to that effect had been conveyed to them by natives.

There did not seem to be a great deal that Stanley could do to remedy this disaster. He fed the survivors healthful food (many had died because, too weak even to cook their meals, they had eaten raw manioc, or cassava, which is poisonous) and set out again a few days later with those who could walk; the dying—forty out of a hundred—were left to their inevitable fate. The march back—not too challenging, considering that it ran through a well-known territory—cost another 106 dead, 38 of them members of the unfortunate rear guard.

On December 20, they reached Fort Bodo, the camp that Stanley had established two hundred miles short of Lake Albert. There, the rest of his men were awaiting him, along with a whole new set of concerns: for some time now, there had been no reports of Emin and Jephson (the latter an officer that Stanley had sent to accompany the pasha on a review of the garrisons of Equatoria, to round up any of the men who wished to leave). And once again, there was no alternative but to go size up the situation in person. Stanley allowed himself three days of rest, then marched toward the lake with all his men, 412 in all, leaving Fort Bodo in flames behind them.

On January 16, 1889, just a single day's march from Lake Albert, the explorer was handed three letters from Emin and two more from Jephson. Jephson's letter made a "mortal shiver" run down Stanley's spine. The discord that had been sown was bearing its bitter fruit. Convinced somehow that their governor meant to abandon them all in order to follow Stanley, selling off Equatoria to the English for a song, the Egyptian soldiers and their officers had mutinied. Emin, Jephson, and Casati were all being held prisoner. And the Mahdists—after a four-year truce—had suddenly attacked, seizing the fort of Regiaf; the fort's garrison had fled to the south, bearing accounts of outright massacres. Panic began to spread. There was, however, a bright side: the panic led the Egyptian mutineers to free the pasha and the others. The rebellious troops no longer knew what to do; they now begged Stanley's pardon.

Stanley seized the moment and laid out the solution he had been proposing all along: they should evacuate Equatoria and march east toward the coast. The officers submitted to his will. They asked for, and were accorded, three weeks to return to their garrisons and round them up, all then to converge on Kavalli, at the northeastern extremity of Lake Albert, chosen as a marshaling site. But a month passed, and there was no sign of the troops—fifteen hundred regular and three thousand irregular soldiers. Long familiar with the delays of the Middle East, Emin found the missed deadline a routine event. The mistrustful Stanley, instead, thought he smelled a rat. He began to suspect a betrayal. Stanley decided that those devious "Turks" were planning a massacre. He managed to lay his hands on letters, and in them he found phrases that were anything but reassuring; the American explorer put the worst possible interpretation on them. At long last, he felt he could completely overrule Emin, who was by now despondent: during his long rule over the province, the death penalty had never been required. The implacable Stanley ordered the arrest of the supposed leader of the conspiracy, Rehan. After a rapid show trial, Rehan was hanged, his body left to the hyenas.

Now—in spite of Emin's and Casati's lingering doubts, reluctant as they were to abandon those of their men who remained loyal to Egypt—Stanley the Rescuer, who had the situation firmly in hand, ordered an immediate departure. Ten thousand people (soldiers, officials, and family members) had been expected; only a twentieth of that number—570 men, women, and children—showed up at Kavalli on April 15, 1889. From there to Bagamoyo was a distance of fifteen hundred miles: almost 300 of the trekkers were lost over that distance. A total of 290 people arrived safely. All the rest died along the way; most fell victim to general hardship rather than hostile natives. In fact, Stanley's regular and vigorous use of the Maxim machine gun easily swept aside all opposition in the restless region of Unyoro and in the bandit-ridden Usukuma. When they reached Mpuapua, just two thirds of the way to the coast, they encountered a German expedition that had been sent too late to rescue the pasha. The Germans had not had the slightest intention of using force to free him. Dr. Karl Peters was the leader of the expedition, and in spite of his disappointment, he regaled the equatorial refugees with fine ham, champagne, and cigars.

A journalist traveling with Peters described their picturesque meeting with the survivors:

> They marched in an endless Indian file along the twisting trail. All of the styles typical of that part of Africa were worn by one or another of the group, and there were more than a few dressed in nothing but their own skin, in keeping with the unassuming fashion sense of the Africans. Thirty or forty men of the expedition had been paid for their services with bright-red blankets transformed into gala outfits, and they had been detailed to

> the transport of Stanley's tent and personal effects. Stanley himself rode on a handsome donkey led by a young man who wore a red turban, red breeches, and a red shirt. The youth seemed proud of his special task, attained for personal merit. Behind the mule came the great explorer's special corps, bearing crates, tents, and other objects on their heads. These men were enveloped in red blankets draping down to their heels. This scarlet brigade, along with Stanley and his donkey, trotted along, passing the others the way that an express train passes an omnibus. It reached the encampment first. If the sun was too hot, then Stanley would open a green umbrella.
>
> Of the Europeans, Emin Pasha, Captain Casati, Jephson, and Bonny rode on donkeys, but Captain Nelson, Lieutenant Stairs, and Doctor Parke walked. The courageous surgeon had not ridden a yard on an animal's back the entire way. Two powerful servants carried Emin's little daughter in a litter, and some of the Egyptian and half-breed women rode donkeys, while others walked, and others still were carried on straps [sic]. Men and women carried their children on their shoulders, but not always. One of the saddest sights of the entire march were the poor little six- and seven-year-old children, tired and broken-footed, who limped along, crying to be picked up and carried. Famished, thirsty, tired, limping because of the thorns piercing their feet, they sobbed at every step, whenever they lost sight of their mothers. Shoved along, brutally pushed by rough men who would rather have seen them lost in the woods or dead, these little voyagers truly faced a fate that inspired a profound pity.

The biblical exodus ended on December 4, 1889, in Bagamoyo, which now housed a German garrison. In a recent partitioning of

Africa among the colonial powers, Germany had been awarded Tanganyika and was gradually taking possession of its new colony. At the banquet that evening, many champagne toasts were raised, and the German subject, Emin Schnitzler, received a personal telegram from the kaiser, which appeared to have moved him deeply. Then came a dramatic turn of events that was never made entirely clear. The pasha, who was very nearsighted and may have raised several toasts too many, left the room and fell from a veranda, fracturing his skull. Some conjectured that Emin might have tried to kill himself over the humiliations that Stanley had inflicted upon him and out of shame at having allowed the American to impose his will. For that matter, back at Mpuapua, Emin had confessed to Peters his great regrets at having abandoned most of his men.

None of this disturbed the Great Rescuer's triumph. Stanley was covered with victor's laurels upon his return to England; shortly thereafter he was happily wed to the painter Dorothy Tennant. In the park of the stately home purchased by the couple, the pond was named Stanley Pool, while a little hummock was dubbed Mountains of the Moon. There Stanley, also called Bula Matari, Breaker of Rocks, died on May 9, 1904.

When Emin recovered from his fall, he left the service of the khedive and took a post in the administration of the nascent German East Africa. In 1891 he set out with a Dr. Stuhlmann for Equatoria, his own land, from which he had been dragged by force. It would appear that he hoped to persuade the survivors to join with him in the service of Germany. But his reunion with his old subjects in Kavalli was not a happy one, and he decided not to continue any farther north; 126 Sudanese men, women, and children went with him. The caravan, ravaged by smallpox, split in two. Stuhlmann set out on his own to return to the coast in January 1892; Emin headed west, toward the great jungle, and vanished. It was not until much later that news came of his death: he had been killed and eaten by a band of cannibals not far from Lualaba, possibly on January 26, 1893.

Selim Bey, Emin's second in command, remained back in Equatoria. He and his men had arrived too late to reach the impatient Stanley, who was anxious to depart immediately. Now the American accused Selim Bey of a far worse crime than tardiness, intentional or otherwise. The treacherous Selim, Stanley claimed, had set afoot a shadowy plot to hand over all Equatoria to the Mahdists. Emin vehemently denied the accusation. Indeed, in 1891 Selim repelled an attack by those very followers of the Mahdi with whom he had supposedly been conspiring. His troops had been reinforced by the chance discovery of a cache of numerous crates of ammunition and arms that Stanley had buried before leaving for the coast.

When a Captain Lugard reached Selim, speaking in the name of the British East Africa Company, Selim agreed to turn over to him command of his remaining troops. The troops were garrisoned in Uganda and the Unyoro. Those "sweepings of the Sudan" proved to be exceedingly courageous, and Lugard succeeded in evacuating them back to Egypt via Mombasa. There were nine thousand of them, including men, women, and children: twenty times as many as had marched in Stanley's caravan. In June 1892, almost all of them returned safe and sound to Cairo. Selim Bey, however, was not with them. He had remained in Uganda, where he died in the summer of 1893.

16
Heart of Darkness

On December 17, 1865, when he appeared before the parliament of Brussels to read in a slow and confident voice the constitutional oath that made him king of the Belgians by the will of the nation, Leopold II of Saxe-Coburg-Gotha had some very clear ideas about the future of that country, too small for his great ambitions. Already, several years previous, when he was still a prince and heir-apparent, upon his return from a trip to Greece, he had brought back a curious gift for the man who would become his most trusted minister, Frère-Orban, which was meant to be both prophetic and talismanic: a fragment of ancient marble upon which he had had carved the phrase: "Belgium must have a colony." He would have to wait quite a while; in fact, it was not until 1876 that he was finally able to lay the foundations of an edifice that was destined to grow well beyond his wildest dreams. On September 12 of that year, King Leopold II inaugurated in Brussels an international conference of geographers and explorers. After seven days of debates over the scientific importance of exploration and the humanitarian importance of halting the slave trade, the conference resolved to create the African International Association. The king was elected president. The association's avowed goal was to open the "unexplored and barbarous" regions of Central Africa to civilization, establishing a network of "scientific and hospital stations."

A few months later, a first Belgian expedition set out for Zanzibar; from there it would head to Lake Tanganyika to explore the region. Almost all of the members of the expedition would be cut down by tropical diseases, some of them even before setting foot on the Dark Continent. In the fall of 1877, the ship had just set sail from Antwerp when Leopold II, reading the *Daily Telegraph,* learned that Stanley had emerged safe and sound at the mouth of the Congo, having followed its entire course, crossing Central Africa from one ocean to the other. That was the man that he needed. The king sent two emissaries, General Sanford (former American ambassador to Belgium) and Baron Greindl, to await the returning explorer in Marseilles. When Stanley landed in the French port in January 1878, they invited him to enter the service of the International Association—in reality, the service of King Leopold II. Deep in his heart of hearts, however, even though Stanley had become an American citizen, he remained a devoted subject of Her Majesty Queen Victoria, and he planned to offer the giant mouthful of Congo to her; he felt the Congo was too much for a small country like Belgium. In London, however, despite his efforts, political and financial potentates turned a deaf ear to his entreaties. Some treated him "like Don Quixote, others even worse, as an adventurer and buccaneer," as his wife wrote years later, her indignation scarcely lessened. He saw no other option than to accept destiny and the king's invitation. And so, on November 28 of that year, the Committee to Study the Upper Congo was formed in the Royal Palace in Brussels. The name of this committee was deceptive because its immediate purpose was the conquest of the Lower Congo. Stanley was commanded to lead an expedition that would plant the light blue flag with a single gold star of the Association at all the stations that would be established along the river "for commercial purposes," purchasing land from the natives and organizing a network of communications, by road, railroad, and steamboat. He left in January 1879 for Zanzibar, where he enlisted his faithful veterans in the new enterprise. At the end of May he set sail from the island, heading for the mouth of the Congo. A few days later, on June 1, Zanzibar—in those days a mecca for African explorers—began to buzz with rumors about the strangest expedition that had ever been seen on the island, this one, too, fruit of the fertile imagination of King Leopold II.

In his youth, during a trip to Ceylon, Leopold had been impressed by the great services performed by the Indian elephant and the ease with which it could be tamed and trained. In that long-ago memory, the enterprising sovereign sought the solution to the immense problem of transportation in the equatorial regions, where horses, donkeys, mules, and oxen all succumbed inevitably to the tsetse fly, while camels could not travel on damp ground and zebras—suggested as beasts of burden by one optimistic zoologist—had proven to be too wild, too impossible to domesticate.

On that morning of June 1, the steamboat *Chinsura*, hailing from Bombay, dropped anchor in the Bay of Sadani, south of Dar es Salaam. It carried an exceedingly valuable cargo: four Indian elephants purchased by the king of the Belgians—two males, Sundergand and Naderbux, and two females, Sosankalli and Pulmalla—accompanied by a splendid general staff of thirteen mahouts and *cornacs*, who seemed like so many rajas with their iridescent silk garb and turbans, their gem-studded daggers, their necklaces and embroidered sashes.

Landing the pachyderms was no easy task on a coast entirely lacking harbor facilitities. Fortunately, the water was deep, and the *Chinsura* was able to anchor just three hundred yards from the coast. There the huge animals were hauled up from the hold and lowered into the sea by means of pulleys fastened to the mainmast. Then, *cornacs* riding on their necks, the elephants swam ashore, clambering onto the African beach, their trunks held rigid as if in triumph. The people of the coast hurried to Dar es Salaam to admire the prodigious sight: elephants that would kneel, raise one leg, then the other, dance, walk, and stop at the signals of men that they gladly tolerated, sitting astride their necks. They not only tolerated the men, they seemed fond of them.

The departure toward the interior began as a triumphant procession; the Africans who witnessed it fell to their knees and cried out at the sight of what seemed to them to be magic. Once they were a few miles inland, however, troubles began. In the marshy terrain, the giant beasts sank up to their bellies in mud. In the steep highlands and the dense and intricate forests, axes and sabers had to be used to cut a path for them. From the sheer sides of deep river valleys, it was necessary to lower the elephants with cables, dozens and dozens of men tugging desperately to keep the elephants from plummeting down. Things were even worse when the elephants had to be hoisted up on the other side of the river. The poor beasts, accustomed in India to being coddled with sweet buns and candies, to being refreshed with water and rum, suffered true privation in that land of hunger. Finally, all the difficulties were overcome, and in Mpuapua, a long rest allowed man and beast to recover.

All the same, ten days later, Sundergrand fell to the earth, victim of an apoplectic fit. This happens all the time to tame elephants, say the mahouts. It has nothing to do with Africa. And on they went, toward the legendary Tabora, while all of the small-time sultans of Ugogo clustered around to see the gods come from the sea, who have the magical power to ride an elephant as it were an ordinary donkey. And as their admiration increased, so rose the price of the tribute to be paid for passage, because admiration had a price too, and divine beings should not lower their dignity by haggling over a few extra bits of cotton.

Shortly before leaving Ugogo, Naderbux became unsteady on his legs and suddenly crumpled to the ground. He died the same day. He had already been sick, claimed the mahouts. And they buried him in great secret, by night, because magical elephants simply do not die. The enormous grave was discovered after the caravan left, and from that day on travelers from the coast were required to pay an exorbitant tribute, because the natives claimed that the stealth of the burial had damaged the harvest.

In Mgunda-Mknali, a sinister region lacking supplies and water, even harder times awaited the expedition. Labyrinths of razor-edged rocks alternated with patches of acacia with needle-sharp thorns, forming an interminable vault of stingers arching overhead. The elephants stopped constantly, trapped amid the stinging branches with their heavy loads. It became necessary to send fifty men ahead to cut a high gallery through the forest, knocking down plants and sawing through branches. The porters suffered greatly, however, forced as they were to march on bare feet over a carpet of thorns. God is merciful, and all tribulations come to an end; they were finally rewarded by their reception in Tabora, where Pulmalla and Sosankalli entered, trunks held stiff and high, trumpeting in triumph, covered with their most garish scarlet and black blankets. On the back of each of the two surviving elephants was a palanquin, in which the Europeans sat in comfort, and all around were mahouts and *cornacs,* glittering in silk: a glorious entrance that seemed to promise the success of the expedition. But the timing was not as good as it seemed at first: surrounding Tabora, all of the Unyamwezi was in flames. The great chief Mirambo, who had become Stanley's blood brother some time before, was determined to build a huge and powerful state in order to oppose the raids of the Arabs. Mirambo had nothing against the Europeans—on the contrary, he considered them his friends. But his men, who often acted on their own initiative, saw danger in that enchanted caravan. Danger, and the possibility of considerable plunder. The caravan fell victim to an ambush in the village of Pimbuè, and whites, blacks, and Indians alike were slaughtered, following a long, drawn-out siege. There is some controversy over the fate of the two female elephants. Some say they were killed in the attack; others say that they were freed by the victors and joined their African counterparts in the forest, where they returned to life in the wild, with occasional longings for the good old days in India, with sweet buns and glasses of rum.

Meanwhile, on the far side of the continent, Henry Morton Stanley was hard at work introducing civilization into the Congo on behalf of King Leopold II. The first station along the river was founded on October 1, 1879: Vivi, about 100 miles from the mouth. Then came the most difficult and important part of the program: the construction of a road stretching over 125 miles, running alongside the Congo past the stretch of river made impracticable by cataracts, making it possible to transport a veritable fleet of steamboats beyond the rough water into navigable waters upstream. It was a colossal undertaking, involving dynamite blasts and men wielding picks. And that was when Stanley won the appellation by which he would go down in history: when the natives saw him shattering small boulders with a sledgehammer, they called him Bula Matari, Breaker of Rocks. And so Bula Matari, relying in part on his reputation as a demolisher of obstacles, stipulated dozens of treaties with tribal chiefs in the name of Leopold II of Belgium, who bartered their lands in exchange for "an ample supply of fine clothes, flunkey coats, and tinsel-braided uniforms, with a rich assortment of diverse marketable wares . . . not omitting a couple of bottles of gin."

But all the while that the American explorer was leveling forests and punching through mountainsides and transporting wholesale into equatorial Africa entire warehouses of used clothing, there was someone on the other side of the river, preparing to undermine his conquests. A small French expedition led by a naval officer named Pierre Savorgnan de Brazza (Italian by extraction, born in Rio de Janeiro, he had rejected the blandishments of the king of the Belgians in the name of his loyalty to France) was just then marching from Gabon toward the Congo along the course of the Ogooué. And there he founded the trading station of Franceville in June 1880. Brazza, who was twenty-eight at the time, had already explored the same district a few years before.

In that same area, another Frenchman (he, too, later to become an American citizen) roamed freely. Paul du Chaillu, the son of a merchant who had set up shop at the mouth of the Gabon River, had roved this region from 1850 to 1858, enjoying a series of adventures—some real, some imagined—that first made him famous, later notorious. Following his return to Europe, he published a book that made him the rage of London's drawing rooms. He rarely had to be asked twice to show off the skins of gorillas he had killed, inevitably in tension-filled scenes of hunting, because du Chaillu, we may say, was the inventor of the gorilla, an animal about which the naturalists of the time knew little indeed. It was he—and he had killed twenty-two of the beasts—who first told stories that would survive in a European mythology of Darkest Africa, in which gorillas became a sort of half-human tribe, only a little hairier and a little more primitive than the other inhabitants of the continent. The Victorian public went wild over the incredibly spicy tale of gorillas in heat who from time to time descend upon a sleeping village to kidnap some black beauties, hustling them back to some treetop where they would ravish them. At the foot of the same trees lived the fabulous pygmies—another du Chaillu specialty, until then the only European who had seen a Pygmy—kindly gnomes of the rain forest.

These amusing fairy tales were met immediately with the approval of the European readership—especially the ladies—but in time they came under the sharper examination of exceedingly serious zoologists and anthropologists, indignant at the presumption of this dilettante, prying into things best left to their scholarly competence. Everything was invented out of whole cloth, they accused him. He had never traveled more than a few miles inland; he had passed off gorilla skins purchased from the natives as trophies of his unerring aim. At this point, angry and venomous with resentment, du Chaillu decided to prove his stories with a second expedition. Indeed, this time he would cross Africa, from west to east.

In 1863 he set out for his beloved Gabon, where he would begin his trek. But an epidemic of smallpox was ravaging the land, and a number of tribal chiefs in the interior seemed to think that this white intruder had brought the pestilence with him (this diagnosis was substantially accurate, even though it could not perhaps be referred to this particular, and unfortunate, explorer). Du Chaillu stumbled into full-fledged disaster some 440 miles inland when one of his men, while cleaning his rifle, accidentally fired a shot that killed a native bystander. The caravan barely saved itself from the wrath of the natives by fleeing as fast as their respective legs would carry them, leaving everything that they had brought with them strewn on the ground, including the invaluable scientific instruments. Having failed to cross the continent, du Chaillu had no alternative but to return to the friendly tribes on the coast.

Those lands were ruled by many lesser monarchs. One, however, was a great ruler, indeed, a great king, so great that he called himself N'Combé, that is, the Sun King. N'Combé held sway over the left bank of the Ogooué, and he was a jolly old monarch, vast in bulk with a jovial face, dressed in a huge white shirt upon which sparkled a brooch and three diamonds manufactured in Hamburg for three pence the pair. He wrapped himself in an immense gown of Scottish poplin with black checks. Around his neck was a cravat cut from an old tent, in his hand he held a drum major's baton, and on his head he wore a top hat adorned with a splendid golden sun. He loved white men because they brought him barrels of rum, and he always held a bottle of rum in his free hand. This obese and good-humored alcoholic was also an atrocious tyrant, heavy-handed with his subjects and his neighbors alike. One day, however, he burned one village too many; one of the survivors performed an act of submission by offering him a gourd brimming over with palm wine. The Sun King drank agreeably, and within a brief while he lay twisting on the ground amid spasms of pain and terrifying hallucinations. Even the medicaments offered by two passing Frenchmen were inadequate, and he died. His funeral cortege, preceded by an accordion and two drums, passed through the streets of the capital amid the inconsolable weeping of his widows.

Savorgnan de Brazza met with another powerful sovereign, Makoko, who ruled over the right bank of the Congo. The French/Italian explorer traveled with a small escort and avoided all conflict with the natives. Brazza was a conqueror but not a conquistador: the exact opposite of Stanley. "Make an effort to understand the blacks," he wrote in instructions to his underlings. "Make an effort to understand not only the words they say, but the way they think. Live amongst them, live the way they live. Visit their villages, question women and children. Bring no weapons! No one should be armed! Don't forget that *you* are intruders, no one invited you here." This attitude won Brazza the sympathy of Makoko; till then all that Makoko knew of white men was that they fired rifles, plundered villages, and forced blacks to serve him as press-ganged bearers. (Makoko had, evidently, heard of Stanley's exploits during his descent of the Congo.)

After a month as a guest at Makoko's court, Brazza signed a treaty with the king putting his country under a French protectorate; the treaty also granted Brazza a plot of land near the riverbank village of M'Fa, and it was there that Brazzaville was later to stand. Brazza left a tiny garrison comprised of a Senegalese corporal named Malamine—promoted to sergeant for the occasion—and two Gabonese sailors; overhead fluttered the inevitable tricolor. Brazza headed back to the coast to procure supplies. It was during this journey, on November 7, 1880, in the village of N'Dambi-Mbongo, on the right bank of the Congo, that the two explorers finally met. They sized each other up, they felt respect for each other, they exchanged courteous greetings, and they disliked each other intensely—they were too different. Brazza said of Stanley that he "made his way with rifleshots and bags of millions." Brazza, instead, was forced to ask his mother for a loan to continue his mission because the French bureaucracy was exceedingly reluctant to make the payments promised.

The presence of that French gentleman in a naval uniform on *his* river made Stanley see red; as soon as he was able, he marched inland. When he reached the large lake now known as Stanley Pool in July 1881, he found Sergeant Malamine on the right bank, with his outsized French flag, "a man of superior capacities, even if he was Senegalese." He then passed over to the left bank, where he assembled his steamboats. On December 1, on a hillside, he founded the city of Léopoldville. Just a month later, however, on New Year's Day 1882, while he was coasting upriver, he discovered that Sergeant Malamine had crossed the river with "his ample tricolor" and was now camped in the village of Kinshasa. The Breaker of Rocks tried to overawe the Iron Sergeant, explaining that he could gobble him up with both his Gabonese for breakfast. Malamine pointed out that he was officially backed by France. Stanley stopped insisting.

But Stanley immediately sent a letter off to Beglium, and from Brussels the long arm of Leopold II reached out to Paris. In May 1882 a quartermaster of the French navy arrived, in a state of exhausted prostration, in Kinshasa and ordered the inflexible sergeant to withdraw to the other side of the river. And so the entire left bank of the Congo, all the way up to the confluence with the Ubangi, became property of the king of the Belgians, and the following year Stanley was able to lead an expedition to the Upper Congo, as far as Stanley Falls. During that journey he made generous use of the ammunition he carried with him.

On April 13, 1885, a twenty-one-cannon salute marked the foundation of the new Free State of the Congo in Vivi, which was to be the capital for the first year. Leopold II was recognized sovereign of the new country by the representatives of the leading powers, who had gathered in Berlin in November 1884 to negotiate the divvying up of Africa. Leopold was more than king of the Congo (he had briefly considered naming himself *emperor* of the Congo); in fact, he owned it: absolute master of a region seventy-six times the size of Belgium. All "free" lands were declared property of the crown; the two leading products of the Congo at that time, ivory and caoutchouc, or rubber, became state monopolies. And in order to harvest those state monopolies, the natives were obliged to provide forced labor: wasn't it their responsibility, after all, to contribute to the triumph of civilization? This was the beginning of a reign of terror that was to last for two decades and kill off half the population of the Congo. It has been calculated that the direct and indirect victims of the new regime amounted to 10 million.

While journalists throughout Europe joined in the collective chorus of praise for the new antislavery campaign being conducted against the Arab slave traders still operating in the eastern provinces, the Congo itself became the most disgraceful slave-holding state ever to have existed on the face of the Earth. Commanded by white officers, the natives enlisted (by force) in the army—called the Force Publique—spread out across the immense nation, spreading terror as they went. The men were forced to abandon their work in the fields to harvest the quotas of raw rubber required by the new government; they toiled month after month in the rain forest. Their stores of foodstuffs were confiscated by the Force Publique; their women and children were held hostage and often died of hunger or diseases caused by malnutrition. All resistance was punished by death, and whenever a rebel was killed his or her right hand was lopped off to show that ammunition was not being wasted. The Belgian bureaucrats demanded that the soldiers turn in one hand for every bullet used. Baskets full of chopped-off hands gathered in front of the residences of Belgian bureaucrats. There were some, like Captain Léon Rom, who preferred a decapitated head as proof. He actually used them to decorate the gardens of his station. These are the heads that we read about in *Heart of Darkness,* surrounding the house of Kurtz. Joseph Conrad worked briefly in those years as a river pilot on the Congo, and the book is simply an account of his experience. There is nothing fanciful about the story.

If Conrad transfigured the tragedy of the Congo into literature, there were others who denounced the crimes of the Belgians in vehement publications aimed at world opinion. In vain, Leopold the Great Civilizer tried to react by smearing the authors. Feeling the pressure of a press campaign that unearthed increasingly atrocious episodes, the king was forced to name a commission of inquest in 1904. Tame though that commission may have been, it was obliged to recognize that the accusations were based in reality.

The reign of terror, however, was not limited to the personal dominion of King Leopold II. Press reports noted that rubber was being gathered with the same horrible techniques in the French Congo. The president of the French Republic responded by entrusting the investigation to the man who had won that territory for the French with his gentle ways: Savorgnan de Brazza. When they learned of his imminent arrival, the colonial authorities of course hurried to conceal their misdeeds and abuses, common in the French Congo though not as widespread as in the Belgian neighbor, the Congo Free State. At first Brazza and his fellow investigators failed to uncover irregularities. But one day, while staying at a rubber marshaling station as they made their way up the course of the Congo, an episode occurred that opened their eyes.

"During a banquet held for the Commission, the chief of the post, in order to distract the attention of the diners, had organized a performance of Negro dances, during the course of which there was one particularly noteworthy exhibition by a large Negro, with remarkable poses and bizarre acrobatics. As he watched the spectacle, Brazza did not smile—quite the contrary, his face darkened. All of a sudden, white as a sheet, he leapt up, placed a protective hand on the Negro's shoulder, and asked the Negro to guide him in his investigation. Then, with an authoritative gesture, he ordered his entourage to follow him. In the Negro's contorsions, he had recognized a message couched in mime: 'Not far from here are prisoners and hostages.' "

It was true. The commission found genuine concentration camps, where the black laborers had been chained to keep them from speaking to the investigators. Leopold II may have been a monster, but he was not a unique monster: forced labor and thinly disguised slavery were common practice in the French colony as well, though hands and heads were not lopped off. And they seemed to be intrinsic to the harvesting of rubber. Horrified at his discovery and worn out by the privations of the journey, the fifty-three-year-old Brazza fell gravely ill and was forced to return to the coast. The kindly conqueror died in the hospital of Dakar on September 14, 1905. The rhetorical flourishes and grace notes that accompanied the great state funeral that was held for him in Paris also helped to tamp down the scandal.

Four years later, in December 1909, Leopold II died, too, at the age of seventy-four. He was no longer the king/owner of the Congo: the year before he had handed over the Congo Free State in exchange for a considerable sum. With the king off the international stage and the transformation of a personal dominion into a standard African colony, there was less international concern for events in the Congo. It appeared that in the end justice had triumphed. In reality, the atrocities continued as before, a little less ferocious, a bit more sporadic, a bit less open. For many years thereafter, the Congolese, feared generically by the Europeans as cannibals, refused to eat tinned beef. They were certain that those cans contained the chopped hands of their massacred fellow Congolese.

PART IV

Asia/Oceania

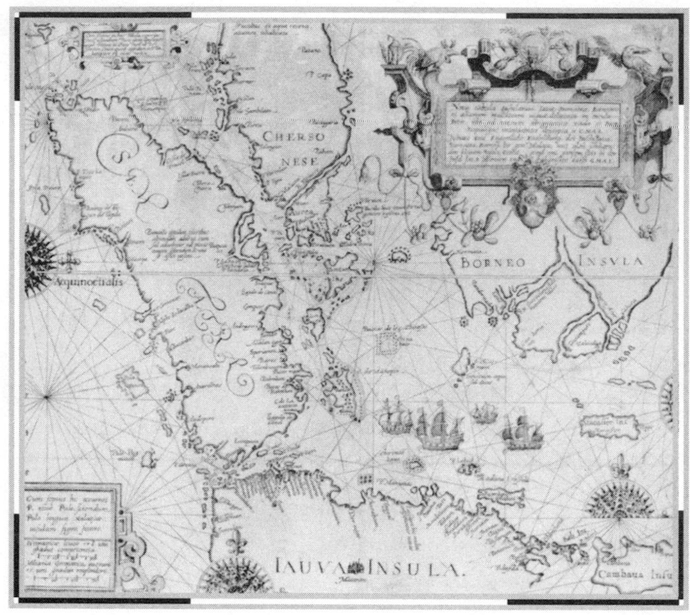

This map of Southeast Asia, by Theodore De Bry, features Borneo, Java, and Sumatra. —Image from Thomas Suarez, *Early Mapping of Southeast Asia,* Periplus Editions, 1999.

Perhaps it is the bracing air of the Pacific Ocean, but it seems that the tales from the Equator in Oceania and Asia are somehow cleaner, less depressing.

The first European adventurer to make his way across the Equator in the Pacific is Ferdinand Magellan, a Portuguese navigator in the service of the Spanish. Magellan was sailing at a time when that distinction was more than a minor one: just a few years after Columbus discovered the New World, Pope Alexander VI (father of Lucrezia Borgia, immortalized for his evil ways in the pages of Machiavelli) had drawn a line north to south dividing the entire planet into two parts, half going to Spain and half going to Portugal. The papal decree came into effect before Europeans were fully aware of just how far east South America bulges, and so Brazil became Portuguese. On the other side of the planet, the Spice Islands, source of the most valuable substances on Earth—cloves, nutmeg, and cinnamon—fell into the Portuguese half. Magellan was sailing the long way around to see if he could obtain spices without trespassing (or at least without being caught trespassing) in Portuguese territory. This first circumnavigation of the globe is one of the great maritime feats of all time.

Our second story skips ahead more than three and a half centuries. Sir James Brooke, an Englishman in search of adventure, became raja of the island of Sarawak, owing allegiance simultaneously to the sultan of Brunei and to the empress and queen Victoria I. Rarely has a thirst for adventure and advancement been so richly rewarded.

We conclude with two stories of the South Seas: the eruption of Krakatoa (*west* of Java, by the way) in 1883, the greatest geological event in recorded history, and, less violent and more evocative, the time that Robert Louis Stevenson spent convalescing in the Gilbert Islands around 1890.

With that, we end our tales of the Equator, on a lyrical, hopeful note.

17
Maluku

On November 28, 1520, springtime in the Southern Hemisphere, three ships emerged from a mazelike strait that had just been named the Strait of All Saints, and ventured forth into an ocean that would prove far more vast than anyone aboard those ships could have imagined. The ships were named *Victoria, Trinidad,* and *Concepción,* and they had set sail from the Spanish port of Sanlúcar de Barrameda, at the mouth of the Guadalquivir River, more than a year earlier, on September 20, 1519. Indeed, five ships had set out, under the command of the captain general Ferdinand Magellan. Besides the three mentioned above, the *San Antonio* and the *Santiago* had set sail.

"They are very old ships, battered and tattered," a Portuguese diplomat who had watched the departure later wrote to his king, clearly hopeful that they would not make it far. "I would be afraid to try to sail one of them as far as the Canary Islands; their ribbings are as soft as butter." Captain Magellan was a Portuguese subject who had placed himself in service to the Spanish, having given up hope of sailing to discover new lands for his own king. The purpose of the expedition was to deprive Portugal of the jewel of its overseas empire, built over twenty years of swordplay and cannonfire in the East Indies: Maluku, or the Moluccas, a group of islands straddling the Equator, comprising a small but incredibly precious archipelago where spices grew in great abundance, spices that, in that period, were worth far more than their weight in gold.

In 1493, when Portuguese and Spanish navigators had first begun to venture into distant seas, a Spanish pope, Alexander VI Borgia, drew a line from Pole to Pole on a *mappemonde*, splitting the Earth into two hemispheres, giving the Eastern Hemisphere to Portugal and the Western one to Spain. He hoped in this way to prevent future squabbles between the two chief seafaring nations of the time. In the wake of the Great Discoveries, of course, squabbles and disputes broke out all the same. First of all, those who had been excluded from that division of worldwide spoils objected vociferously ("Show me Adam's will!" Francis I, king of France, was reported to have exclaimed). Second, it was no easy matter to determine, with the geographic knowledge of the day, precisely where the famous north-south line ran.

Maluku, for instance, was perhaps the most appetizing geographic mouthful of the entire global cake, and it lay precisely athwart the dividing line: but which side was it on? After seeing his ambitions thwarted in Portugal and moving on to the Spanish court, Magellan maintained and "proved" to the seventeen-year-old King Charles that the Moluccas lay in the Western, or Spanish, Hemisphere. And Magellan went on to make an even more significant statement: he claimed that he knew how to find the long-sought-after and still-elusive passage to Asia through the American continent. Thus, the entire voyage would take place in waters assigned to Spain by the pope, and Portugal could neither hinder him before his departure nor protest after his successful return.

Magellan's confident words persuaded the king and his royal council. The explorer finally obtained the funding he had sought, and, with the ill wishes of the Portuguese ambassador, he set sail, firmly convinced that he would perform the astonishing deed that

Columbus had failed to accomplish. The great Italian navigator had been frustrated by the unexpected existence of the vast American continent, but Magellan would successfully sail west to reach the Far East, that same Far East in which he had navigated and fought for his ungrateful monarch, King Manuel I of Portugal.

Sailing with Magellan in positions of command were many other Portuguese renegades. In the end, the presence of so many Portuguese commanders would arouse the envy and rivalry of the Spanish officers and crew, causing serious problems for the expedition. The crew was polyglot, as were so many crews of the day: Spaniards were in the majority, Portuguese, Italians, Frenchmen, Flemish, Germans, one Englishman, Arabs, and blacks, for a total of 380 men.

Six days after setting sail, the fleet reached the Canaries, where they took on the last provisions of food and fresh water before embarking on the great voyage across the Atlantic. And there, in the shadow of the Pico de Tenerife, a fast caravel that had set out after them from Spain pulled level with the flagship to deliver a message to Magellan. Written and sealed by his brother-in-law, Diogo Barbosa, the message apparently warned him to be particularly wary of the commander of the *San Antonio,* Don Juan de Cartagena, who was taking part in the expedition with the official rank of *veedor,* which we might translate as "the eyes of the king." Don Juan had been named by the Spanish monarch to oversee the progress of the voyage and monitor the captain general's performance of his duties. He was officially subordinate to Magellan, yet he was a harsh and arrogant hidalgo, and he did little to conceal his dislike of and contempt for Portuguese in general.

The ships set sail once again, sailing close in along the African coast, an unusual route. Perhaps Magellan was hoping to avoid confrontations with the Portuguese, perhaps he was simply searching for new trade winds with which to cross the Atlantic farther south. In any case, the fleet was soon languishing in the equatorial doldrums, and there it lay for fifteen days, motionless beneath a scalding sun. It was during this two-week delay that the first frictions emerged. Cartagena expressed his concerns, and he was promptly rocked back on his heels by Magellan, who said that he would have no explanations to offer his *veedor*. Every member of his crew and of his fleet need do nothing more than obey him.

In time, the wind freshened and the ships began to move, but harmony failed to return. The hidalgo enjoyed his revenge, with a subtle slight to his captain. Speaking the flagship was a daily ritual, and the *veedor* was expected personally to call the official greeting to Captain General Magellan; instead, Cartagena had a subordinate call the greeting, in a clear sign of disrespect.

Four days later came the inevitable confrontation. During a meeting of ship captains aboard the *Trinidad*, Cartagena asked for an explanation of the unorthodox route "in the name of the king." Magellan replied once again that he could expect orders, and nothing more. Imperiously, Cartagena repeated his demand, whereupon Magellan ordered him arrested, to the astonishment and dismay of the other commanders. In mid-December, with Cartagena under arrest, foaming with indignation at the insult he had suffered at the hands of that Portuguese sailor, the fleet entered the stupendous bay where Rio de Janeiro would one day stand. This was paradise: friendly Indios, banquets of pineapples and suckling pig, native maidens willing to trade their charms for a folding knife.

The celebrations went on for two weeks, until Christmas Day. On December 26, Magellan ordered the anchors weighed and began the long sail southward, searching for the passage of whose existence he seemed so oddly positive. He suffered, however, a bitter disappointment, when he mistook the estuary at the mouth of the Río de la Plata for the strait; after sailing upstream for a while, it proved to be only a river, however broad a river. The fleet would have to sail much farther south, deep into the Southern Hemisphere, amid blowing gales, lashed by hail and storms, the yardarms and masts coated with ice. At the end of March 1520, the strait was still elusive, and winter was drawing closer and closer.

The captain general decided to give his men a break; they were suffering from the cold and increasingly restive. The fleet would winter in a bay that appeared suitable to Magellan; he named it Porto San Julián. It would be hard to imagine a site less equatorial. San Julián lay nearly fifty degrees south of the Equator. There was nothing but desolation, gray cliffs, and rocky beaches, a desert of frozen rock pits. There they built some huts and settled down to wait for spring. The Spanish captains, however, grew increasingly impatient. They wanted to sail back home, and set out the following year with a bigger fleet, better equipped to deal with the harsh cold. In fact, Magellan had never expected to be forced to sail so far to the south. Cartagena poured oil on the flames, claiming that the Portuguese commander was intentionally sailing them into disaster, and was secretly working for King Manuel I of Portugal, not King Charles of Spain!

Mutiny was now inevitable, and it came one foggy night. Three Spanish captains—Cartagena, Mendoza, and Quesada—with their followers seized command of three ships and then issued an ultimatum to Magellan, demanding that he immediately set sail back to Spain.

Magellan was not at all cowed; he immediately launched a counterattack, sending two launches full of loyal sailors to retake Mendoza's ship. The mutinous captain was killed in the fray. Then, master of three ships out of five, Magellan barred the entrance to the bay. After a short exchange of cannon fire, the mutineers were overwhelmed and surrendered.

The following day, a court-martial judged the rebels, issuing forty death sentences. An example was made of the dead captain Mendoza: his corpse was first hanged, then quartered by the windlasses of various ships. The four pieces of his dead body were raised high on stakes, the crowning indignity reserved for traitors.

Quesada was beheaded by his own servant, Luis de Molina, who had agreed to perform the macabre task to save his own life; otherwise he, too, would have had his head lopped off. This arrangement was in part suggested by Magellan's sense of poetic justice; in part it was a simple practical necessity. The expedition lacked an official executioner.

All of the others, including Cartagena, were spared, by Magellan's orders. Their death sentences were commuted to hard labor. All of the mutineers, except Cartagena, were put in chains, and for the rest of the winter they had to chop down trees and pump bilge.

One day, a man appeared in that frozen desert. Actually, he was a giant. Naked, in the bitter cold, he danced and sang on the seashore, scattering sand and dirt over his head. The sailors cautiously approached him and persuaded him to come present himself to their captain general. He was so tall that the Europeans only reached to his waist. The giant continued pointing at the sky, because he thought that the white men had come from there. The Europeans placed a large mirror in front of him. When he saw his reflection, the giant leapt backward and knocked four men to the ground. They offered him food and drink: he ate hardtack by the sack and drank water by the bucketful. Magellan called him Patagón, or Bigfoot. And so Patagonia became the name of that land. The first gentle giant was followed by others in the days that followed; they came to exchange guanaco meat for the usual trading goods: combs, mirrors, beads. Women came as well: they were "loaded down like asses" and "their breasts were as long as half an armslength," according to Antonio Pigafetta, chronicler of the expedition.

They took two of the natives prisoner with a trick—filling their arms with gifts until they could scarcely move and then quickly clapping irons on their ankles—and held them captive on the flagship. Magellan planned to show off those specimens of outsized humanity when he returned to Spain.

In the meanwhile, Magellan had sent the *Santiago* south to reconnoiter. The ship, however, was wrecked when a tempest drove it onto the rocks. The crew survived and made it back to Porto San Julián on foot, announcing that they had found a better anchorage.

So, in late August the fleet made south, remaining in the new mooring site until mid-October. They left Cartagena and an accomplice, a priest, amid the skeletal remains of Mendoza and Quesada, with a little water and hardtack, never to be heard of again.

On October 18, with the first signs of a southern spring, they set out again in search of the elusive strait. On the twenty-first, after sailing for about a hundred miles, they discovered what seemed to be a closed bay. Without great hopes, but determined to overlook no possibility, Magellan sent the *San Antonio* and the *Concepción* ahead to see whether there might be a western outlet. A tempest suddenly struck, dragging the two ships away and preventing the others from following. For two anxious days, the captain general waited; finally the two ships reappeared. They had raised the Great Banner and they were firing salvos of joy. The wind had driven them into a narrow, very deep channel. The water had been salt the whole distance. This was no river mouth. Could it finally be the strait?

His heart brimming over with hope, Magellan gave the order to venture into that labyrinth of rocks and towering mountains where the sea meandered in a bramble patch of channels, forks, small and large gulfs, and dead ends. They saw forests and glaciers; they saw a native cemetery with mummified bodies laid out on high grates; they saw a vessel of some sort that vanished among the rocks; they saw countless fires burning in the night on a large island, which they duly named Tierra del Fuego.

The ships split up in order to find the right way through the maze. The answer to the riddle and the first glimpse of the western ocean was found by a launch from the *Trinidad.* The ship's head gunner, a Flemish sailor named Roldán de Argote (clearly a Hispanicized version of the name), climbed up onto a headland and from there looked out over a vast, unknown ocean, with calm and peaceful waters. When he heard the news, Magellan wept with joy.

Then he waited for the other ships, out scouting the twists and turns of the strait, to return. When they did, he would begin making preparations for the last leg of their voyage to the Moluccas.

Concepción and *Victoria* arrived quickly, but *San Antonio* failed to appear, though the captain general waited for a full week. Magellan's pilot, Andrés de San Martín, who knew how to read the stars as well as nautical charts, told him, after consulting the constellations, that he saw the ship sailing back to Spain, its captain in chains. Magellan, who had been expecting a second mutiny, believed him. With the three ships that remained to him, he set out into the vast ocean, which he named the Pacific.

"We sailed for three months and twenty days without fresh provisions, and we ate biscuit, and when there was no more of that, we ate the dried stale crumbs, which were full of maggots and smelled strongly of mouse urine. We drank yellow water, already several days putrid. We also ate some of the hides which were wrapped around the main yardarm to keep it from cutting the shrouds. These hides were very much hardened by the sun, rain, and winds. We would let them soak in the sea for four or five days, and then we would put them over the fire for a bit, and so eat them; sometimes we would eat sawdust. Mice could be sold for half a ducat apiece, and still many who would have paid could not get them," Pigafetta wrote. Four thousand leagues of starvation without the slightest sign of land, except for two desert islands on which they saw nothing but "birds and trees, and for this reason we called them the Unfortunate Isles."

They passed near the archipelagos of Tuamotu, the Marquesas, and the Marshall Islands without actually sighting them; in a way, that may have been lucky, because they might well have hit any of a number of coral reefs surrounding these atolls and wrecked their hulls. They passed northward over the Equator.

Hunger, in any case, was only part of the problem; they also suffered from scurvy: "Of all our misfortunes, this was the worst: the gums of some of the men swelled over their upper and lower teeth, so that they could not eat and so died." Nineteen men died, along with the poor giants captured from Patagonia.

On March 6, 1521, one of the few sailors of the *Trinidad*'s crew with enough strength left to clamber up to the crow's nest sighted land. It was the island of Guam, the southernmost of the group that is now called the Marianas. But Magellan dubbed them the Ladrones, or Islands of Thieves, because when they stood in to land, they were immediately boarded by swarms of natives who took everything that wasn't nailed down. This encounter—the first meeting between Europeans and people of Oceania—culminated in cannon fire, which chased off the frightened natives, though they did manage to take a launch as they went. The following day, forty sailors armed with crossbows went ashore, and after killing seven natives, burning the village, and recovering the stolen launch, they took all the food they could lay their hands on: fruit, hogs, chickens, rice, yams, fresh water. With those stolen provisions, the health of the crews improved considerably.

Once they had recovered their strength and morale, the surviving members of the expedition set out to find Maluku, which could not be far off now. Ten days later, they happened upon a large group of islands that half a century later would be named after King Philip II of Spain; and in those inhabited waters Magellan finally had proof that he was close to his goal. His slave, Enrique, a Malaysian who had been with Magellan since the long-ago years in which he had fought in the Far East for the king of Portugal, spoke to a group of natives paddling a canoe and they answered him in Malaysian, which Enrique could interpret.

Instead of heading directly for the Moluccas, however, the captain general decided to explore the Philippines at greater length. He claimed them for the Spanish crown and for Christendom in general, dubbing them the Islands of Saint Lazarus, because he had reached them on Saint Lazarus's Day. The minor local sultans of such places as Limasáwa and Cebu, after initial reluctance, allowed themselves to be won over by the usual trinkets and, especially, by the clear demonstrations of the Europeans' might. One particularly effective show came when Magellan donned his metal breastplate and had one of his men stab him repeatedly with a dagger. He wanted the chiefs to understand that he was wearing armor that made him invulnerable.

Magellan began to preach Christianity to the natives, delivering impromptu sermons that were translated into Malaysian by Enrique, erecting crosses, and distributing holy images, until the local rulers finally agreed to convert to the new religion, along with their wives and dignitaries and subjects. They burned the idols they used to worship and swore allegiance to the king of Spain. They may have been encouraged to do so by the Europeans' long-standing reputation for the arbitrary use of their power, dating back to the arrival of the first Portuguese traders years earlier.

At this point, however, Magellan overplayed his hand. To show the natives that his arrival was truly providential and that conversion to Christianity and a Spanish alliance would bring considerable advantages, Magellan decided to attack the sultan of Mactan, a minor enemy of the sultan of Cebu. It appears, among other things, that the sultan of Cebu did not much care about this attack, but was willing to go along.

Just after midnight on April 27, 1521, some twenty dugouts loaded with warriors from Cebu and two launches with sixty Europeans approached Mactan. They waited till dawn to land.

After intimating that the sultan, Silipulapu, would be wise to surrender and convert to Christianity—a suggestion that the sultan rejected with scorn—Magellan plunged into the water, followed by forty-nine men in full armor, armed with harquebuses and crossbows, and splashed clumsily toward the beach, moving gingerly over a seabed covered with sharp coral. The warriors of Mactan, who appeared not to be frightened in the slightest, showered the invaders with "arrows, spears, lances with their sharp tips hardened in the fire, stones, and projectiles of all sorts, in such quantities that we could not defend ourselves against them." The harquebuses fired, it is true, but it took two men to work one, and the ground was so uneven that none of the shots went home. The European attackers managed to reach the village, whereupon the defenders of

Mactan redoubled their hail of projectiles, advancing from all directions. Suddenly a wave of panic swept through the European attackers, who had just realized they were about to be surrounded. One or two Europeans fell dead. A headlong retreat began. They ran toward the beach, tossing their breastplates onto the ground as they went so that they could run faster. From the boats, men began firing mortars, but they could not stand in close to the beach because of the sharp coral. Thus, the mortar fire was falling short, and they were afraid that they would do more damage to friend than foe. Magellan tried to cover the disorderly retreat and stood and fought with a small party of fellow soldiers. At last, he was wounded in the leg, and then a native stabbed him in the face with a spear. "He immediately killed the same native with his own spear, and left the weapon in the native's body. Then he tried to draw his sword, but he could not entirely unsheath it, because of a spear-cut that he had in his arm. When the natives saw this, they all leapt at him: one stabbed him in the leg with a huge javelin, and he fell to the ground, face down. At that, the natives all fell on him at once, with iron and bamboo spears and javelins; and so they killed our mirror, our light, our staff and our true guide. As they stabbed him, he looked back repeatedly to see if we had all safely reached the boats."

The Portuguese Duarte Barbosa, a relative of Magellan's, was named captain general by the men, shaken and upset by the death of their leader. The situation required great care: after the disastrous and shameful failure of the invasion of Mactan, the prestige of the Europeans had fallen very low. They had showed that they were anything but invincible and, moreover, that they were not very bright. The landing had been a very badly managed affair.

Humiliation was followed by betrayal. Magellan had promised his faithful Malaysian slave Enrique that, when Magellan died, he would have his freedom. Enrique refused to serve as he had done when his master was alive. Barbosa laughed at this, slapping and threatening the Malaysian. Deeply offended, Enrique decided to take revenge; he suggested to the sultan of Cebu that together they could seize the ships with all their cargo. The idea appealed to the sultan; a few days later he invited the Europeans to a great banquet. Twenty-seven of them accepted—officers and crew, including Barbosa. Two of the men were surprised at the strange looks the natives were giving them; suspecting that something was in the air, they returned to the ships. This was a wise move because that night all the others were either killed or taken prisoner, later sold as slaves to Chinese merchants. Of the avenging Enrique, we know nothing more. If he did return to his native Malacca, then he was the first man to sail around the world.

The three ships left Cebu, the site of so many misfortunes, to seek a quiet spot on the nearby island of Bohol where they could decide what to do next. The new captain general, the pilot João Carvalho, who was also Portuguese, clearly understood that the 110 men who remained were too few to sail three ships. He decided to sacrifice the ship that was worst off, *Concepción.* He ordered the ship emptied and stripped of everything that could be useful; then it was burned to the waterline. For six months, *Victoria* and *Trinidad* wandered around the Philippines and Borneo, dabbling in a bit of trade, a bit of theft, and a bit of piracy; at every opportunity, they asked about Maluku. At last, the pilots of a large junk that the Europeans had captured told them exactly how to get to the Moluccas. They were very well-informed: they even knew that on the island of Ternate, there was a Portuguese named Francisco Serrão. Serrão had been a friend of Magellan's and had sailed and fought with him when they were both young men. It was he who had suggested that Magellan conquer the Moluccas for Spain, and he had been waiting there for him for years.

Serrão first encountered the Moluccas when he was shipwrecked there, but over time he had gained a considerable ascendancy over the small local court; in 1514 he had written Magellan from there, suggesting that he come join him.

Now that they finally knew where to go, the crews of the two ships headed straight for the Moluccas. Carvalho, who had shown himself to be incompetent, had been ousted as captain general. He was replaced by the Spaniard Gonzalo Gómes de Espinosa.

At dawn on November 8, flags flying in the breeze, *Trinidad* and *Victoria* sailed into the port of Tidore, "firing all their artillery" in a sign of joy. One of the captured pilots who had been forced to come with them announced that "those five islands, Ternate, Tidore, Matir, Machian, and Bachian, were Maluku." And, as Pigafetta wrote, "it was no wonder that we were all overjoyed, since we had spent twenty-seven months less two days looking for Maluku."

The next day, the local sultan came to greet them, aboard a *praho.* He sailed from one ship to another, "seated under a silk parasol. Before him stood one of his sons holding the royal sceptre, two other sons holding two golden urns with water for his hands, and two more sons holding two gilded boxes full of betel nuts." He gave them an official welcome and announced that he had seen them in his dreams, "coming from afar."

Then he came aboard the flagship, where he was honored with many gifts, including a robe made of yellow "Turkish-style" velvet. The sultan was so pleased that he announced that from that day forth, his island would no longer be called Tidore, but Castile.

One week later, a Portuguese mercenary named Afonso da Lorosa arrived from Ternate; he and Magellan's friend Serrão had been soldiers together. He informed them that Serrão had died seven months before, probably poisoned by the sultan of Tidore, who had been defeated by Serrão and forced to give one of his daughters as a bride to the sultan of Ternate.

The two months that followed were spent purchasing and loading spices, primarily cloves and nutmeg. Indeed, the Europeans purchased too much—almost seven tons of spices had to be left on the beach because the ships were overloaded. In fact, the poor *Trinidad* was coming apart at the seams and leaking badly; she had to be dragged onto the beach and heeled over for repairs to her hull before attempting the voyage back to Spain. And so the *Victoria* set sail alone, on December 21, 1521, with forty-seven men of her original crew and thirteen Moluccans taken aboard as simple seamen. Nine months later, she arrived in Spain with only eighteen of the forty-seven original crew and only three of the thirteen Moluccans. It was September 8, 1522. The next day, the survivors walked barefoot, in procession, into the church of Santa Maria de la Victoria in Seville, each one lighting a candle at the altar where Magellan had been accustomed to kneel in prayer.

The trip back had been just as troubled as the trip out; the new commander, Elcano, was not popular with the men, in part because he had been involved in the mutiny at Porto San Julián; but he proved to be almost as skillful a navigator as Magellan. He sailed the *Victoria* through the islands of the Indonesian archipelago, which were swarming with Portuguese ships that would have gladly attacked and sunk the *Victoria.* He crossed the southern Indian Ocean, rounded the Cape of Good Hope, sailed along the western coast of Africa, losing men to scurvy and starvation as he went. The lack of provisions forced him to make a desperate move: he landed in the Cape Verde Islands, which were Portuguese. He declared that he was arriving from America, but the thirteen men that he sent ashore to buy supplies offered packets of cloves in exchange because they had no money, and Portuguese officials immediately had them arrested. Spices were a monopoly of the Portuguese crown; they believed the ship must have arrived from the East Indies. Elcano managed to weigh anchor just as armed boats were approaching to surround and capture the Spanish ship. The last leg of the trip was incredibly hard: the twenty-one surviving crew members had to do the work of fifty men, but the odyssey came to a happy end when they finally sighted the port of Sanlúcar de Barrameda, from which they had set sail exactly three years before.

Trinidad had a much worse time of it. She left Tidore on April 6, 1522, heading east for America, following a northern route, which proved impracticable because of contrary winds and fierce storms. In November the badly battered ship returned to the Moluccas. In the meantime, the islands had been occupied by the Portuguese.

Trinidad was confiscated, her cargo was seized by Portuguese officials, and her crew was imprisoned. Only four men, many years later, made it back to Spain.

As for the deserters aboard *San Antonio*, after making a quick stopover at Porto San Julián to try to embark Don Juan de Cartagena and his accomplice the priest (the deserters found not a sign of either man), they reached Seville without incident on May 6, 1521. They accused Magellan of every sort of infamy and were so successful in painting a picture of innocence that the only one to wind up behind bars was Captain Mezquita (Portuguese, and a relative of Magellan), against whom they had in fact mutinied. It was not until *Victoria* returned and the truth came out that Mezquita was released and rehabilitated.

In the meanwhile, Magellan's widow, who was waiting for him in Seville, was placed under guard, her every possession sequestered until judgment could be passed. She died of heartbreak and humiliation, before she could learn her husband's fate; shortly after she died, their two children died as well.

Elcano, together with a few crew members from *Victoria*, was received in Valladolid in the court of King Charles who was now Holy Roman emperor as well. Elcano was awarded an annual pension of five hundred golden ducats and a coat of arms: the terraqueous globe, with the motto *Primus circumdedisti me* ("You were the first to circumnavigate me").

Those who had financed the enterprise became even wealthier than they had been before, because the single cargo of spices delivered by the one surviving ship was enough to pay for all the expenses and to supply them with a handsome profit as well.

Many of the surviving crew, on the other hand, did not even receive back pay, or if they did, it was not until years later, because the coffers of the king of Spain were chronically empty. None of Magellan's heirs ever saw a penny, either.

18

The White Raja

After Magellan's death, the two surviving ships of the expedition left the Philippines—burial site of their beloved commander—and navigated southwestward, a bit haphazardly, coasting around the immense island of Borneo. This was the largest known island on Earth, leaving aside New Guinea, as yet undiscovered. They sighted the port of Brunei, entered the harbor, and dropped anchor. The sultan immediately sent a *praho* embellished with gilded carvings to greet his unexpected guests. Aboard the *praho* was a full orchestra of horns and drums. A few days later he invited the voyagers to his court.

The Europeans crossed the vast wooden city—the first city they had seen since leaving Spain—mounted on elephants sent for them by the island sovereign. They made their way through the crowded streets, escorted by two lines of soldiers armed with swords, spears, and shields. Clearly, the escort was a tribute, but also a subtle form of intimidation. These new arrivals, the sultan clearly thought, might well be cut from the same cloth as those Portuguese mariners who had been lording it over these islands and waters in recent years; it was well, he must have decided, to show them immediately who was stronger.

The sultan of Brunei was mighty indeed. He dominated the whole northwest coast of the huge island; his royal palace was girded by strong walls and defended by heavy cannons. The rooms of the palace were decorated with carpets, silks, and brocades and were crowded with courtiers dressed in precious cloth embroidered in gold, armed with jewel-encrusted daggers.

In the throne room, the sultan sat cross-legged, chewing betel nuts. Behind him stood the women of his harem. The Europeans were warned that under no circumstances must they speak directly to the sultan. If they wished to say something to him, they should speak to a courtier, who would in turn convey the message to a courtier of higher rank. That courtier would then repeat the words to the brother of the city's governor, who would then whisper the request through a blowgun into the ear of the grand vizier, who would finally murmur it to the great monarch. The response would then make its way back to the Europeans by the same, reverse succession of interlocutors. The Europeans thus received permission to trade with the subjects of the powerful sultan.

The sultan, however, refused to show the curious interlopers the prize possession of his treasury that they had heard described in the city: two perfectly round pearls the size of hens' eggs.

This fabulously wealthy personage and his long line of successors negotiated and bargained with all the white traders who came to seek their fortunes in the East Indies: Portuguese and Spaniards in the early years, Dutchmen and Britons later on. The Europeans would bargain and negotiate, cheat and be cheated; in the end, they were often robbed of everything they had. These waters, with their constellations of tiny islands, islets, and reefs, were a mecca for pirates, a perfect labyrinth in which to lay ambushes. The coastline was covered with dense tropical vegetation, beyond which ran rivers. Pirates loved to venture upstream, waiting just inland, then sail downriver and burst into open waters at the right moment.

The most fearsome of the pirates of Borneo were the Illanun, based variously in northern Borneo, on the Sulu islands, and at

Mindanao. The Illanun were fond of encouraging the tendency of equatorial nature toward chaotic exuberance by planting the coastal lagoons with mangrove trees. These trees would take root in water two or three yards deep. Their arching roots would form a labyrinth of channels and basins where the pirates could conceal their *prahos,* tucked away beneath the leaves, while lookouts perched high in the branches, scanning the sea in search of likely prey. The *prahos* of these cunning and ferocious brigands were the largest pirate vessels in the East Indies. They were some thirty yards in length, displaced about sixty tons, and were propelled by a broad sail as well as the forced labor of one hundred galley slaves, chained to their oars. The chief pirate had a large cabin astern; a deckhouse ran the full length of the ship, its roof forming a deck upon which the armed pirates would line up, ready to fight and board.

The Illanun had a decided passion for showy elegance; they would wear scarlet jackets, chainmail breastplates, and majestic headgear adorned with brightly colored plumes. Like old-fashioned paladins of the sea, they scorned firearms and loved hand-to-hand battle. They fought with lances and the notorious kris (a heavy dagger with a wavy blade). Their favorite weapon, however, was the *kampilan,* a huge two-handled sword; it was a point of pride with any Illanun pirate to be able to cleave a victim's skull in two with a single blow of his *kampilan.*

The Illanun would set out on long cruises with fleets of 40 or 50 *prahos* and, in some unusual cases, as many as 150 or even 200. On these cruises, they would venture as far as the coasts of Java and Sumatra, and even the Bay of Bengal (a range of almost two thousand miles).

They would lay in ambush among the islands, as described above, and Malaysian sampans, Chinese junks, and European masted ships all fell victim to their sudden attacks. They would strip the vessels of everything of value and sell passengers and crew into slavery.

If the Illanun constituted the aristocracy of the pirates of Borneo, it would also be fair to say that all the coastal peoples of the great island practiced that profitable profession. In the sultanate of Brunei, the Sea Dayaks stood out for their fierce aggressivity; they were called the Sea Dayaks to distinguish them from their poor cousins, the Land Dayaks. The Land Dayaks lived on the interior of the island, in the mountains, and they hunted and farmed. In contrast, the Sea Dayaks lived along the rivers and were exceedingly skillful in handling canoes, in which they ventured out into the open sea. The Malaysian pirates, sensing raw talent, had enlisted the Sea Dayaks en masse, and piracy was now their chief occupation.

Sea Dayaks and Land Dayaks practiced a custom that was to give Borneo a grim reputation: they were headhunters. The custom began simply enough, when the Dayaks beheaded the enemy killed on the battlefield or in single combat; the heads were then hung up in the large multifamily dwellings that European anthropologists later dubbed *longhouses.* The greater the number of heads captured, the higher the prestige of the village, and probably the greater its prosperity. Those macabre trophies were thought to be good-luck charms.

In time, it was inevitable that the practice would transmute from a custom of warfare into a form of sport. Young men who wished to obtain fame and honor, and especially those who wanted to make a good impression on some young woman whom they wished to marry, would leave their village and venture alone into the deep recesses of the jungle, presumably returning some time later with booty that proved their courage and skill. The victim could be anybody: an inhabitant of an enemy village, an incautious wandering peddler who had ventured too far inland, a wayfarer ambushed on a trail, a farmer working in his field, a woman, or even a child. In contrast with what we might expect, the heads of women and children were the most valued trophies; they were proof that the headhunter had ventured dangerously close to a longhouse to capture his prey and had thus shown great daring and courage.

The entire island of Borneo was torn by a permanent state of warfare, pitting neighbor against neighbor. Every so often, the villages would call a truce in order to exchange their respective heads: they were needed because without the head, it was impossible to perform a proper funeral for the decapitated body. From time to time, these mass exchanges were necessary to placate the spirits of the underworld. If the number of heads exchanged failed to match, then a slave or two would promptly be decapitated to make up the discrepancy.

Sultan Omar Ali Saifuddin had ruled over these gentlemen of land and sea since 1828. The sultan was mentally retarded and had succeeded to the throne due to the achievements of his mother, not through any merits or accomplishments of his own. His mother had arranged for the assassination of her own brother, Mohammed Alam, also known as Api, or "Fire," who had ruled over Brunei with the most bloodthirsty tyranny.

Before being strangled—the traditional way of death for a deposed sultan—Api had had the presence of mind to ask his executioners to make careful note of the direction in which his lifeless body fell. If it slumped to the left, that would signify great misfortune for his nephew, son of his sister, who was about to succeed him as sultan of Brunei. Indeed, after he was strangled, his body fell to the left.

Omar Ali became sultan, but he was not accorded the title of Iang Partua, "the lord who governs," because he was mentally retarded. Even worse, he had a physical defect that was unsuitable for the sovereign of an Asian monarchy: on his right hand, he had a tiny second thumb. The real power was held by another of his uncles, his mother's second brother, Hasim. Hasim was named Raja Muda, or heir to the throne, as well as regent.

In 1837, Hasim was obliged to leave his palace in Brunei to see to matters in the province of Sarawak, where a rebellion was raging that threatened to become extremely serious.

The Malaysian aristocracy that ruled the island of Borneo inflicted a systematic form of depredation upon its native subjects.

They demanded tribute, but they also enforced *serah*, a term we might translate as "involuntary trade." Each village was required to offer all its goods for sale to the Malaysian aristocrat to which it reported: these goods included rice, wax, honey, and bird's nests, which the Malaysian noblemen would then resell to Chinese merchants. The Malaysians had the right to set whatever price they preferred; they always set ridiculously low prices. And if the village was unable to provide the quantity of goods demanded, the villagers were forced to give their own children as slaves.

As if the obligation of "involuntary trade" were not sufficiently onerous, the natives were also required to engage in "involuntary shopping": the Malayasian chief could send any object he chose to the village, and the villagers were obliged to purchase it. In this case, of course, the price was always staggeringly high.

The tribes that were most oppressed and abused by this system, of course, were the meekest and most peaceable tribes, such as the Land Dayaks and the Murut. Once they had been forced into bleak desperation, the only way they knew to escape their plight was to run, fleeing the territories of Brunei and heading inland, toward the more mountainous areas of the island.

With less mild-mannered tribes, such as the Sea Dayaks and the Kayan, the Malaysian chiefs would use a different method: they would sell the tribes weapons and then urge them to commit acts of piracy and make raids on the territories of neighboring tribes. They would then take half of the plunder as tribute.

In 1837, this mixed regime of extortion and outright theft had intensified into a state of crisis through its own greed and lack of restraint. The new governor of the province, Makota, had so exaggerated in his haste to pile up wealth that there was nothing left for the Malaysian nobles to steal. Worse, the Malaysian nobles, almost all of whom were relatives of the ruling dynasty in Brunei, were deeply offended by the scornful treatment they received from the new governor. The Malaysians actually led a revolt of the exasperated natives, who in turn were glad to kill any Malaysians available, whatever faction they might belong to. And so the mutiny spread, a field day for the native headhunters. The mutiny, worrisome enough on its own, became even more of a headache for the monarch in Brunei because of what we might call international complications. The mutineers asked for the help of the Dutch, who had settled in the southern part of the island of Borneo. Hasim saw the danger of losing Sarawak, and perhaps even his throne; he therefore hurried down to the province to take the situation personally in hand.

Like all of the princelings of the vast Asian archipelago, Hasim knew that the best way to counter the moves of a European power was to call for the help of another, rival European power, in this case the British. They had established a base twenty years previous in Singapore, and they were anxious to seize any opportunity to expand their political and commercial influence. Circumstances came to their assistance: in 1838, a British ship was wrecked at the mouth of the Sarawak River. Hasim came to the mariners' rescue, and housed and fed them until he could send them back to Singapore at his own expense.

This gesture of royal munificence made an excellent impression on the colonial authorities. The governor, Bonham, decided to send a mission to Raja Muda Hasim to express his gratitude; a secondary consideration was that such a mission could open the court of Brunei to British influence.

Governor Bonham had just the right person at hand for the task: a bit of an eccentric, obsessed with Borneo and the urgent need to displace the Dutch from the East Indies, establishing British colonies in their place. His name was James Brooke, and he had recently arrived in Singapore aboard his own schooner, the *Royalist.* He was a gentleman, good-looking and well-mannered; Bonham chose to send him as the proper emissary to convey Her Majesty Queen Victoria's compliments to Hasim.

The fortunate chargé d'affaires of this diplomatic maneuver could not have hoped for anything better. James Brooke was thirty-five years old. He had been born in 1803 in a suburb of Benares, where his father, Thomas Brooke, was serving as judge of the supreme court of the East India Company. James was the fifth of six children, two boys and four girls, and at the age of twelve he was sent to study in England; after completing his studies, he returned to India and enlisted in the Bengal army. In 1852 he fought in the First Burmese War as a cavalry officer, distinguishing himself by his outstanding bravery. He was shot in the lung and left for dead on the battlefield; it was not until the next day that his comrades in arms, removing corpses for burial, discovered that he was still alive. He gradually convalesced back in England and then went by ship once again for Bengal in 1830; his passage was delayed by severe weather, and when he finally arrived, the five-year term that the East India Company allowed to return to service had just expired. He pleaded for an extension but was coldly denied. And so he tendered his resignation in a fit of anger and bore a lifelong grudge against the Company for its arrogance and rigidity. He continued on to China and finally returned to England, but he had fallen helplessly in love with the Far East, and especially with the Indonesian archipelago. He spent all his time reading everything he could find about the islands. He dreamed of buying a ship and trading in the East Indies.

In 1834, he thought that his chance had come. In Liverpool, a fine brigantine, the *Findlay,* was for sale at an excellent price. At first, his father refused to lend him the money, but he finally yielded to James's entreaties. Dreaming of glory, James sailed for the East Indies with his new ship loaded with fine cargo and trading goods. The trip was a bitter disappointment. The entire voyage was practically one unbroken quarrel with the captain of the *Findlay,* a certain Kennedy—it was hard to say which of the two men had the more fiery temper. When they finally arrived, James discovered that he had brought the wrong merchandise. Nobody wanted his cargo. He was forced to unload his cargo at a steep loss and to sell the ship at Macao. He returned home, humiliated. Still, the experience was to prove invaluable in the future.

His father died in 1835. With his share of the inheritance, James decided to try his fortune again, this time with a smaller ship, the schooner *Royalist.* He set sail in October 1838 and arrived in Singapore in May 1839, just in time to offer his services to Governor Bonham.

On August 12 of that year, the *Royalist* was dropping anchor at the mouth of the Sarawak River, and three days later the ship was sailing upriver to reach Kuching, newly founded by the governor, Makota. The Dayaki rebels had just burned the previous provincial capital, Katubong. Kuching was a small cluster of wooden stilt-dwellings, like any other settlement along the coastline; it was inhabited by about a thousand people, all Malaysians except for a group of Chinese merchants.

The Raja Muda and the governor received him in formal audience under an awning; but that evening they had a private meeting, and Hasim expressed his concern about Dutch ambitions. Hasim asked Brooke whether Great Britain would be willing to help.

The Englishman, who was only a private citizen and could not make commitments on behalf of his country, evaded the question with generic assurances and pointed criticisms of the Dutch. In the days that followed, he scouted the surrounding countryside extensively, getting to know Sarawak. And he liked what he saw. He liked the place and he liked the people—though he was a little perplexed at the sight of thirty or so dried human heads hanging up in a Dayaki longhouse. If he liked them, they certainly liked him in return—the natives, the Malaysians, and the Chinese. Hasim, in particular, liked James Brooke, and he liked him even better a month and a half later when, as he was preparing to leave Sarawak, he repelled a group of pirates who had incautiously attacked the *Royalist.* Raja Muda invited him back to Kuching and honored him, regaling him with a sumptuous banquet and giving him a gift orangutan.

Back in Singapore, Brooke's welcome was somewhat chillier and less festive. The British merchants congratulated him, it is true, as they hoped that he would open the gates of Brunei to British goods.

Governor Bonham, on the other hand, was vexed and irritated when he learned that Brooke had touched on political matters, however tangentially. He feared complications with the Dutch, who were inordinately suspicious of every British move in what they considered to be their private reserve.

Annoyed, Brooke sailed off to circumnavigate Celebes, and on his way back he stopped off again at Kuching. This time Hasim welcomed him as a savior. The rebel forces weren't far from the city; would the English gentleman be so kind as to pay a visit to the government troops that were holding off the mutineers, if only to encourage the troops, and perhaps to intimidate the enemy with the mysterious presence of a white man?

James Brooke, courteous and accommodating as always, agreed and sailed upriver as far as the camp of the sultan's army, surrounded by a bamboo stockade. Within shouting range was another stockade, and behind it were the enemy forces. Daily combat consisted of nothing more than the exchange of murderous insults between the two forces. Makota, who was in command of the sultan's army, had no intention of risking a battle; he remained inactive even after Brooke had several heavy cannons brought up the Sarawak River from the *Royalist.* Nor was Makota willing to negotiate terms with the mutinous tribes, who were beginning to tire of their rebellion. He simply waited, with classic Eastern calm.

At this point, the Englishman decided to leave once and for all. Hasim, however, pleaded with him to stay a little longer, and in the face of Brooke's misgivings he made an extraordinary offer. Not only would he accord him exclusive trading rights to the province of Sarawak, but he would make him the provincial governor. He even dropped hints about the title of raja.

Decidedly titillated at the prospect, Brooke sailed up the river and took the situation firmly in hand, unleashing an offensive that overwhelmed the rebels, who sued for peace. They were willing to negotiate terms only with the assurances of the Englishman, who had won their confidence.

Hasim promised that he would obtain from his demented nephew, the sultan of Brunei, the necessary document naming Brooke governor. The Englishman sailed off to obtain a load of goods in Singapore so that he could begin regular trade. He was told that, upon his return, he could expect to find a house and a shipload of antimony, as well as his appointment as governor.

When he returned, he found nothing. Since he had purchased another schooner, the *Swift*, which had been exceedingly costly, he flew into a towering rage. Adding to his fury was the discovery that the infamous Makota was plotting with a band of Sea Dayaks to attack the Land Dayaks and the Chinese merchants.

So great was the effect of Brooke's rage that Hasim locked himself in his house for several days, claiming to be deathly ill. In the end, however, the angry Englishman obtained what he wanted: a house was quickly built for him, a bit of antimony arrived, and Makota's raid was canceled, making Brooke the beloved protector of the Land Dayaks and the Chinese merchants.

His prestige grew even greater when he remained, intrepid and alone, in Kuching, while he sent all his men off, either with the *Swift* to deliver the antimony to Singapore, or with the *Royalist* to Brunei, to negotiate the release of the crew of an English ship that had been wrecked in nearby waters.

The *Royalist* was unsuccessful in its mission, but shortly after negotiations broke down, a British ship-of-war of the Royal Navy sailed into the harbor, and the terrified authorities of the sultanate hastily released the imprisoned crew, now convinced that Brooke had all of Great Britain behind him, armed to the teeth.

In the meantime, Makota, like the grand villain of this equatorial set piece that he had become, was plotting and conniving. He went so far as to try to poison Brooke's Malaysian interpreter with a dose of arsenic in his rice. The Englishman, who lost his temper for much, much less, sailed up the river in the *Royalist* and anchored at Kuching, trained his cannon on Hasim's palace, landed with an armed squad, and laid into the Raja Muda with a violent diatribe leveled at Makota, traitor to all: traitor to himself, James Brooke, traitor to Hasim, traitor to the distant and disordered sultan of Brunei, traitor to the long-suffering Land Dayaks, to the peaceful Chinese merchants, to the Malaysian nobility, and in short, traitor to the entire created world. Would Raja Muda Hasim like another fine rebellion? This time he, James Brooke, in person, would lead that rebellion; and he would be followed, because he was now the only man considered trustworthy by all of Sarawak. He would lead the rebellion right up to the gates of Brunei, and he would destroy anything and anybody that stood in his way, a latter-day Attila of Borneo.

Brooke emerged from that impromptu and terrifying audience with a document naming him governor of Sarawak and adjoining regions, in exchange for a small annual tribute to the sultan and the promise that he would respect local laws and religions. On November 24, 1841, James Brooke was publicly proclaimed the new raja of Sarawak, a white man, an Englishman, a "conniving adventurer," as the outraged Dutch immediately denounced him.

The Dutch had every reason to hope that this adventurer's adventure would soon be over, if their intrigues and those of Makota succeeded. In fact, Brooke's situation was fairly precarious. He was isolated, accompanied by just a handful of Europeans—the crewmen of his two ships—on a remote Asiatic island. What was more, his ships were often away, coming and going to Singapore.

Brooke, however, would soon show his mettle. He quickly understood that he needed to win the support and love of his new subjects, and that in order to do so, he needed to pursue two objectives. He needed to create an honest administration that would eliminate the abuses of past governments, and he needed to develop trade in order to bring prosperity to his province. That meant that he would have to protect the Land Dayaks, restrain the Malaysians without arousing their resentment, and encourage and favor the Chinese merchants. One more thing: he would have to eradicate the pirates. He began to inflict small lessons on them, while waiting for his chance to erase them once and for all from the face of Sarawak.

Another important question remained: the title of raja and governor assigned to him by the terrified Hasim still needed to be confirmed and recognized by the sultan of Brunei. Heir to the throne and regent though Hasim might be, he had not set foot in the capital for years. He was, indeed, afraid to go there. He was afraid of palace intrigues set in motion during his absence by his various relatives; he expected daggers from behind curtains, poison drops in his drinks. Hasim's presence in Kuching was an embarrassment for Brooke, because the raja Muda formally had an authority greater than his own. When the governor issued an order, his subjects seemed to wait for confirmation, or at least silent assent, from Hasim.

At last, after trying in vain to persuade the regent to return to Brunei and resume command of the government, the exasperated Englishman left for the capital of the sultanate in July 1842, accompanied by two of Hasim's numerous brothers. As they departed, Hasim embraced his brothers tearfully, certain as he was that only one would emerge alive from the viper's nest that Brunei had become.

Instead, Brooke received a cordial welcome from the retarded but extremely amiable Omar Ali. The sultan was pleased at Brooke's gifts, he openly referred to Brooke as *amigo sua* in the patois left behind by the Portuguese as the only relic of their rule in those waters, and he was particularly pleased at Brooke's suggestion that the tribute of Sarawak be paid in British goods. Omar Ali wrote a letter to his uncle, inviting him to come home, and he issued to the Englishman a handsome parchment with numerous official seals, declaring him a legitimate and official raja. Menacing shadows of discontent loomed in the halls of the palace, but no one dared to oppose the sultan's decisions openly.

The same thing happened back in Kuching, when Brooke returned and Hasim read the fateful document to the entire assembled court. As he read, Hasim glared meaningfully at the glowering Makota; after he finished reading, he announced that anyone who dared to disobey would have their skull cleft in twain by a single blow from a *kampilan.* As Makota hung his head in resignation, Hasim's ten brothers danced around him, their swords wheeling and flashing.

Now solidly in command, Raja Brooke decided to organize an expedition against the pirates, taking advantage of the presence of the British warship *Dido,* under the command of Captain Keppel, who had arrived in the waters off Borneo in May 1843. A flotilla of launches and canoes loaded with British marines and Malaysian and Dayaki warriors rowed and paddled up the Saribas River. They overcame the obstructions built by the pirates in the middle of the river, attacked their log fortresses, and burned their villages until they finally received tokens of surrender and submission from the vanquished brigands. This was the first in a series of campaigns, always conducted with the same tactical approach. During one campaign, old incorrigible Makota was caught red-handed stirring up hostility and treason against his hated rival. Neither Brooke nor Hasim had the courage to execute Makota, because he still had too many confederates and sympathizers in the province of Sarawak. But they did banish him, and Makota made his way back to Brunei.

Hasim, too, finally left, taking with him his vast family and clan: brothers, wives, children, courtiers, servants, an entire tribe that filled a ship, all welcomed warmly in Brunei by the sultan, their nephew.

Free of both his sworn enemy and the friend who had overstayed his welcome, James Brooke finally felt that he truly was the raja of Sarawak. In the months that followed, he visited his various possessions, writing a treatise on piracy and trying to obtain from Her Britannic Majesty's government some recognition of his role and his rank. He was unable to win anything more than an appointment as "confidential agent"; in the meanwhile, Captain Keppel returned to England and published part of the diaries that Brooke had entrusted to him. The book was enormously popular and the White Raja, as he was now known commonly throughout Borneo, became a national hero in Britain: a good and romantic adventurer who struggled to bring the benefits of British civilization to a savage land, fighting pirates and headhunters.

Still, the time had not yet come to enjoy his glory in peace. After all, the cautious Hasim had not been entirely wrong to fear Brooke's return to Brunei. Sultan Omar Ali had fallen under the evil influence of a new grand villain called Haji Seman, the sultan allowing Haji Seman to organize a palace coup in which nearly all of the royal princes were murdered. Poor Hasim had managed to escape the initial slaughter but then, tracked down and surrounded, killed himself with a pistol shot to the head. When news of the massacre reached Singapore, exaggerated with false reports that the victorious conspirators were attacking Kuching to massacre Brooke and all the whites in Borneo, the Royal Navy came sailing to the rescue. In July 1846, a squadron picked up Brooke at Kuching, which was not, fortunately, under attack, and then sailed up the river that led to Brunei. The squadron came under cannon fire from the batteries arrayed along the riverbanks, but no harm was done to it. British marines occupied the town of Brunei. The sultan, his court, and most of the populace had fled in great haste. An expedition set out into the jungle in search of Omar Ali, but returned empty-handed. Another expedition sent to capture Haji Seman in his residence at Kimanis was equally unsuccessful: the devious conspirator had escaped, and all that the British marines managed to seize was Haji Seman's sizable collection of human heads.

A few days later, Sultan Omar Ali was persuaded to return to the capital. He declared that he had been deceived and that he now repented his actions. He paid homage at the graves of the murdered uncles; he confirmed Brooke as governor of Sarawak, renouncing the payment of tribute. As punishment, he was obliged to cede the island of Labuan to Queen Victoria. The White Raja brought back with him to Kuching the wives and children of Hasim who had survived the slaughter. Later, Haji Seman was finally captured.

Once the crisis was resolved, and after carrying out a number of minor expeditions against the perennial pirates, Brooke returned to England after what had now become an absence of seven years. He enjoyed a triumphant welcome, including a reception by Queen Victoria and the Prince Consort Albert. He was made an honorary citizen of London and named governor of the newly British island of Labuan, as well as consul general to Borneo.

He also began to think of the problem of succession. He took a good look at his nephews, the two sons of his sister, Emma Johnson. He asked their parents to make sure that they received a "suitable education."

When he returned to Borneo he found that, in his absence, his old enemies had raised their heads. The pirates had resumed their misdeeds, and in Brunei old Makota had reappeared, like a phantom that would not be laid to rest. A new chief, Laksamana, had taken leadership of the Sea Dayaks of Saribas. In March 1849, with a fleet of eighty *prahos,* the Sea Dayaks laid waste to the banks of the Sadong River, taking advantage of the absence of the men, who were away harvesting crops. They decapitated about a hundred women and children, triumphantly carrying off their heads.

In July, Brooke organized a crushing reprisal, setting out from Kuching with a mixed fleet of British warships and Malaysian *prahos,* with a crew totaling twenty-five hundred men. When Brooke's fleet reached the various pirate bases, it found that the entire pirate fleet—over 150 vessels—had gone to sea. And so Brooke and his men lay in ambush at the mouths of the various rivers along which the pirates would have to return. When the pirates arrived, Brooke's men slaughtered them. The survivors fled to their villages, which the British/Malaysian expedition then burned. The lesson was so harsh that many of the tribes renounced piracy for good.

The great battle was the talk of the island for months, and it marked the beginning of the end of piracy in northwest Borneo. It had unpleasant consequences for Brooke, however. Back in England, a few sensitive souls accused him of murdering innocent savages and claiming that they were pirates, with the sole purpose of seizing their lands, and of doing so with the unwitting complicity of the Royal Navy. Parliament named a commission of inquiry; the inquest dragged out but in the end found in favor of the White Raja.

In the meanwhile, Brooke, or the White Raja, assisted by his two nephews—Charles, now called Tuan Muda, or "Young Lord," and Brooke, now called Tuan Besar, or "Great Lord"—further enlarged his dominion by annexing the districts of Skrang and Saribas to the province of Sarawak with the approval of the new sultan, Munim, who had succeeded to the throne when Omar Ali died in 1852.

Munim, who had married one of the late sultan's sisters, belonged to a cadet branch of the ruling family and felt that his grip on the throne was somewhat precarious. With that gracious concession of territory, Munim wanted to assure himself the support of the powerful White Raja.

Powerful and famous, in those years Sarawak had won the attention of the world, with its raja and its pirates. The province attracted scientists such as the Englishman Alfred Wallace and the Italian Odoardo Beccari, who came to study the flora and fauna of Borneo, especially the orangutan. They were treated courteously by Brooke or, when he was away, by his nephews who were learning the arts of government. Another visitor was the most famous traveler of the period, the Austrian woman Ida Pfeiffer, who traveled around the world twice. She ventured deep into the jungle in search of excitement. She found it: the hospitable Dayaks prepared a bed for her in the place of honor in their longhouse, under a line of freshly cut heads.

This period of relative peace ended suddenly in 1857 with a terrible sequence of events that came close to plunging Sarawak into total violent chaos. The Chinese workers at a large gold-mining camp at Bau, on the upper reaches of the Sarawak River, had been incited for some time by a xenophobic secret society that preached hatred for the English. The British empire, said the preachers of the society, had inflicted one burning humiliation after another upon the Celestial Empire in recent years. The Chinese gold miners especially resented a heavy fine inflicted upon them for contraband of opium (not because it was illegal to smoke it, but because it was a government monopoly), and so they conspired to exterminate the white Europeans and their Malaysian allies and to take control of Kuching.

During the night of February 18 and the early morning of the next day, hundreds of armed Chinese silently descended the Sarawak in boats with muffled oars and entered the city. One group of Chinese headed rapidly toward Brooke's home and entered it surreptitiously. They did make some noise, however, and the White Raja awakened from a bad attack of malaria to the sight of one of his officials being murdered. He miraculously made it out of the house without being seen, while the attackers were setting fire to the building. He dove into the river and swam away, passing close to the Chinese boats. Meanwhile, the attackers were fanning out through Kuching, breaking into the homes of Europeans and burning them.

Brooke tried to assemble the loyal Malaysians and organize a counterattack, but they were outnumbered. He left the town and sent a message to Tuan Muda Charles, who was at Skrang, asking him to come quickly with his Dayaks.

The surviving Europeans, in the meanwhile, awakened by the clamor and the glare of the flames, took refuge in the headquarters of the Protestant mission and prepared to defend themselves to the death. The Chinese, however, instead of simply attacking that last outpost of resistance, sent representatives to the bishop, saying that they had no quarrel with the mission, but only with the raja and his officials, and asked him to come care for their wounded. Bishop McDougall agreed, and he was led before the Chinese commander, who sat on the raja's throne, showing his men a head on a stake, claiming that it was Brooke's. In fact it belonged to the official killed in Brooke's residence.

McDougall, who must have been a courageous man, pointed out to the Chinese that before long Tuan Muda would arrive, hungering for revenge, and that his Dayaks would chop the Chinese into little pieces. This reasonable observation sufficed to dampen the rebels' enthusiasm. They decided to return to the gold field at Bau.

On February 21, the Chinese started upriver, their boats loaded with plunder. A number of Malaysians attacked the rear guard, whereupon the Chinese returned and burned the Malaysian quarter to the ground. The enterprising Bishop McDougall caught up with the White Raja, after conveying the women and children to safety by sending them downriver aboard a boat. The bishop urged him to seize the moment and overwhelm the enemy. Brooke, however, was truly outnumbered; he attacked, reluctantly, and he and his men were knocked about badly. He was still suffering from his attack of malaria, and it would seem that he was discouraged as well. According to one witness, he talked about simply handing the country over to the Dutch.

Tuan Muda, at Skrang, was also abed with malarial fever when a servant burst into his room with the news that his uncle had just been killed at Kuching by Chinese mutineers. Tuan Muda tottered to his feet, and even before he could clearly understand what had happened, he saw dozens of Dayaki *prahos* arriving, all crowded with men anxious to avenge the death of their raja. The flotilla set off at once, and along the way met up with the boatload of women and children; the Dayaks and Tuan Muda learned that Brooke was still alive. Brooke himself, traveling downstream toward the rescuers, saw the steamer *Sir James Brooke* on its way back from Singapore. He was taken aboard and, followed by the Dayaki *prahos,* reached the burning capital, Kuching, and began bombarding the Chinese with the shipboard cannon.

The Dayaks poured out of their *prahos* like so many avenging furies and destroyed the Chinese boats; the rebels then fled into the jungle, where they were chased for miles and miles and killed by the hundreds. The surviving Chinese rebels fled inland to the interior of Borneo, abandoning Sarawak forever. In the days that followed, even the Chinese who had had nothing to do with the uprising left en masse, fearful of reprisals. Their departure badly undermined the country's prosperity for many years to come.

The year 1858 was marked by the loss of an old enemy and the unexpected addition of a new figure to the general cast of characters. In Brunei, Makota died. Back in England, where Raja Brooke had gone to try to persuade the British government to make Sarawak a protectorate, an illegitimate son materialized out of thin air: Reuben George Brooke, twenty-four years old. Sir James Brooke, the White Raja, officially recognized him as his son and informed his nephews of the development. Charles and Brooke, fearing that they would soon be written out of their uncle's will, had reactions that verged on hysteria.

Reuben George, however, never set foot in Sarawak, and after a year vanished from the scene. He died in a shipwreck in 1874. Little is known or understood about his role. Some thought that he was a pious fraud and that he had taken advantage of James Brooke's good faith. Others believed that Brooke himself had met the young man, decided that he was better suited to govern Sarawak than his nephews, and decided to pass him off as his son. Perhaps this second hypothesis is accurate, because there are no reports of Brooke ever having relations with women. One biographer, based on confidential reports from close friends of Brooke, states that the bullet that supposedly penetrated his lung on that battlefield in Burma in 1825 actually damaged another, lower organ.

In any case, there was one woman who played an important role in the White Raja's life: Miss Angela Burdett-Coutts, whom he had met in his youth at Bath, while convalescing from that 1825 wound. She corresponded with him for years, becoming a most loyal friend and trusted adviser, and when she inherited a considerable fortune, she invested a great deal of money in Sarawak and helped James financially.

The young lady intensely disliked James Brooke's relatives, a fact that greatly complicated the question of the successor to the throne of Sarawak. That question obsessed James Brooke more and more as his health declined. In 1861, he had proclaimed his nephew, Brooke, Raja Muda, or presumptive heir. He had promised the young Brooke more than once that he would soon abdicate. When his uncle was negotiating with the British government for the establishment of a protectorate, young Brooke misunderstood the situation and thought that the White Raja was preparing to hand the country over to the British. He wrote theatening and ill-advised letters to his uncle in an attempt to dissuade him. If there was one thing the White Raja would not tolerate, it was insubordination, least of all from a nephew upon whom he had lavished generosity and opportunities. He immediately hastened back to Kuching (at the advice of Miss Burdett-Coutts, and with a loan from her to pay his way) and finally did write poor Brooke out of his will, ordering him into exile. Charles—who had always sided with his uncle—thus became the next heir to the throne, though he too was a favorite target for the barbs of his uncle's friend.

Despite all that, Charles did finally become the second White Raja of Sarawak when Sir James Brooke died on the morning of June 11, 1868, in Burrator, England, where he had spent the last five years of his life.

For years afterward, the inhabitants of Kuching would point to the mountain of Santubong, saying that God had so willed it that the mountain resembled the profile of the founder of their state, his eyes fixed on Sarawak to protect it forever.

19
Around the World in Thirty-five Hours

On May 27, 1883, a cheerful little excursion group boarded a steamship in the Pacific port of Batavia, the handsome capital of the Dutch East Indies. They were heading out on a very special day-trip. The ladies wore crinoline and held charming and colorful little parasols edged with lace, to protect themselves against the powerful equatorial sun; the gentlemen wore jackets and ties. They were all venturing out into the Sunda Strait to the desert island of Krakatoa, where a volcano that had been dormant since 1680 had suddenly awoken, spitting ash and lapilli.

The island had, until recently, been covered by dense green forest, but now everything was a uniform shade of gray. A thick layer of cinders had smothered all vegetation, killing color and life. The steady gray rain had been dropping for a week now. The most daring members of the party took the exhausting climb to the summit of Mount Perboewatan. There they could look over the edge of the crater and see an immense column of steam that poured with a tremendous racket out of a crevasse that yawned almost three hundred yards across.

The ladies and gentlemen climbed back down and returned to

their boat. The ladies were suffused with a becoming pallor of excitement under their now-gray parasols; the gentlemen were adjusting their ties, proud of the courage they had shown in the face of the forces of nature.

In the days that followed, the explosions that had lured the curious sightseers out from Batavia slowly subsided; there was a new burst of activity around June 19, which in turn died down. On August 11, another boatload of visitors discovered that there were now three volcanic mouths, all issuing eruptive material, while the island's main peak, the volcano Rakata, which towered 915 feet tall, showed absolutely no sign of life.

All of this was a source of good fun for the Dutch diplomatic families at Batavia, a way of thrilling the ladies and causing the unmarried daughters to clutch appealingly at the sleeves of their gentleman companions. But it was hardly an uncommon occurrence in the archipelago, studded as it was with volcanoes large and small, some of them active at any given point. Within a matter of weeks the island of Krakatoa would erupt in what one observer described as "the greatest geological phenomenon in history."

On August 26, after the first in a series of violent explosions, a column of black smoke rose straight up from the small island to an altitude of over fifteen miles. The tremendous explosions continued through the night without pause, and along the neighboring coastlines of Java and Sumatra no one slept a wink that night. In Batavia, one hundred miles away, the windows shook as if there were a major bombardment under way. At ten in the morning on the following day, August 27, the eruption came to a head, with the sudden expulsion of a cloud of ash that filled the sky, casting a dense shadow over the entire region. The cataclysmic explosion was heard more than twenty-five hundred miles away: in Ceylon, Burma, New Guinea, and Australia. In French Indochina, coastal observation posts telegraphed to headquarters in Saigon that a naval battle seemed to be in progress out at sea. The most distant point that recorded the noise was the island of Rodriguez in the Indian Ocean, 2,990 miles to the west of Krakatoa, where a member of the coast guard heard it exactly four hours after the eruption and noted it in his diary.

In Batavia, where many windows were shattered by the shock of the explosion, the light of day did not return until after three in the afternoon, when the rain of ash finally stopped coming down. In the meanwhile, however, half an hour after the immense explosion, a wall of water 115 feet high had swept over the surrounding shorelines, destroying 295 towns and villages and quickly killing more than forty thousand people. For a range of sixty miles from the epicenter, nothing remained standing. Two thirds of Krakatoa, a surface area of eight square miles, had simply plunged into the ocean, causing an enormous backwash of water. Giant tidal waves thundered onto the shorelines, uprooting trees and crushing houses several miles inland. All that remained of the island of Sebesi, twenty miles from Krakatoa, was a flat surface. Every last one of its three thousand inhabitants was dead. Two hours later, the tidal wave was flooding the low-lying areas of Batavia and then rolling onward to China and Japan, in one direction, and Madagascar in the other, finally skirting the Cape of Good Hope, penetrating into the Atlantic Ocean, and rolling northward. The next day, the tidal level at La Rochelle, on the French coast, rose sharply. And the atmospheric reverberations from the explosive jet of steam traveled around the world in thirty-five hours.

A number of eyewitnesses told apocalyptic stories. A Dutch engineer, Van Sandick of the Dutch Civil Engineering Corps, was on board the steamship *General Loudon,* at anchor in the bay of Lampong, Sumatra. He said that ash dropped onto the deck of the ship by the ton, turning into a mud pack that covered the ship's deck to a depth of two feet.

The foul-smelling muck made its way everywhere on the ship, even belowdecks. It got into the eyes and the nose, it made breathing difficult, and it stank of sulfur. The ears buzzed, a strange sleepiness seemed to grip everyone on board, and the compass was spinning crazily. Pumice stones of all sizes fell from the sky, and lightning struck the mainmast seven times, crackling the length of the ship and flickering off into the ocean with a "diabolical noise."

Suddenly, the sea rose to an astounding height, and an immense wave came rushing toward the steamship at unbelievable speed. The ship had just enough time to turn her bow toward the onrushing tsunami. An instant later, the *General Loudon* was lifted straight up like a piece of straw, and then was sent plunging down into the successive trough, as the mountain of water went thundering on to strike the coast, erasing from the face of the Earth the Sumatran city of Telok-Betong in the blink of an eye. The lighthouse went over like a tenpin, houses crumbled, trees were uprooted, and a steamer, *Barouw,* was lifted over the pier and deposited two miles inland. When the water retreated, it had changed the face of Sumatra, and it dragged with it thousands of corpses, scattering them throughout the strait. In the days that followed, ships encountered banks of human bodies pushed together by the currents. In early September, a German ocean liner was almost blocked by an island of floating cadavers. No one ate fish for months, after a story made the rounds about local fishermen finding human fingers in the belly of one of their catches. For six months, the bay of Lampong was blocked by a bank of pumice a thousand yards across, twenty miles long, and fifteen feet high; in time, wind and currents broke it up and dispersed the floating rocks.

Krakatoa itself was unrecognizable: two thirds of the island had vanished, dropping into the sea. Where the land had once risen from four hundred to fourteen hundred feet above sea level, there was now a crater some nine hundred feet *below* sea level. Over a radius of some sixty miles from the island, nothing survived except those who had been on ships or boats, and not all of them made it. Hundreds of small vessels were swallowed up by the waves, hurled against the rocks, or shattered on the beach.

One year after the eruption, in May 1884, a French scientific mission visited the devastated archipelago. They were not able even to set foot on what remained of Krakatoa. Enveloped in a whitish plume of smoke, the crater of Rakata bombarded their boat with a continuous shower of stones the size of oranges, whistling and cracking like a shooting gallery. One projectile, "about the size of a mortar shell," just grazed the boat, causing it to ship water and persuading the scientists to shift rapidly from daring to extreme caution. "It seemed as if the god of the volcano, still angry, refused to be examined by these powerless little humans who had come from the far side of Earth to admire his displays of might." The scientists retreated to Sebuku, where nothing was left of a once-lovely forest except a jumble of tree trunks, whitened and scattered along the hillside, largely buried under drifting ash.

They sailed over to Sebesi, where they found an island Pompeii. Buried beneath a layer of ash and pumice towering more than thirty feet in the air, the island had preserved its previous shape, but seemed to have risen into the air. Its coastline was a "perfidious terrain," because the upper layer of ash had dried under the equatorial sun and seemed solid. But it was actually just a thin crust, which could suddenly give way, plummeting the incautious stroller down into a cinder-studded muck, where he could easily suffocate as if caught in quicksand.

Farther along, at the foot of the slopes of the volcanic cone that constituted the island, the scientists stumbled across a daunting spectacle. The torrential rains that had fallen during the season of the monsoons had carved deep gullies into the layers of detritus, washing down from the volcano. The rains had thus uncovered the original ground level; and there, at the bottom of those gullies, stacked one atop the other, lay hundreds of mummified corpses of the former inhabitants, amid the pathetic remains of their houses. They had died even before they could drown in the great tidal wave; they had been suffocated by the rain of sulfur and ash.

20

Tusitala in Equator Town

The island of Apemama, in an archipelago that white navigators called the Gilbert Islands after an English sea captain who had passed that way in 1788, was under the rule of the terrifying King Tembinok' when a schooner entered the atoll's lagoon through the north passage on September 1, 1889, a blazingly hot equatorial Sunday.

King Tembinok' was a feared and respected personage in the Gilbert Islands, the hero of songs and the subject of much conversation. He was the last absolute monarch of the islands, a holdout from an array of royal dynasties that had been crushed and destroyed by the white interlopers. On all the other islands of this archipelago that straddled the Equator, the whites had taken over, building bungalows, drinking gin, and treating the natives—royalty included—like domestic animals of limited intelligence and questionable usefulness.

But not on Apemama. On the island of Apemama, there was only one white man, tolerated but not well liked, unwelcome at court and constantly spied upon, like a mouse in a house full of cats. Apemama was the last island off limits to European hegemony. On all the other islands of the chain, whites came and went whenever they chose, and stayed just as long as they pleased. But on Apemama, nothing could be done without the permission of the king, who scrutinized his visitors with the clinical distaste of a bad-tempered customs officer. Now, the mighty Tembinok' had failed to achieve his ambition of becoming emperor of the entire archipelago, though not through any fault of his own; just as he was preparing to sail out and conquer the neighboring islands, a British man-of-war had appeared in the lagoon, cannons primed, and Tembinok' had been obliged to dump all the weapons he had amassed into the clear blue water. Still, fear of Tembinok's long, strong arm still troubled the sleep of his fellow kinglets on the other islands of the Gilbert chain.

Nowhere but Apemama could the ancient customs of the Gilberts still be found. Only there did unwed girls still go naked; only there did widows keep their late husbands' skulls next to them in their beds as they slept, carrying the sun-bleached craniums around with them by day.

The seventy-ton schooner, the *Equator*, was piloted by Captain Dennis Reid. It sailed into the breeze-ruffled lagoon and anchored just off a shelf of white coral rising seven or eight feet above the water. A little way inland lay the chaotic jumble of buildings that constituted the royal palace; next to it was a village of *maniap'*, steep-roofed houses with open walls.

On the beach, several serious-looking men hurried to launch an outrigger, which they paddled quickly to the ship's side, bringing the king's ladder. Tembinok' had once had an unpleasant experience with one of the fragile gangplanks employed by many of the freighters of the South Seas, and since that day he had refused to board a ship on any ladder but his own. Once the stout structure, really more staircase than ladder, had been affixed to the side of the *Equator*, the natives withdrew. A long wait ensued, according to island protocol, before the mighty equatorial sovereign finally appeared, followed by an entourage of courtiers and several of his wives; they clambered into the lifeboat of a British battleship, kindly donated by the Royal Navy. Heavy-footed, King Tembinok' climbed the stairs and stalked onto the deck. He was tall, powerful, and heavy, with long black hair and malevolent, challenging eyes. That day, he was dressed in his favorite clothes: green corduroy trousers and a cardinal-red silk jacket to which the tails of a white shirt had been sewn. On other occasions, he liked to wear a navy uniform or a colorful woman's dress.

Boarding the ships that visited his island harbor was not only the king's favorite pastime; it was also his chief occupation. While King Tembinok' was the absolute ruler of the threefold island kingdom of Apemama, Aranuka, and Kuria, he was also the only merchant in the realm. He held a monopoly on the island's turtles as well as the entire harvest of copra, the sun-dried coconuts that were the single most important article of trade in the Pacific Ocean. While King Tembinok' sat negotiating with the ship's captain at a table groaning with delicacies (his reputation as a gourmand had spread well beyond the Gilberts), his substantial and garrulous wives had also boarded the schooner to do a little shopping, with his royal indulgence. Each wife had received a ration of copra as pocket money for her shopping spree. The island queens turned up their noses at the trinkets that the captain laid out for them: bonnets, bows, corsets, crinolines, scents, and tins of salmon. Instead, they scooped up packets of tobacco, which was the prized commodity of Apemama, the basic unit of legal tender.

The king, in contrast to his discerning wives, was a glutton when it came to shopping. His *maniap'* were heaped with treasures of every improbable sort: crates of clocks and watches, boxes full of harmonicas, sunglasses, umbrellas, soldiers' dress jackets, hunting rifles, sewing machines, vials of medicine, canned foods, balls of wool, cakes of scented soap, and an amazing number of cast-iron potbelly stoves. That day in 1889 King Tembinok' purchased the entire contents of the schooner's hold, right down to the last case of a liqueur that vaguely resembled kirsch, of which he was a great consumer and perhaps the world's most devoted connoisseur.

The *Equator*, however, had not brought only sundry merchandise to Apemama. On board the ship were passengers of note: Robert Louis Stevenson; his wife, Fanny; her brother, Lloyd Osbourne; and their Chinese domestic, Ah Fu.

For more than a year now, the Scottish author—a well-paid celebrity following the success of *Treasure Island* and *The Strange Case of Dr Jekyll and Mr Hyde*—had been roaming through the South Seas. A sizable inheritance had fleshed out Stevenson's considerable royalties, and he had used the money to charter the yacht *Casco*, commanded by a Captain Otis. He and his little clan had sailed from San Francisco in June 1888. Stevenson was only thirty-eight years old, but he was already a "walking spectre," the victim of pulmonary tuberculosis, a disease that had plagued him since childhood. "I believed that my life was at an end, and that nothing awaited me but nurses or undertakers." Before he died, he wanted at least to see the islands of the South Seas, which had so excited his youthful imagination.

The *Casco* was a splendid ship, seventy-four tons displacement, a luxury yacht with wall-to-wall carpeting, a large library, barrels of vintage wines, and cases of champagne. Everywhere the yacht moored, she aroused admiration, just as her eccentric and ghostly passenger aroused surprise and amazement.

The yacht's first destination was the Marquesas Islands, the first encounter with a different world, with men "who have never read Vergil, who were never conquered by Julius Caesar, who were never governed by the wisdom of Papinian." Stevenson and entourage stayed there from July until September; then they sailed to Tahiti. Stevenson fell ill in Papeete, a place he disliked. But when he decided to move to Tautira, on the Taiarapu Peninsula, he discovered "the loveliest place on earth." In the two months that he stayed there, he recovered his health and good humor.

At the beginning of 1889, the *Casco* reached the Hawaiian Islands, mooring in Honolulu; Stevenson's charter was up, and he and the family were forced to leave the ship. But the writer did not have the heart to return to "my life as a recluse and my sickroom," and he wanted to "sail before the wind" once again. He took passage for himself and his entourage on the *Equator*, and a few months later the ship was mooring in Apemama Lagoon.

Because Apemama seemed to be a refuge of native customs, which had been eroded on the other islands by white interlopers, Stevenson greatly wished to spend time there. He expressed his desire to the majestic King Tembinok'. Tembinok' promised that he would think it over. He then descended his personal gangway and arranged himself in the royal lifeboat. Three sweeps of the oars took him to the beach, across which he was carried on the shoulders of his loyal subjects, into his palace crowded with clocks and cast-iron stoves.

Two days later, a messenger brought the royal decision. Tembinok', who spoke a fractured but clearly understandable English, had carefully watched Stevenson's *eyes* and especially his *mouth* during their brief conversation; he had decided that the writer was trustworthy. Especially his *mouth*, which meant that the writer must have spoken well, *but not excessively.* If there was one thing that His Apemamian Majesty could not abide, it was idle chatter. King Tembinok' liked to say that his subjects did not need to speak, they needed only to obey orders. He had once ventured—out of pure curiosity—to allow a few missionaries to land in his island realm, but he sent them packing once he had seen them preach. The same thing had happened to all the whites who had come to Apemama: sent away, passage provided gratis as far as the nearest island. Only one fortunate European had escaped the fate of this royal deportation, silent, sober, solitary. Of him, the king said: "I think he good; he no 'peak."

And so the laconic Stevenson and followers were graciously allowed to stay on Apemama, until the return of the *Equator* from its customary trading cruise, provided that they chose a site where the king would build a "town" in which they would agree to live. The second article of the royal treaty dictated that one of King

Tembinok's cooks would come each day to take lessons from Stevenson's cook, Ah Fu. The third article required that the monarch could come for lunch whenever he liked, and on days that he stayed home, a dish would be sent over from Stevenson's table. Lastly, Stevenson was required to solemnly swear that he would never give any of King Tembinok's subjects liquor, money, or tobacco. The liquor and the money were forbidden; the third could be distributed only by the king himself.

Once the location of Equator Town had been chosen—the site was named after the schooner, but also after the Line, only a few dozen miles away—on a small rise covered with a grove of pandanus, King Tembinok' promised that the city would be ready the following day.

The next morning Lloyd Osbourne came ashore; he found nothing and he went to ask King Tembinok' for an explanation. The king called for his Winchester, stepped out into his courtyard, and fired two shots in the air. That was a royal proclamation, on this island where talk was considered superfluous. In less than half an hour the subjects had assembled and work had begun; when the future citizens of Equator Town arrived in the early afternoon with their luggage, where the lovely grove of pandanus had once stood there now stood a single *maniap'* and a little enclosed house, while a second *maniap'* was slowly and silently climbing the little slope, as some thirty bare feet moved in step beneath it.

The king looked on, seated on a mat, wearing his cardinal-red jacket, a cuirassier's helmet on his head, a meerschaum pipe in his mouth, one of his wives standing behind him. When the king withdrew at sunset, Equator Town had been founded. The construction was completed the following morning with a hanging palisade of garlands of palm leaves strung from the branches of the palm trees, entirely surrounding the buildings. This marked the area that was taboo to all the Apemamians.

There was a daily relay of succulent delicacies prepared by Ah Fu for King Tembinok', who returned the kindness by coming over every evening for endless games of poker with Stevenson and family and the king's wives. Every night, the king's wives lost all the spending tobacco they had received that day, because the rules of poker by which they played had been subtly altered. The rules of Apemamian poker required total respect for the king's skill at cards.

The days passed slowly and serenely, without noteworthy events.

Once Stevenson complained to the king about the lazy disobedience of a housekeeper that Tembinok' had sent over; the king encouraged the guilty party to redouble his scanty efforts by firing two shots from his Winchester over the man's head and two shots just below his feet, from a distance of fifty paces. For the occasion, Tembinok' had dressed in his garish woman's dress and had worn his cuirassier's helmet, his customary garb for inflicting punishment.

Another time, when the invalid author had actually managed to catch a cold at the Equator, he decided to take the opportunity to test the effectiveness of the local medicos. Stevenson was entrusted to the care of two shamans, Tamaiti and Terutak'. Tamaiti built a bonfire of palm leaves and fanned the smoke into Stevenson's face. Terutak' attempted to hypnotize him, but only succeeded in putting the Scotsman to sleep. When Stevenson awoke, however, his cold was gone.

At last, the schooner returned, considerably later than agreed—a delay that was a source of pleasure, not concern. The short-lived but glorious existence of Equator Town—the highest city above sea level on the island of Apemama—came to an end. Its buildings walked back down the hill and returned to their previous locations. The royal lifeboat, with Tembinok' at the helm in his full navy regalia, escorted the Stevenson entourage to the *Equator.* The king made a short speech of farewell, shook hands all around, and returned to the beach. The *Equator* set sail, and the tips of the palm trees of Apemama vanished over the horizon.

The South Sea wanderings of the Stevenson family finally came to an end in 1890 in Samoa, after one last cruise aboard the steamship *Janet Nicoll.* The Stevensons paid twenty thousand dollars for fifty acres of land in Vailima, near Apia, and they settled there, making it their *Buen Retiro.* It was there that the Samoans, fascinated by Stevenson's ability to invent and recount fabulous narratives, gave him the name of Tusitala, "teller of tales."

The diplomat and author Henry Adams, descended from two American presidents, passed through Apia in December 1890; he described Stevenson as having adapted wholeheartedly to Samoan ways, including Samoan dress. He wore one brown wool stocking on his left foot and one gray wool stocking on his right foot. He wore them in the house as slippers. Both stockings had completely worn through at the heel. In consideration of the sensibilities of his American guests, Stevenson had put on a shirt.

Tusitala, the magical narrator, died at Vailima a few years later, in 1894. He was buried, as he had asked, at the summit of Mount Vaea, which overlooks the town of Apia. His stories still travel around the world.

A Note on the Sources

We based this book almost entirely on the original accounts of the various adventures, explorations, and events.

Antiquity

We took material from *Les Contes populaires de l'Egypte ancienne* by the great Egyptologist Gaston Maspéro, published in 1889; from the excellent English translation by M. N. Adler of *The Itinerary of Benjamin of Tudela* (1907); the fanciful Arabic tales assembled in *Le Isole mirabili,* by Angelo Arioli (1989); and from the Chinese accounts quoted in *Viaggiatori del Regno di Mezzo,* by Gabriele Foccardi (1992).

Orellana's expedition was described by Gaspar de Carvajal in his *Descubrimiento del Río de las Amazonas,* the text of which was used by Gonzalo Fernándo de Oviedo in his *Historia general y natural de las Indias* (1535), published in its entirety under the editorship of José Toribio Medina in 1894. Concerning the tragic adventure of Lope de Aguirre, the fundamental—and exceedingly hostile—account is that of Francisco Vásquez, *Relación verdadera de todo lo que sucedió en la jornada de Omagua y Dorado,* published in the collection of the

Historiadores de Indias (1909). The story of Bernard O'Brien is told in *Red Gold* by John Hemming (1978). Charles Marie de La Condamine published in 1751 his *Journal du Voyage faict par ordre du Roi à l'équateur;* subsequent editions include a letter written to the author by Godin des Odonais concerning the perils undergone by his wife. For the story of the Baroness Elisa von Wagner, we based our account on *Gli Efferati* by Emilio de' Rossignoli (1978).

Africa

The Italian missionary Padre Antonio Zucchelli wrote at considerable length about the Congolese prophetess Dona Beatriz in his *Relazioni del Viaggio e Missione di Congo* (1712); this book also includes eyewitness accounts by fellow members of his order.

Concerning the discovery of the source of the Nile and related adventures and exploits in the region, we utilized works by the protagonists themselves: Sir Richard Burton's *The Lake Region of Central Africa* (1860); John Hanning Speke's *Journal of the Discovery of the Source of the Nile* (1863); Samuel Baker's *The Albert Nyanza, Great Basin of the Nile* (1866); Carlo Piaggia's *Dall'Arrivo fra I Niam-Niam alle sponde del lago Tana* (1877); Georg Schweinfurth's *The Heart of Africa* (1873); Samuel Baker's *Ismailia, a Narrative of the Expedition to Central Africa for the Suppression of the Slave Trade* (1874); Henry Morton Stanley's *How I Found Livingstone* (1872); and again Stanley's *Through the Dark Continent* (1878). Of course we could not ignore the fundamental work by Alan Moorehead, *The White Nile* (1960); we also made use of Adam Hochschild's recent book, *King Leopold's Ghost* (1998).

For the Belgians and the French in Central Africa, we relied principally upon Jean Becker's *La troisième expédition belge au Pays Noir* (1886); Elio Zorzi's *Al Congo con Brazzà* (1940); and Paul du Chaillu's *Adventures in the Great Forest of Equatorial Africa and the Country of the Dwarfs* (1890).

Concerning Equatoria and the controversial rescue of Emin Pasha, we used Romolo Gessi's *Sette anni nel Sudan egiziano* (1891); Gaetano Casati's *Dieci anni in Equatoria e ritorno con Emin Pascià*

(1892); Henry Morton Stanley's *In Darkest Africa or the Quest, Rescue and Retreat of Emin, Governor of Equatoria* (1890); A. J. Monteney-Jephson's *Emin Pasha and the Rebellion at the Equator* (1890); Karl Peters's *Die Deutsche Emin Pasha Expedition* (1891); and Georg Schweitzer's *Emin Pasha: Eine Darstellung seines Lebens und Wirkens* (1898).

Asia

For Magellan's expedition, we made use of the eyewitness account of Antonio Pigafetta, *Il primo viaggio intorno al mondo,* in the edition edited by Camillo Manfroni (1929). For the story of Sir James Brooke, we used *The White Rajahs* (1960). For the eruption of Krakatoa, we used *Les Volcans,* by Arnold Boscowitz (1886), and *Krakatau et le détroit de la Sonde,* by Edmond Cotteau (1884).

Oceania

The source for the voyage of Robert Louis Stevenson and family to Apemama is his book, *In the South Seas.*